My Way: The Way of the White Clouds

Osho taught philosophy at the University of Jabalpur
before establishing the commune in Poona, India, which
has become famous all over the world as a mecca for
seekers wanting to experience meditation and transformation. His teachings have influenced millions of
people of all ages and from all walks of life. He has
been described by *The Sunday Times* as one of the 1,000
Makers of the Twentieth Century, and by *The Sunday
Mid-Day* (India) as one of the ten people – along with
Gandhi, Nehru and Buddha – who have changed the
destiny of India.

MY WAY

THE WAY OF THE
WHITE
CLOUDS

OSHO

ELEMENT

Shaftesbury, Dorset • Boston, Massachusetts
Melbourne, Victoria

Fifth edition

This edition published in the UK in 1995 by
Element Books Limited
Shaftesbury, Dorset SP7 8BP

Published in the USA in 1995 by
Element Books, Inc.
160 North Washington Street
Boston, MA 02114

Published in Australia in 1995 by
Element Books and distributed
by Penguin Australia Limited
487 Maroondah Highway, Ringwood,
Victoria 3134

Reprinted 1999

Design by Ma Deva Sandipa

Printed and bound in Great Britain by
JW Arrowsmith, Bristol

British Library Cataloguing in Publication
data available

Library of Congress Cataloging in Publication
data available

ISBN 1–85230–699–8

Spontaneous discourses
given by Osho
to disciples and friends
in Lao Tzu House,
Poona, India.

CONTENTS

INTRODUCTION

ON FIFTEEN MAY MORNINGS in Poona, a large Indian city near Bombay, a group of Western followers gathers at Osho Commune International to ask Osho a series of questions about himself and his path to enlightenment.

The questions have been chosen with a specific purpose: to prepare a book introducing Osho and his work to the thousands of visitors and people looking for a new way of life.

With a clarity available only to a man of supreme consciousness, Osho here gives a comprehensive blueprint of his vision for a troubled humanity as it moves into the twenty-first century.

The symbol of the white clouds is chosen to represent the way a seeker moves on the path...and this book addresses all the states – storms, winds, sun, rain and rainbows – that are part of the adventure called life.

*A white cloud is a mystery – the coming, the going, the very
being of it. A white cloud exists without any roots – an unrooted
phenomenon, grounded nowhere, or, grounded in the nowhere.
But still it exists, and exists abundantly.*

*The whole of existence is like that – without any roots,
without any causality, without any ultimate cause, it exists.
It exists as a mystery.*

*A cloud has nowhere to go. It moves, it moves everywhere.
All dimensions belong to it, all directions belong to it.
Nothing is rejected. Everything is, exists, in a total acceptability.*

*The clouds have no way of their own – they drift.
A way means reaching somewhere. The real way is a wayless way.
Moving, but not with a fixed mind – moving without a mind.*

*Meditation basically means a state of no-mind –
 where you are, but not going anywhere:
 where just being, just to be, is the goal.*

*Hence I call my way, the way of the white clouds.
I would like you also to become white clouds drifting in the sky.
Drifting, not moving to a point.*

*Wheresoever you happen to be, that is the goal.
The goal is every moment. The journey is the goal.
Become white clouds – just being there, no resistance, no fight:
just enjoying the very existence, celebrating the moment,
the joy, the ecstasy of it.*

The Way
of the
White
Clouds

CHAPTER ONE

Beloved Osho,
Why is your way called
The Way of the White Clouds?

J UST BEFORE BUDDHA DIED somebody asked him: When a buddha dies where does he go? Does he survive or simply disappear into nothingness? This is not a new question, it is one of the oldest, many times repeated and asked. Buddha is reported to have said: Just like a white cloud disappearing....

This very morning there were white clouds in the sky. Now they are there no more. Where have they gone? From where do they come? How do they evolve, and how do they dissolve again? A white cloud is a mystery, the coming, the going, the very being of it. That's the first reason why I call my way The Way of the White Clouds.

But there are many reasons, and it is good to ponder, to meditate upon them. A white cloud exists without any roots. It is an unrooted phenomenon, grounded nowhere or grounded in the nowhere. But still it exists. The whole of existence is like a white cloud: without any roots, without any causality, without any ultimate cause, it exists. It exists as a mystery.

A white cloud really has no way of its own. It drifts. It has nowhere to reach, no destination, no destiny to be fulfilled, no end. You cannot frustrate a white cloud because wherever it reaches is the goal. If you have a goal you are bound to get frustrated. The more goal-oriented a mind is the more anguish, anxiety and frustration there will be, because once you have a goal you are moving with a fixed destination. And the whole exists without any destiny. The whole is not moving anywhere; there is no goal to it, no purpose.

Once you have a purpose you are against the whole – remember this – then you will get frustrated. You cannot win against the whole. Your existence is so tiny – you cannot fight, you cannot conquer. It is impossible to conceive how an individual unit can conquer the whole. And if the whole is purposeless and you are with purpose you are going to be defeated.

A white cloud drifts wherever the wind leads – it doesn't resist, it doesn't fight. A white cloud is not a conqueror, and still it hovers over everything. You cannot conquer it, you cannot defeat it. It has no mind to conquer – that's why you cannot defeat it. Once you are fixed to a goal, purpose, destiny, meaning, once you have got that madness of reaching somewhere, then problems will arise. And you will be defeated, that is certain. Your defeat is in the very nature of existence itself.

A white cloud has nowhere to go. It moves, it moves everywhere. All dimensions belong to it, all directions belong to it. Nothing is rejected. Everything is, exists, in a total acceptance. Hence I call my way The Way of the White Clouds.

The white clouds have no way of their own – they drift. A way means reaching somewhere. The white clouds' way means a pathless path, a wayless way. Moving, but not with a fixed mind – moving without a mind. This has to be understood, because purpose is synonymous with mind. That's why you cannot conceive how to live without purpose...because the mind cannot exist without purpose.

And people are so absurd – they even come to me and ask: What is the purpose of meditation? Meditation cannot have any purpose because meditation basically means a state of no-mind. It is where you are, not going anywhere; where just being, just to be, is the goal.

The goal is here and now. Once the goal is somewhere else, mind starts its journey. Then the mind starts thinking, then the mind starts a process. If future is there then mind can flow, then mind can have its course, then mind has space to move. With purpose comes future, with future comes time.

A white cloud hovers in the sky, timeless – because there is no future and no mind to it. It is here and now. Each moment is total eternity. But the mind cannot exist without purpose, so mind goes on creating purposes. If the so-called worldly purposes are lost then the mind creates religious purposes, otherworldly purposes. If money has become useless, then meditation becomes useful. If the so-called world of competition, politics, has become useless, then another world of new competition, of religion, achievement, becomes meaningful. But mind always hankers for some meaning, some purpose. And to me only that mind is religious which is purposeless. But that means that mind is no more a mind at all. Think of yourself just like a white cloud, with no mind.

In Tibet they have a meditation: monks sitting on the hills, lonely, absolutely in aloneness, just meditating on white clouds drifting in the sky, continuously contemplating, and by and by being merged. Then they become white clouds – just perching on a hill like a white cloud. No mind, just being there. No resistance, no fight, nothing to be achieved, nothing to be lost. Just enjoying the very existence, celebrating the moment – the joy, the ecstasy of it.

Hence I call my way The Way of the White Clouds. And I would like you also to become white clouds drifting in the sky. I say drifting, not moving, not moving to a point – just drifting wheresoever the winds lead you. Wheresoever you happen to be, that is the goal. So the goal is not something ending somewhere, the end of the line. The goal is every moment.

Here you are *siddhas* to me, enlightened ones. Here you have achieved. Here you are as perfect as you can be, just like a Buddha, a Mahavira, or a Krishna. There is nothing else to be achieved. Right this very moment everything is there, only you are not alert. And you are not alert because your mind is in the future. You are not here. You are not aware of what is happening to you this very moment. And this has been happening always and always. For many, many millions of lives this has been happening. Every moment you have been a buddha. Not for a single moment has it been missed. It cannot be missed, that is how nature itself is, how things are. You cannot miss it!

But you are not alert and you cannot be alert because of a goal somewhere, something that has to be achieved. Because of that a barrier is created and that which you are already is missed. Once this is revealed, once this is realized, once you become aware of this, the greatest mystery of being is revealed, that everyone is perfect. That's what we mean when we say everyone is Brahman – everyone is the soul, the ultimate soul, the divine. That's what we mean when we say *tattwamasi* – you are that. Not that you have to become that, because if you have to become that, then you are not that. And if you are not that already, how can you become? The seed becomes the tree because the seed is already that. A stone cannot become a tree. The seed becomes the tree because the seed is already that!

So the question is not of becoming, the question is only of revelation. The seed is revealed this moment as a seed, next moment as a tree. So this is only a question of revelation. And if you can penetrate deeply, the seed is the tree this very moment.

Tibetan mystics or Zen masters or Sufi dervishes, they have all talked about the white clouds. The white clouds have been catching many people's inner being. A rapport is achieved, it seems, with the white clouds. Make it a meditation and then many things will come to you.

Life should not be taken as a problem. Once you start that way you are lost. Once you think life is a problem it can never be solved. That's how philosophy moves – and that's how philosophy always moves wrongly. There are no right philosophies: there cannot be. All philosophies are wrong. Philosophizing is wrong, because philosophy takes the wrong basic step of thinking of life as a problem. Once life is a problem there is no solution to it. Life is not a problem but a mystery, which is how religion takes it.

A white cloud is the most mysterious thing, suddenly appearing, suddenly disappearing. Have you ever thought at any time that clouds have no *nam-roop* – no name, no form? Even for a single moment the form is not the same. It is changing, it is becoming, it is a riverlike flow. You can give a form to the cloud, but that is your projection. A cloud has no form; it is formless or continuously being formed, it is a flux. And that's how life is. All forms are projected.

This life you call yourself a man and just one life before you could have been a woman. This life you are white and the next life you can be black. This moment you are intelligent and the next moment you behave in a stupid way. This moment you are silent and the next moment you become mad, fiery, aggressive. Have you got a form? Or are you continuously changing? You are a flux, a cloud. Have you got a name, any identity? Can you call yourself this or that? The moment you say you are this, that very moment you become aware that you are the contrary also.

You say to someone: I love you – and that very moment hate is there. You say you are a friend to someone and that very moment the enemy is laughing inside you, waiting for its moment. Some moment you say you are happy and that very moment happiness is lost and you have become unhappy. You have no identity. If you realize this you become a cloud with no form, with no name. And then drifting starts.

To me, the life of a white cloud is the life of a sannyasin, of a man who has renounced. The life of a householder is a fixed routine. It is a dead thing, it is a pattern. It has a name, it has a form. It moves on a particular track like railway lines. On the track trains are moving; they have a goal, they have to reach somewhere. But a sannyasin is like a cloud drifting in the sky – no iron tracks for him, no routes, no identities. He is no one and lives the life of a non-being, lives as if he is not.

If you can live a life as if you are not, you are on my way. And the more you are, the more disease will be there; the less you are, the more healthy you will be. The less you are, the more weightless you will be. The less you are, the more you will be divine and blissful.

When I say life is not a problem but a mystery, I mean you cannot solve it, you can become it. A problem is something to be solved intellectually; but even if you solve it nothing is achieved.

You have gathered a little more knowledge, but no ecstasy out of it. A mystery is something you can become. You can be one with it, merged. Then ecstasy arises, then bliss – then the ultimate that can happen to a being, the ultimate joy.

Religion takes life as a mystery. What can you do about a mystery? You cannot do anything about the mystery but you can do something about *you*. You can become more mysterious. And then the similar can meet with the similar, the same can meet with the same.

Look for the mysterious in life. Wherever you look – in the white clouds, in the stars in the night, in the flowers, in a flowing river – wherever you look, look for the mystery. And whenever you find that a mystery is there, meditate on it.

Meditation means: dissolve yourself before that mystery, annihilate yourself before that mystery, disperse yourself before that mystery. Be no more, and let the mystery be so total that you are absorbed in it. And suddenly a new door opens, a new perception is achieved. Suddenly the mundane world of division, of separation has disappeared, and a different, totally different world of oneness comes before you. Everything loses its boundary; everything is with others, is not divided, but one.

This can be done only if you do something with you. If you have to solve a problem, you have to do something with the problem. You have to find a key, a clue. You have to work on the problem; you have to move in a laboratory – you have to do something. If you have to encounter a mystery, you have to do something with you; with the mystery nothing can be done.

We are impotent before a mystery. That's why we go on changing mysteries into problems, because with problems we are potent, with problems we feel we are in control. With mysteries we are impotent, we cannot do anything. With mysteries we face death and we cannot manipulate.

That's why the more human intellect grows mathematical, logical, the less and less possibility of ecstasy is open before the human mind; less and less poetry is possible. Romance is lost;

life becomes factual, not symbolic.

So when I say my way is The Way of the White Clouds, it is just a symbol. The white cloud is not being used as a fact, it is used as a symbol, as a poetic symbol – as an indication of a deep merger into the mysterious and the miraculous.

Beloved Osho,
Would you tell us what
your relationship is to the white clouds?

I AM A WHITE CLOUD. There is no relationship and there cannot be. Relationship exists when you are two, divided. So relationship is really not a relationship. Wherever relationship exists there is separation. I am a white cloud. You cannot be related to a white cloud. You can become one with it and allow the white cloud to become one with you, but relationship is not possible. In relationship you remain separate, and in relationship you go on manipulating.

This is one of the miseries of human life, that even in love we create relationship. Then the love is missed. Love should not be a relationship. You should become the lover or the beloved. You should become the other and let the other become you. There should be a merger, only then conflict ceases; otherwise love becomes a conflict, a struggle. If you are, then you will try to manipulate, then you would like to possess, then you would like to be the master, then exploitation comes in. Then the other will be used as a means, not as an end.

With white clouds you cannot do that, you cannot make them wives and husbands. You cannot chain them or persuade them into a relationship. They won't allow it, they won't listen to you. They have had enough of it – that's why now they have become white clouds. You can be one with them, and then their hearts are open.

But human mind cannot think beyond relationship, because we cannot think of ourselves as if we are not. We are: howsoever we hide it, we are there. Deep down the ego is there and deep down the ego goes on manipulating.

With a white cloud this is not possible. With your ego you can look at the white cloud, think about it, but the mysteries will not be opened. The doors will remain closed. You will remain in a dark night. If your ego disappears you have become the white cloud.

In Zen they have one of the oldest traditions of painting. One Zen master had a disciple who was learning to paint, and through painting, of course, meditation. The disciple was obsessed with bamboos; he was continuously drawing and painting bamboos. The master is reported to have said to his disciple: Unless you become a bamboo nothing is going to happen.

For ten years the disciple had been drawing bamboos. He had become so efficient that even with closed eyes on a dark night without light he could draw bamboos. And his bamboos were so perfect and so alive.

But the master would not approve. He said: No, unless you become a bamboo, how can you draw it? You remain separate, you remain an onlooker, you remain a spectator. So you may have known the bamboo from without, but that is the periphery, not the soul of the bamboo. Unless you become one, unless you become a bamboo, how can you know it from within?

Ten years the disciple struggled but the master would not approve. So the disciple disappeared into the forest, into a bamboo forest. For three years nothing was heard of him. Then news started coming that he had become a bamboo. Now he doesn't draw. He lives with bamboos, he stands with bamboos. Winds blow, bamboos dance – he also dances.

Then the master went to find out. And really, the disciple had become a bamboo. The master said: Now forget all about you and bamboo.

The disciple said: But you told me to become the bamboo and I have become it.

The master said: Now forget this also, because now this is the only barrier. Deep down somewhere you are still separate and remembering that you have become the bamboo. So you are not yet a perfect bamboo, because a bamboo would not remember this. So forget it.

For ten years the bamboos were not discussed. Then one day the master called the disciple and said: Now you can draw. First become the bamboos, then forget the bamboos, so you become so perfect a bamboo that the drawing is not a drawing but a growth.

I am not related with white clouds at all. I *am* a white cloud. I would like you also to be white clouds, not related. Enough of relationship – you have suffered enough. Many, many lives you have been related with this or that, and you have suffered enough, more than enough. You have suffered more than you deserve. The suffering has been centered on the wrong concept of relationship. The wrong concept is: you have to be yourself and then related. Then there is tension, conflict, violence, aggression, and the whole hell follows.

Sartre says somewhere: The other is hell. But really, the other is not hell – the other is the other because you are the ego. If you are no more, the other has disappeared. Whenever this happens – between a man and a tree, between a man and a cloud, between a man and a woman, or between a man and a rock – whenever it happens that you are not, hell disappears. Suddenly you are trans-figured, you have entered paradise.

The old biblical story is beautiful: Adam and Eve were thrown out of the garden of Eden because they had eaten a forbidden fruit, the fruit of the tree of knowledge. This is one of the most wonderful parables ever devised. Why was the fruit of the tree of knowledge forbidden? – because the moment knowledge enters, the ego is there. The moment you know you are, you have fallen. This is the original sin.

Nobody threw Adam and Eve out of heaven. The moment they became aware that they were, the garden of Eden disappeared. For such eyes, which are filled with ego, the garden cannot exist. It is not that they have been thrown out of the garden – the garden is here and now, it is just by your side. It has always been following you wherever you go but you cannot see it. If the ego is not there you enter again, the garden is revealed. You have never been out of it.

Try this: sitting under a tree, forget yourself. Let only the tree be there. This happened to Buddha under the bodhi tree. He was not, and in that moment everything happened. Only the bodhi tree was there.

You may not be aware that for five hundred years after Buddha his statue was not created, his picture was not painted. For five hundred years continuously, whenever a Buddhist temple was created, only the picture of the bodhi tree was there. That was beautiful – because in that moment when Gautam Siddhartha became Buddha he was not there, only the tree was there. He had disappeared for a moment – only the tree was there.

Find moments when you are not, and those will be the moments when you will for the first time really be.

So I am the white cloud, and the whole effort is to make you also white clouds drifting in the sky. Nowhere to go, coming from nowhere, just being here this very moment – perfect. I don't teach you any ideals, I don't teach you any oughts. I don't say to you be this, become that. My whole teaching is simply this: Whatsoever you are, accept it so totally that nothing is left to be achieved and you will become a white cloud.

Beloved Osho,
Is it true that to really break through,
to become totally present,
to become a white cloud,
we have to live through all our dreams,
all our fantasies?
And how can that reality be as real
in response to
'Hare Krishna, Hare Rama' in Poona
as it would be in the garden of Eden
in the heart of nature?

T HE QUESTION IS NOT whether one has to live through all the dreams and fantasies or not. You *are* living in them. You are already in them. And it is not a question of choice – you cannot choose. Can you choose? Can you drop your dreams? Can you drop your fantasies? If you try to drop your dreams you will have to substitute them with other dreams. If you try to change your fantasies they will change into another type of fantasy – but they will remain dreams and fantasies.

So what is to be done? Accept them. Why be against them? This tree has red flowers, that tree has yellow flowers. So it's okay. You have certain dreams – yellow dreams. Somebody else has other dreams – blue dreams, red dreams. So it's okay. Why fight with dreams, why try to change them? When you try to change them, you believe them too much. You don't think they are dreams, you think they are real and that changing them will be significant. If dreams are dreams, why not accept them?

The moment you accept them they disappear, this is the secret. The moment you accept them they disappear – because the dreaming mind exists through rejection. The very phenomenon of a dreaming mind is rejection.

You have been rejecting many things – that's why they pop up in your dreams. You are moving on a street; you look at a beautiful woman or man. Desire arises. Suddenly you drop it: This is wrong! You reject it. Tradition, culture, society, morality say: This is not good!

You can look at a beautiful flower, nothing is bad in it. But when you look at a beautiful face something immediately goes wrong – you reject it. Now this face will become a dream. The rejected becomes the dream. Now this face will haunt you. Now in the night this face will come around you. Now this body will be hovering. The desire that you have rejected will become a dream. Desires that you have repressed will become dreams and fantasies.

So how to create a dream? The secret is: reject. The more you reject, the more dreams will be there. Those who go to the hills, those who reject life, they are filled with too many dreams. Their dreams become so real, hallucinatory, that they cannot make any distinction as to whether this is a dream or a reality.

Don't reject, otherwise you will create more dreams. Accept. Whatsoever happens to you, accept it as part of your being. Don't condemn it. The moment you become more accepting dreams will dissolve. A person who accepts his life totally becomes dreamless, because the very base has been cut. That's one thing.

Secondly, the whole is nature – the whole I say. Not only the trees, not only the clouds – the whole. Whatsoever has happened has happened because of nature. There is nothing unnatural – cannot be; otherwise how could it have happened? Everything is natural. So don't create a division – this is natural and this is unnatural. Whatsoever is, is natural. But the mind lives on distinctions, divisions. Don't allow divisions; accept whatsoever is, and accept without any analysis.

Whether you are in the market or in the hills you are in the same nature. Somewhere nature has become hills and trees, and somewhere it has become shops in the market.

Once you know the secret of accepting, even the market becomes beautiful. The market has a beauty – the life there, the activity, the beautiful madness that goes on around. It has its own beauty! And hills would not be so beautiful if there were no markets, remember. The hills are so beautiful and so silent *because* the market exists. The market gives silence to the hills.

So everywhere – whether you are in the market, or doing 'Hare Krishna, Hare Rama', or sitting under a tree silently – take it as one expanse, don't divide it. And when you are dancing, doing 'Hare Krishna, Hare Rama', enjoy it! It is the way you are flowering, this very moment. 'Hare Krishna, Hare Rama' can become a flowering in you; it has become a flowering for many. When Mahaprabhu Chaitanya was dancing in the villages of Bengal and doing his kirtan, 'Hare Krishna, Hare Rama', it was a flowering. It was one of the most beautiful things that has ever happened. Not only is Buddha sitting under a bodhi tree beautiful, a Chaitanya Mahaprabhu dancing in the streets with 'Hare Krishna, Hare Rama' is also beautiful – the same, just the other extreme.

You can sit under a tree and can forget yourself so completely that you have disappeared. You can dance in a street and be absorbed in your kirtan, in your singing, in your dancing, so totally that you have disappeared. The secret is total absorption wherever it happens.

It happens to different people in different ways. We cannot conceive of Buddha dancing; he was not that type, not a dancing type. You may be a dancing type, so don't force yourself under a bodhi tree or you will be in trouble. Just forcing yourself, stilling yourself, will be violent. Then your face will not become like a Buddha; it will be tortured, it will be a self-torture. You may be like Chaitanya, you may be like Meera....

Find out the way *your* cloud moves, where it drifts, and allow it full freedom to move and drift. Wherever it goes it will reach to the divine. Just don't fight, flow. Don't push the river, flow with it. A dance is beautiful, but you must be totally in it – that's the point. Don't reject anything, rejection is irreligious. Accept totally, acceptance is prayer.

Enough for today.

The Mystery

CHAPTER TWO

Beloved Osho,
Beautiful white cloud,
Why are we so fortunate to have you with us –
and why are we with you?

HYS ARE ALWAYS UNANSWERABLE. To the mind it seems that whenever you can ask a why it can be answered. But that is one of the fallacious assumptions. No why has ever been answered or can be answered. Existence is – no why about it. If you ask, if you persist, you may create an answer – but that answer will be a created one; it will not really be an answer. Questioning itself is foundationally absurd.

The trees are – you cannot ask why.

The sky is – you cannot ask why.

Existence exists, rivers flow, clouds float – you cannot ask why.

The mind asks why, I know it. Mind is curious; it wants to know the why of everything. But this is a disease in the mind, and it is something which cannot be satisfied because if you answer one why, then another arises immediately. Every answer only creates more questions. And the mind will not be satisfied unless the ultimate answer has been given to you – and there can be no ultimate answer. By ultimate answer, I mean that you cannot ask any why anymore. But there is no possibility of such a state. Whatsoever is said, why again becomes relevant.

This has been the whole absurd effort of philosophies: Why is this world? So they thought and they created a theory about it: God created it. But why did God create it? Then again more theories and then finally: Why is God? So the first thing to know about is this quality of the mind which goes on asking whys. Just as leaves grow out of trees, whys grow out of the mind – you cut one, many more grow. You may collect many answers but *the* answer will not be there. And unless the answer is there the mind goes on, restless in its search. So this is the first thing I would like to say to you: Don't insist much on whys.

Why do we insist? Why do we want to know the cause? Why do we want to go deep into a thing and come to the very base of it? Why? ...Because if you know every why, if you know every answer about a thing, you have become the master of it. Then the thing can be manipulated. Then the thing is not a mystery; there is no awe, no wonder about it. You have known it, you have killed the mystery.

The mind is a killer, a murderer – the murderer of all mysteries. And mind is always at ease with anything dead. With anything alive mind feels uneasy, because you cannot be the total master. The living is always there – unpredictable. The future cannot be fixed with a living thing, and you don't know where it will go, where it will lead. With a dead thing everything is certain and fixed. You are at ease. You are not worried about it, you are certain.

To make everything certain is a deep urge in the mind because mind is afraid of life. Mind creates science just to kill every possibility of life. Mind tries to find explanations. Once an explanation is found the mystery is dissolved. You ask a why and it is answered, then the mind is at ease. What have you achieved through it? You have not achieved anything, you have lost something – a mystery has been lost.

Mystery makes you uneasy because it is something greater than you, something which you cannot manipulate, something which you cannot use as a thing; something which overwhelms, something which overpowers, something before which you are naked and impotent – something before which you simply dissolve. Mystery gives you a feeling of death; hence so much inquiry about whys – why this, why that. This is the first thing to be remembered.

But don't think that I am avoiding your question. I am not avoiding it, I am telling you something about the mind – why it asks.

And if you can retain the feeling of mystery, I am going to answer. If the feeling of mystery is retained then answering is not dangerous, it can be useful. Then every answer leads you into a deeper mystery. Then the whole thing becomes qualitatively different. Then you ask not to get an explanation, then you ask to get deeper into the mystery. Then the curiosity is not mental, then it becomes an inquiry – a deep inquiry of being.

See the difference? If you are hankering after an explanation then it is bad, and I will be the last one to fulfill it because then I become an enemy to you, then I make things dead around you. Theologians have made even God a dead thing – they have explained it so much, they have answered so many things about God, that's why God is dead. Humanity has not killed him – the priests, they have killed him. They explained him so much that no mystery has remained. And what is God if there is no mystery in it? If it is just a theory you can discuss, a doctrine you can analyze, a belief you can accept or deny, then you are greater and this God is just part of the furniture of your mind – it is a dead thing.

Whenever I am talking to you remember this always: whatsoever I say is not to kill your inquiry, is not to give you explanations. I am not interested in giving you answers. Rather, on the contrary, it is to make you more inquiring, deeply penetrating into the mysteries. My answers will give you deeper questions, and a moment will come when all questioning will drop – not that you have received all the answers, but because every answer is futile. And then the mystery is total, then it is all around, without and within. Then you have become part of it, then you float in it, then you have also become a mysterious being, and only then do the doors open.

Now I can answer why I am with you, and why you are with me here.

The first thing: it is not only here this moment that you are with me – you have been before. Life is so interrelated, it is a riverlike flow. We divide it into past, present and future, but the division is just utilitarian. Life is not divided. The flow of life is contemporaneous.

The river Ganges at the very source, the river Ganges passing through the Himalayas, the river Ganges on the plains, the river Ganges falling into the ocean – this is one. It is contemporaneous. The origin and the end, the beginning and the end, are not two separate things – it is one flow. It is not past and future, it is eternal present. This has to be understood very deeply.

You have been with me. You are with me. It is not a question of past. If you can be silent, if you can put your mind aside a little, if you can become a white cloud perched on a hill, not thinking, just being, you will feel it. You have been with me, you are with me, you will be with me. This being with me is not a question of time.

Somebody asked Jesus: You talk about Abraham – how do you know? ...Because there is a long gap between the days of Abraham and Jesus, thousands of years. And Jesus said a very mysterious sentence, the most mysterious that Jesus ever asserted. He said: Before Abraham was, I am. Before Abraham was, I am. Time dissolved.

Life is eternal present. We have been here and now always – forever, forever. Different shapes, different forms, of course, different situations. But we have been always and always.

Individuals are fictions. Life is not divided. We are not like islands, we are one. This oneness has to be felt, and once you feel this oneness time disappears, space becomes meaningless. Suddenly you are transported from both time and space. Then you are – simply you are.

Somebody asked Buddha: Who are you? And Buddha said: I belong to no rank. I just am. I am, but I don't belong to any rank.

Right now you can have the glimpse. If you are not thinking, then who are you? Where is time? Is there any past? Is there any future then? Then this moment becomes the eternity. The whole time process is just a long extended now. The whole of space is just expanded here.

So when you ask why I am here, or why you are here, it is because this is the only way of being. I cannot be anywhere else, you cannot be anywhere else. This is how we have become joined together. You may not be able to see it right now. The links are not so clear for you because your own unconscious is not clear for you, because you don't know yourself in your totality. One-tenth of your being is known to you, nine-tenths is just in darkness.

You are like a forest with a little clearing. Trees have been cut, and a small place has been created in which to live. But just beyond that small clearing the dark forest exists. You don't know the boundaries of it. And you are so afraid of darkness and the wild animals that you never leave your clearing. But your clearing is just part of this dark forest. You know only a part of your being.

I see you as your total darkness, the whole forest of you. And once I see a single individual in his totality all individuals are involved, because that forest is not separate. In that darkness boundaries meet, mingle and become one.

You are here. If I become too attentive to one individual, then I am focusing myself. But still, even focusing, I continually feel your boundaries are mingling with the other. So for certain purposes I may take you as an individual, but in reality it is not so. When I am not focused I simply look at you without seeing you – just a look, then you are no more there. Your boundaries are meeting with everyone else's, and not only with man and human beings – with trees, with rocks, with sky...everything. Boundaries are fictions, hence individuals are fictitious.

I am here because I cannot be anywhere else. This is how life has happened. You are here because you cannot be anywhere else. This is how life has happened to you. But it is difficult to accept it. Why is it difficult to accept it? – because then you cannot manipulate it, then life becomes greater than you.

If I say you are here because you are a great seeker of truth, then you are at ease. If you are here because you are a great seeker, then the ego is fulfilled. Then if you choose, you can go. Then you are the chooser. Then you are controlling life, not controlled by life. But I don't say that, I say you are here because life has happened this way. You could not have chosen, it is not your choice. Even if you leave that will not be your choice. Again, that will be how life happens to you. If you choose to remain, that too is not a choice.

Choice is not possible. Choice is possible only with the ego.

Whenever ego is not fed, uneasiness, discomfort, is felt. So there are two ways to be at ease: one is to go on feeding the ego, another is simply to drop it. And remember, the first way is temporary. The more you feed the ego the more it demands, and there is no end to it.

So I tell you: life has happened in such a way that I am here and you are here. And it has happened many times before, and it will continue happening the same way. If you can realize this, much more will immediately become possible. If you realize this you will be more open, less closed, more vulnerable, more receptive. Then you are not afraid. Then life can pass through you. Then life becomes just a breeze, and you become an empty room, and life comes and goes...and you allow it. Allowing is the secret – the secret of all secrets.

Hence I emphasize, insist, that you are not here because of any choice on your part. I am not here because of any choice on my part. As far as I am concerned there cannot be any choice, because I am not. As far as you are concerned, you may be under the delusion that you are here because of your choice, but that is not a fact.

And I am not going to feed your egos because they have to be destroyed. That's what the whole effort is: how to destroy you – because once your boundaries are destroyed you are infinite. Right this moment this can happen. There is no barrier to it – there is only your clinging.

Many people come to me and ask: Have we been with you before? If I say yes, they feel very good. If I say no, they feel dejected, depressed. Why? We live in fictions. You are here with me – that is not so significant; you were with me in the past – that seems to be more significant. And you are missing this moment when you can really be with me – because to be with me is not a physical phenomenon. You can sit by my side and you may not be with me. You can cling to me for years and you may not be with me for a single moment – because to be with me only means that you are not.

I am not, and if even for a single moment you are also not there, there will be a meeting – then two emptinesses meet. Remember, only two emptinesses can meet, there is no other meeting possible. Whenever you have a meeting, it means two emptinesses merging.

The ego is very solid, too substantial to merge. So you can struggle, clash, but you cannot meet. You may think that this clash of two egos is a meeting; it *is* a sort of meeting. You come together, but you are never together. You meet and still you don't meet. You touch each other and still you remain untouched. Your inner emptiness remains a virgin land, it has not been penetrated.

But when the ego is not there, when you are not feeling much I, when you are not thinking about yourself at all, when there is no self, that's what Buddha calls *anatta* – no-selfness. He was very much misunderstood. In India people were talking of *atman* – the self, the supreme self. Everybody was searching for the supreme self – how to become the ultimate self. And then Buddha comes and he says: There is no self to be attained; rather, please, be a no-self. His teaching could not be accepted. Buddha was thrown out of this country. He was not accepted anywhere. A Buddha is always thrown out. Wherever he goes he will be thrown out, because he hits on you so deeply you cannot tolerate it. He says you are not.

When you are empty, when just a vacuum exists, meeting happens. Anybody who is capable of being empty will merge. And this is the only way to become one with existence. You may call it love, you may call it prayer, you may call it meditation, or whatsoever you like.

You are here because life has happened that way.

I am here because this is how life has happened to me.

And this possibility of your being near me can be used, can be misused, can be missed altogether. If you miss, then too it will not be for the first time. Many times you have been with me. It may not have been exactly with me; many times you were with a Buddha and that was to be with me. Many times you were with a *jinna*, with a Mahavira, and that was to be with me. Many times you were around Jesus or Moses or Lao Tzu – that was being with me. A Lao Tzu or a Buddha cannot be defined in any way; they are two emptinesses, and two emptinesses have no qualities to differ. You may have been with a Lao Tzu and I say you were with me, because there is nothing to make any distinction. A Lao Tzu is an emptiness. Two emptinesses are just the same, you cannot make any distinction. But you missed. You have been missing many times. You can miss again.

And remember, you are wise, clever, calculating. Even if you miss you will miss very wisely. You will rationalize it. You will say there was nothing to be gained. Or you will find arguments that hide the fact. If you become alert to this possibility of missing, then meeting is immediately possible. And I say immediately – there is no need to postpone it.

And this is significant, that life has happened in such a way that you are here. Millions are there and life has not happened in such a way. You are fortunate, but don't make that point an ego food – because if your ego takes anything out of it and becomes stronger, you have missed that fortune. You are fortunate, but it remains an open possibility. You can grow into it, you can drop out of it. And this is rare – rare for many reasons.

First, it is very difficult to be attracted to a person who is empty – very difficult, because emptiness is not such a magnetic force. You are attracted to a man who has got something. Why are we attracted to a man who has got something? – because we have desires. We also want to get something. You are attracted to a politician who has power because you are power-oriented, you want power. So whosoever has it becomes the idol, the hero. You are attracted to a person who has fabulous riches. Because you are poor, deep down you hanker after riches. So whosoever has them becomes the ideal. But why should one be attracted to a person who has nothing?

This is fortunate, a rare possibility. Sometimes life happens in such a way that you become attracted to a person who has got nothing, who is empty. You are not going to gain anything out of him; rather, everything has to be lost with him. It is a gamble. So you are gamblers – that's why you are here. And unless you gamble totally you will miss, because this gambling cannot be partial – parts cannot be accepted. That is not the rule of this game.

So don't hold back, put in everything you have. It is dangerous and risky. That's why I say it is rare to be attracted to a Buddha or to a Jesus. Very few are attracted. You know about Jesus...very few, only twelve disciples. And very ordinary men: some fisherman, some woodcutter, some farmer – not significant in any way, just common people. Why are such common people attracted to Buddha or Jesus? To be common is a very uncommon quality, because those who are not common, they are after some ego-trip – riches, power, status. A farmer, a fisherman, a woodcutter – insignificant people, absolutely ordinary, not looking for any achievement – they become attracted to Jesus.

To be common is rare; to be absolutely ordinary is really extraordinary. Zen masters are reported to have said continuously: Become ordinary and then you become extraordinary. Every ordinary being is trying to be extraordinary – that is the ordinary thing. Just remain ordinary. That means not searching for anything, not seeking any achievement, really, not in any way goal-oriented, just living moment-to-moment, drifting. That's what I was saying to you – drifting like a white cloud.

Your being here is rare for other reasons also...because human mind is always afraid of death. It clings to life, a lust for life is there. Even in misery it clings to life – a deep fear of death. And when a person comes to me he is coming, really, to die, he is coming to dissolve. I will be an abyss to him, a bottomless abyss in which he will fall and fall and fall and reach nowhere! If you look into me you will feel dizzy. If you stare into my eyes you will see the abyss, and then the fear will grip you – and the falling and falling.... Just think of a leaf falling into an abyss – and the abyss is infinite and there is no bottom to it so it cannot reach anywhere, it can only disappear; falling, falling, falling, it will disappear.

The religious journey begins but never ends. You come to me, you fall into me, you disappear, you never reach anywhere. But that disappearance is the delight. No other delight has ever been known, no other delight is there. The delight of total disappearance! Just as a dewdrop in the morning disappears when the sun rises, or just as in the night an earthen lamp burns, the wind comes and the flame goes out and darkness.... The flame has disappeared and you cannot find it anywhere – the same way you disappear.

It is rare to seek suicide: this is suicide, the real suicide! You can kill the body anywhere, but you cannot kill the self anywhere. Here you are ready for the final suicide – to kill the self.

But don't make all these things explanations, they are not. I am always anti-explanation. If all this makes you more mysterious, if all this makes you more vague, so far, so good. If your mind goes up in smoke and you don't know what is what, that's the best condition.

Beloved Osho,
As with all clouds,
white clouds are directed by the wind.
What is the present direction of the wind?
Are there special potentialities in this age?

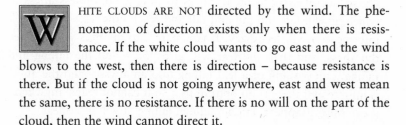 HITE CLOUDS ARE NOT directed by the wind. The phenomenon of direction exists only when there is resistance. If the white cloud wants to go east and the wind blows to the west, then there is direction – because resistance is there. But if the cloud is not going anywhere, east and west mean the same, there is no resistance. If there is no will on the part of the cloud, then the wind cannot direct it.

You can direct only when somebody is not ready to float, to relax, to let go. But the phenomenon of the cloud means it is the very let-go. If the wind says east the cloud is ready; it is already on the move towards the east. There has not been a single thought of no; there has not been a single denial. If the cloud was moving to the west and the wind starts blowing east, the cloud moves to the east. The wind is not directing; direction is needed only when someone is against.

People come to me and they say: Direct us – and I know what they are saying; Guide us – and I know what they are saying. They are not ready; otherwise, what is the need of being directed and guided? It is enough that you are here with me, and everything will happen. The wind blows to the east and you start floating towards the east. But you say: Guide; you say: Direct. You are saying that you are against. You have a denial, you have a rejection; you will fight. And if there is no will on the part of the cloud, how can you make a distinction which is the cloud and which is the wind? The boundary exists with will.

Remember this, this must become your foundational insight: the boundary between you and me exists because of your will. You are there, surrounded by a will. Then I come and there is conflict. A cloud has no will, so where is the boundary? Where does the cloud end and the wind begin? The wind and the cloud are one. The cloud is part of the wind; the wind is part of the cloud. The phenomenon is one, undivided.

And the wind goes on blowing in all directions. So the problem is not to choose the direction; the problem is how to become the cloud. The wind goes on blowing in all directions. It moves, it changes. It is always running from this corner to the other. Really, there is no direction, there is no map; the whole thing is uncharted. There is no one guiding it and saying: Now go to the east, now go to the west. The whole of existence 'waves' it. It is a waving existence – all directions belong to it. And when I say all directions, I mean the good and the bad both, I mean the moral and the immoral both. When I say all directions, I mean *all*.

The wind is blowing in all directions. This has always been so.

So remember: there has not been a specifically religious age nor an anti-religious age, there cannot be. People think this way because that too gives them ego-trips. In India, people think that in the old days, in ancient days, there was a religious age on the earth and now everything has gone rotten – this is the darkest age. This is all nonsense. No age is religious, no age is anti-religious. Religiousness is not concerned with the time, it is concerned with the quality of the mind.

So it is not a question of whether the cloud is going to the east, then it will be religious, or going to the west and it will be anti-religious. No. If the cloud has no will, the cloud is religious wherever it goes. And if the cloud has will then wherever it goes it is irreligious. And there are both types of clouds: very few who are will-less, millions who have their wills and projections and desires and ideas. They fight with the wind. The more they fight, the more anguish is created. And fighting leads nowhere, because nothing can be done. Whether you fight or not the wind will go to the east and you will have to go to the east. You can only carry a notion that you have been fighting and you are a great warrior, that's all.

One who understands stops fighting. He is not even trying to swim, he simply goes with the flood. This very current he uses as a vehicle; he becomes one with it and moves with it. This is what I call surrender, and this is what the old scriptures called the attitude of the devotee. Surrendered, you are not. Then wherever the wind leads you, you will go. You don't have any will of your own. This has always been so.

In the past there were buddhas, floating white clouds; in the present there are buddhas, floating white clouds. In the past there were mad black clouds filled with will, desire, future; they are there today also. With will and desire you are a black cloud – heavy. With no will, no desire, you are a white cloud – weightless. And the possibility for both of these is always open. It is up to you whether to allow the letgo or not.

Don't think of time and age. Time and age are indifferent. They don't force anyone to become a buddha; they don't prevent anyone from becoming a buddha. Time and age are just indifferent. Allow yourself to be empty and this is the golden age. Allow yourself to be too much filled with desire and this is the darkest age possible, the *kali yuga*. You create your time and age around you. You live in your own age and time.

Remember, we are not contemporaries in that way. A person like Jesus is ancient; he may be just here, but he is ancient. He lives so eternally, you cannot call him modern. He lives so totally that you cannot say that he belongs to a fragment of time. He is not part of the world of fashions which come and go. Living with the absolute, you become absolute. Living with the eternal, you become eternal. Living with the timeless, you become timeless.

But the question is still pertinent in another sense also. All over the world people have the feeling that a certain age, a certain time, a certain climax, a crescendo, is nearing – something is going to explode, as if we are reaching a particular point in human evolution. But I would like to say to you: this is again the ego-trip for the age. Every age thinks that way: something is reaching a climax with us; we are here, something special is going to happen on the earth. This has always been so!

It is reported that when Adam and Eve were thrown out of the garden of Eden, Adam said to Eve just as they passed through the door: We are passing through the greatest transformation ever known in history. The very first man saying and thinking: The greatest transformation....

Every age thinks that things are reaching to a crescendo, to an ultimate point, to an omega point, where everything will explode and a new being will be born. But these are hopes, ego-trips, not very meaningful. You will be here for a few years; then others will be here and they will think the same. The crescendo is reached not with the age but with the individual being. The climax *is* reached but it is always reached with consciousness, not with a collective unconscious.

You can become a religious person. And the time is good, the time is always good. Don't think of others too much because this may be just an escape from yourself. Don't think of the age and don't think of humanity – because mind is so cunning, human mind is so cunning, you don't know....

I have been reading a letter from a friend, and he says that he became so frustrated with all his love affairs, whenever he was in love it was such misery, that he stopped loving any individual and started to love the whole of humanity. Now, the whole of humanity is easy to love; and those who cannot love will always love the whole of humanity, there is no problem. To love an individual is very, very difficult; it can be hell itself. It can be hell itself because it can become heaven.

We go on avoiding. People start thinking about others just to avoid thinking about themselves. They start thinking about the age, the time, the planets, and what is going to happen to human consciousness, just to avoid encountering the basic problem: What is going to happen to my consciousness?

Your consciousness should be the target.

Every time is good, all times are good for it.

Enough for today.

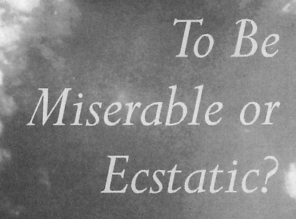

*To Be
Miserable or
Ecstatic?*

CHAPTER THREE

Beloved Osho,
You once told us a story about an old man
who was over one hundred years old.
One day, on his birthday, he was asked
why it was that he was always happy.
He replied: Every morning when I wake up
I have the choice to be happy or unhappy,
and I choose to be happy.
How is it that we usually choose to be unhappy?
How is it that we don't feel aware of the choice?

HIS IS ONE of the most complex human problems. It has to be considered very deeply – and it is not theoretical, it concerns you. This is how everybody is behaving – always choosing the wrong, always choosing the sad, the depressed, the miserable. There must be profound reasons for it, and there are.

The first thing: the way human beings are brought up plays a very definite role in it. If you are unhappy you gain something from it, you always gain. If you are happy you always lose. From the very beginning an alert child starts feeling the distinction. Whenever he is unhappy everybody is sympathetic towards him; he gains sympathy. Everybody tries to be loving towards him; he gains love. And even more than that, whenever he is unhappy everybody is attentive towards him – he gains attention.

Attention works like food for the ego, a very alcoholic stimulant. It gives you energy; you feel you are somebody. Hence so much need, so much desire to get attention. If everybody is looking at you, you become important. If nobody is looking at you, you feel as if you are not there, you are no more, you are a non-being.

People looking at you, people caring about you give you energy.

The ego exists in relationship. The more people pay attention to you the more you gain ego. If nobody looks at you the ego dissolves. If everybody has completely forgotten you, how can the ego exist? How can you feel that you are? Hence the need for societies, associations, clubs. All over the world clubs exist – Rotary, Lions, Masonic Lodges – millions of clubs and societies. These societies and clubs exist only to give attention to people who cannot get attention in other ways.

It is difficult to become a president of a country, it is difficult to become a mayor of a corporation. It is easier to become the president of a Lions Club, then a particular group gives you attention. You are very important – doing nothing! Lions Clubs, Rotary Clubs...doing nothing at all but still they feel they are something important. And the president goes on changing – one this year, another next year. Everybody gets attention. It is a mutual arrangement, and everybody feels important.

From the very beginning the child learns the politics. The politics are: look miserable, then you get sympathy, then everybody is attentive. Look ill – you become important. An ill child becomes dictatorial; the whole family has to follow him – whatsoever he says is the rule. When he is happy nobody listens to him. When he is healthy nobody cares about him. When he is perfect nobody is attentive. From the very beginning we start choosing the miserable, the sad, the pessimistic, the darker side of life. That's one thing.

A second thing related to it is: whenever you are happy, whenever you are joyful, whenever you feel ecstatic and blissful, everybody is jealous of you. Jealousy means that everybody is antagonistic, nobody is friendly; at that moment everybody is an enemy. So you have learned not to be so ecstatic that everybody becomes inimical towards you – not to show your bliss, not to laugh.

Look at people when they laugh. They laugh very calculatingly. It is not a belly laugh, it is not coming from the very depth of their being. They first look at you, then they judge...and then they laugh. And they laugh to a particular extent, the extent you will tolerate, the extent which will not be taken amiss, the extent where nobody will become jealous. Even our smiles are political. Laughter has disappeared, bliss has become absolutely unknown, and to be ecstatic is almost impossible because it is not allowed. If you are miserable nobody will think you are mad. If you are ecstatic and dancing everybody will think you are mad. Dance is rejected, singing is not accepted. A blissful man – and we think something has gone wrong.

What type of society is this? If someone is miserable everything is okay; he fits because the whole society is miserable more or less. He is a member, he belongs to us. If somebody becomes ecstatic we think he has gone berserk, insane. He doesn't belong to us – and we feel jealous, and because of jealousy we condemn him. Because of jealousy we will try in every way to put him back to his old state. We call that old state normality. Psychoanalysts will help, psychiatrists will help to bring that man to the normal misery.

In the West the whole society is turning against psychedelics. The law, the state, the government, the legal experts, the high courts, the legislators, priests, popes – everybody is turning against. They are not really against psychedelics – they are against people being ecstatic. They are not against alcohol, they are not against other things which are drugs, but they are against psychedelics because psychedelics can create a chemical change in you. And the old crust that the society has created around you, the imprisonment in misery, can be broken, there can be a breakthrough. You can come out of it, even for a few moments, and be ecstatic.

Society cannot allow ecstasy. Ecstasy is the greatest revolution.

I repeat it: ecstasy is the greatest revolution.

If people become ecstatic the whole society will have to change, because this society is based on misery. If people are blissful you cannot lead them to war – to Vietnam or to Egypt or to Israel. No. Someone who is blissful will just laugh and say: This is nonsense!

If people are blissful you cannot make them obsessed with money. They will not waste their whole lives just accumulating money. It will look like madness to them that a person is destroying his whole life, just exchanging his life for dead money, dying and accumulating money – and the money will be there when he is. dead. This is absolute madness! But this madness cannot be seen unless you are ecstatic.

If people are ecstatic then the whole pattern of this society will have to change. This society exists on misery. Misery is a great investment for this society. So we bring up children...from the very beginning we create a leaning towards misery. That's why they always choose misery.

In the morning for everybody there is a choice. And not only in the morning – every moment there is a choice to be miserable or to be happy. You always choose to be miserable because there is an investment. You always choose to be miserable because that has become a habit, a pattern, you have always done that. You have become efficient at doing it, it has become a track. The moment your mind has to choose, it immediately flows towards misery.

Misery seems to be downhill, ecstasy seems to be uphill. Ecstasy looks very difficult to reach – but it is not so. The real thing is quite the opposite: ecstasy is downhill, misery is uphill. Misery is a very difficult thing to achieve, but you have achieved it, you have done the impossible – because misery is so anti-nature. Nobody wants to be miserable and everybody is miserable.

Society has done a great job. Education, culture, and the culturing agencies, parents, teachers – they have done a great job. They have made miserable creatures out of ecstatic creators. Every child is born ecstatic. Every child is born a god, and every man dies a madman.

Unless you recover, unless you reclaim your childhood, you will not be able to become the white clouds I am talking about. This is the whole work for you, the whole *sadhana* – how to regain childhood, how to reclaim it. If you can become children again then there is no misery. I don't mean that for a child there are no moments of misery – there are, but still there is no misery.

Try to understand this. A child can become miserable, he can be unhappy, intensely unhappy in a moment, but he is so total in that unhappiness, he is so one with that unhappiness, that there is no division. The child separate from unhappiness is not there. The child is not looking at his unhappiness as separate, divided. The child *is* unhappiness – he is so involved in it. And when you become one with unhappiness, unhappiness is not unhappiness. If you become so one with it, even that has a beauty of its own.

So look at a child – an unspoilt child I mean. If he is angry then his whole energy becomes anger; nothing is left behind, no hold-up. He has moved and become anger; there is nobody manipulating and controlling it. There is no mind. The child has become anger – he is not angry, he has become the anger. And then see the beauty, the flowering of anger. The child never looks ugly – even in anger he looks beautiful. He just looks more intense, more vital, more alive – a volcano ready to erupt. Such a small child, such a great energy, such an atomic being – with the whole universe to explore. And after this anger the child will be silent. After this anger the child will be very peaceful. After this anger the child will relax. We may think it is very miserable to be in that anger, but the child is not miserable – he has enjoyed it.

If you become one with anything you become blissful. If you separate yourself from anything, even if it is happiness, you will become miserable.

So this is the key. To be separate as an ego is the base of all misery; to be one, to be flowing with whatsoever life brings to you, to be in it so intensely, so totally that you are no more, you are lost, then everything is blissful. The choice is there, but you have even become unaware of the choice. You have been choosing the wrong so continuously, it has become such a dead habit, that you simply choose it automatically. There is no choice left.

Become alert. Each moment when you are choosing to be miserable, remember: this is your choice. Even this mindfulness will help – the alertness that this is my choice and I am responsible, and this is what I am doing to myself, this is my doing. Immediately you will feel a difference. The quality of mind will have changed. It will be easier for you to move towards happiness.

And once you know that this is your choice then the whole thing has become a game. Then if you love to be miserable, be miserable, but remember this is your choice and don't complain. There is nobody else who is responsible for it. This is your drama. If you like this way, if you like a miserable way, if you want to pass through life in misery, then this is your choice, your game. You are playing it – play it well! Then don't go and ask people how not to be miserable. That is absurd. Don't go and ask masters and gurus how to be happy. The so-called gurus exist because you are foolish. You create the misery, and then you go and ask others how to uncreate it. And you will go on creating misery because you are not alert to what you are doing.

From this very moment try – try to be happy and blissful.

I will tell you one of the deepest laws of life. You may not have thought about it at all. You have heard – the whole of science depends on it – that cause and effect is the base. You create the cause and the effect follows. Life is a causal link. You put the seed in the soil and it will sprout. If the cause is there then the tree will follow. The fire is there – you put your hand in it and it will burn. The cause is there and the effect will follow. You take poison and you will die. You arrange for the cause and then the effect follows. This is one of the most basic scientific laws, that cause and effect is the innermost link of all processes of life.

Religion knows about a second law which is still deeper than this. But the second law which is deeper than this will look absurd if you don't know it and experiment with it. Religion says: Produce the effect and the cause follows. This is absolutely absurd in scientific terms. Science says: If the cause is there the effect follows. Religion says the converse is also true: you create the effect, and see...the cause follows.

There is a situation in which you feel happy. A friend has come, a beloved has called; a situation is the cause – you feel happy. Happiness is the effect, the coming of the beloved is the cause. Religion says: Be happy and the beloved comes. Create the effect and the cause follows. And this is my own experience, that the second law is more basic than the first. I have been doing it and it has been happening. Just be happy and the beloved comes. Just be happy and friends are there. Just be happy and everything follows.

Jesus says the same thing in different words: Seek ye first the kingdom of God, then all else will follow. But the kingdom of God is the end, the effect. Seek ye first the end – the end means the effect, the result – and the cause will follow. This is as it should be.

It is not only that you place a seed in the soil and the tree follows; let there be a tree and there are millions of seeds. If cause is followed by effect, effect is again followed by cause. This is the chain. Then it becomes a circle – start from anywhere, create the cause or create the effect. And I tell you, it is easier to create the effect because the effect depends totally upon you; the cause may not be so dependent on you. If I say I can only be happy when a certain friend is there, then it depends on a certain friend, whether he is there or not. If I say I cannot be happy until I attain this much wealth, then it depends on the whole world and the economic situation and every-thing. It may not happen, and then I cannot be happy.

Cause is beyond me, effect is within me. Cause is in the sur-roundings, in the situations – cause is without. Effect is me. If I can create the effect the cause will follow. Choose happiness – that means you are choosing the effect – and then see what happens. Choose ecstasy and see what happens. Choose to be blissful and see what happens. Your whole life will change immediately and you will see miracles happening around you – because now you have created the effect and causes will have to follow.

This will look magical; you can even call it the law of magic. The first is the law of science and the second is the law of magic. Reli-gion is magic and you can be the magician. That's what I teach you: to be the magician, to know the secret of magic. Try it. You have been trying the other your whole life – not only this but many other lives also. Now listen to me. Try this magic formula, this mantra I give to you. Create the effect and see what happens. Causes imme-diately surround you, they follow. Don't wait for the causes; you have waited long enough. Choose happiness and you will be happy.

What is the problem? Why can't you choose? Why can't you work on this law? – because your mind, the whole mind, which has been trained by scientific thinking, says that if you are not happy and you try to be happy, that happiness will be artificial. If you are not happy and you try to be happy, that will be just acting, that will not be real. This is what scientific thinking says – that that will not be real, you will be just acting. But you don't know. Life energy has its own ways of working. If you can act totally it will become the real. The only thing is, the actor must not be there. Move totally in it, then there is no difference. If you are acting halfheartedly then it will remain artificial.

If I say to you: Dance and sing and be blissful, and you try half-heartedly just to see what happens, but you remain behind...and you go on thinking: This is just artificial. I am trying but this is not coming, this is not spontaneous – then it will remain acting, a waste of time.

If you try, then try wholeheartedly. Don't remain behind, move into it, become the acting – dissolve the actor into acting and then see what happens. It will become the real and then you will feel it is spontaneous. *You* have not done it, you will know then that it has happened. But unless you are total this cannot happen. Create the effect, be in it completely, see and observe the results.

I can make you kings without kingdoms, only you have to act like kings, and act so totally that before you even a real king will appear as if he is just acting. And when the whole energy has moved into it, it becomes reality! Energy makes anything real. If you wait for kingdoms they never come. Even for a Napoleon, for an Alexander, who had big kingdoms, they never came. They remained miserable because they didn't come to realize the second, more basic and primal law of life. Alexander was trying to create a bigger kingdom, to become a bigger king. His whole life was wasted in creating the kingdom, and then there was no time left for him to be king. He died before the kingdom was complete.

This has happened to many. The kingdom can never be complete. The world is infinite – your kingdom is bound to remain partial. With a partial kingdom how can you be a total king? Your kingdom is bound to be limited, and with a limited kingdom how can you be the emperor? It is impossible. But you *can* be the emperor. Just create the effect.

Swami Ram, one of the mystics of this century, went to America. He used to call himself Badshah Ram – Emperor Ram – and he was a beggar! Somebody said to him: You are just a beggar, but you go on calling yourself the emperor. So Ram said: Don't look at my things, look at me. And he was right, because if you look at things then everybody is a beggar – even an emperor. He may be a bigger beggar, that's all. When Ram said: Look at me! in that moment Ram was the emperor. If you looked, the emperor was there.

Create the effect, become the emperor, be a magician – and from this very moment, because there is no need to wait. One has to wait if the kingdom has to come first. If the cause has to be created first, then one has to wait and wait and wait and postpone. There is no need to wait to create the effect. You can be the emperor this very moment.

When I say: Be! just be the emperor and see – the kingdom follows, I have known it through my experience. I am not talking to you about a theory or a doctrine. Be happy, and in that peak of happiness you will see the whole world is happy with you.

There is an old saying: Weep and you weep alone, laugh and the world laughs with you. Even the trees, the rocks, the sand, the clouds...if you can create the effect and be ecstatic, they will all dance with you. Then the whole existence becomes a dance, a celebration. But it depends on you, if you can create the effect. And I say to you, you *can* create it. It is the easiest thing possible. It looks very difficult because you have not tried it yet.

Give it a try!

Beloved Osho,
We hear what you say, but we in the West
keep the information in our heads.
How can we get out of our heads?
What methods can we use,
and can willpower help us?

N O, WILLPOWER WILL NOT HELP YOU. Willpower is not a power at all, because will depends on the ego – a very tiny phenomenon; it cannot create much power. When you are will-less, then you are powerful – because then you are one with the whole.

Deep down, willpower is a sort of impotence. To hide the fact that we are impotent we create will. We create the opposite to deceive ourselves and others. People who feel they are foolish try to show that they are wise. They are constantly aware that they are foolish so they do everything to look wise. People who are ugly or feel they are ugly always try to beautify themselves – even a painted beauty, just a face, a mask. People who are weak always try to look strong. The opposite is created; that is the only way to hide the reality within. A Hitler is a weakling; that's why he creates so much willpower around himself, just to hide the fact. A person who is really strong will be unaware that he is strong. Strength will be flowing, it will be there, but he will not even be conscious of it.

Says Lao Tzu: A man of real virtue never knows that he is virtuous. A man who is really moral is never aware that he is moral. But a man who is aware that he is moral has immorality hidden deep down. A man who thinks he is good, saintly, a sage, is a sinner – and he knows it! And just to hide the fact he creates the opposite.

Willpower is not really power but weakness. A really powerful man has no will of his own – the whole is his will. He floats like a white cloud, one with existence, in tune with it. Your will will always create conflict. It will shrink you, make you an island, and then the struggle starts.

A will-less person will be naturally headless. And remember, you cannot get out of your head. You can cut it – and that is easier. Getting out of it is almost impossible, because even this concept of getting out is part of it. The head is a mess, it is a chaos. You think, and you also think against thinking. The thinking that is against thinking is also thinking. You are not moving out of it. You can condemn your thoughts, but this condemning is again a thought. Nothing has been achieved, you are moving in a vicious circle. You can go on moving, but you will not be out.

So what to do? How to get out of the head? Only one thing is possible: don't create any fight inside and don't create any effort to come out, because every effort will be suicidal. What can be done then? Simply watch. Be in and watch. Don't try to get out – be in and watch.

If you can watch, in those moments of watchfulness there will be no head. Suddenly you will be beyond. Not out – beyond. Suddenly you will be hovering beyond yourself.

There is one Zen story – very absurd, as all Zen stories are. But they have to be absurd because life is such; they depict life as it is.

One Zen master used to ask his disciples: Some time ago I put a goose in a bottle. Now the goose has grown, and the neck of the bottle is very small so the goose cannot come out. The bottle is very precious and I don't want to break it, so now there is a crisis. If the goose is not allowed out she will die. I can break the bottle and the goose will be out, but I don't want to break the bottle – the bottle is precious. I don't want to kill the goose either. So what would you do?

This is the problem! The goose is in the head and the neck is very narrow. You can break the head, but it is precious. Or you can let the goose die, but that too cannot be allowed – because you are the goose.

That old Zen master continued asking his disciples, and beating them and saying to them: Find a way...because there is no time!

And only once did he allow an answer. One disciple said: The goose is out!

Many answers were tried, but he would always beat the person and say no. Someone would suggest doing something with the bottle, but again the master would say: The bottle will be broken, or something will go wrong, and that cannot be allowed. Or somebody would say: Let the goose die if the bottle is so precious. These were the only two ways; there was no other way. And the master wouldn't give any other clue.

But to this disciple he bowed down and touched his feet and said: He is right – the goose is out! It has never been in.

You are out! You have never been in.

The feeling that you are in is just a false conception.

So there is no real problem of how to bring you out of your head. Just watch. When you watch, what happens? Just close your eyes and watch the thoughts. What happens? Thoughts are there, in, but you are not in. The watcher is always beyond. The watcher is always standing on the hill. Everything moves around and around, and the watcher is beyond.

The watcher can never be the in, can never be the insider – he is always out. Watching means to be out. You may call it witnessing, awareness, mindfulness, or whatsoever you choose to call it, but the secret is – watch! Whenever you feel the head is too much, just sit under a tree and watch, and don't try to come out. Who will come out? No one has been in. The whole effort is futile, because if you have never been in then how can you come out? You may go on trying and trying and getting involved in it, you may get mad but you will never be out.

Once you know that in a moment of watchfulness you are beyond, transcending, you are out. And from that moment you will be headless. The head belongs to the body, not to you. The head is part of the body, it belongs to the body, it has a function in the body; it is beautiful, it is good. The bottle is precious, and if you know the way, the secrets of it, it can be used.

When I am talking to you, what am I doing? Using the bottle. When Buddha is preaching, what is he doing? Using the bottle. The bottle is really precious, worth preserving. But this is no way to preserve it – to get into it and get caught in it, and then make efforts to come out. The whole life becomes chaos.

Once you know that watching you are out, you become headless. Then you move on this earth without any head. What a beautiful phenomenon, a man moving without a head! That's what I mean when I say become a white cloud – a headless phenomenon. You cannot even imagine how much silence can descend upon you when the head is not there. Your physical head will be there, but the involvement, the obsession, is not there. The head is not a problem. It is beautiful, a wonderful device, the greatest computer yet invented, such a complex, such an efficient mechanism. It is beautiful. It can be used, you can enjoy using it. But from where have you got the idea that you are in it? It seems to be just a false teaching.

You may not be aware that in old Japan and still old people in Japan, if you ask them: Where do you think from? they will point to their belly, because in Japan it was taught that the belly is the center of thinking. So when Europeans reached Japan for the first time, they couldn't believe that a whole country thinks that the head is in the belly, not in the head. This is just a Western attitude that you are in the head. In old Japan thinking from the belly really worked, but now they are shifting from the belly to the head. There have been other traditions that have thought from other parts of the body. Lao Tzu says you think from the soles of your feet. So there are techniques in Taoist yoga to get out of the soles of your feet – because there the thinking is going on.

What is the reality? The reality is: you are beyond. But you can get attached to any part of the body – the head is a Western obsession, the belly was the Eastern obsession. You must have heard about D. H. Lawrence. He used to think that one thinks from the sex center, that that is the real thinking center, nowhere else.

And all are equal – equally wrong or equally right. There is nothing to choose because the witness is beyond. It is all around the body and beyond the body. You can get attached to any part of the body and start thinking that this is the part. There is no need to come out because you have never been in. The goose is out – already out!

Watch...and when you watch you have to remember that while watching, don't judge. If you judge, watching is lost. While watching, don't evaluate. If you evaluate, watching is lost. While watching, don't comment. If you comment, you have missed the point. While watching, just watch...a river flowing, the stream of consciousness flowing, atomic thoughts floating like bubbles, and you sitting on the bank watching. The stream goes on and on and on. You don't say this is good, you don't say this is bad, and you don't say this should not have been, and you don't say this should have been. You don't say anything – you simply watch. You are not asked to comment. You are not a judge – just a watcher.

Then see what happens. Watching the river, suddenly you will be beyond...and the goose will be out. Once you know this, that you are out, you can remain out. And then you can move on this earth without a head.

So this is the way to cut the head. Everybody is interested in cutting others' heads – that won't help. You have already done that too much. Cut your own. To be headless is to be in deep meditation.

Enough for today.

All
Hopes
Are False

CHAPTER FOUR

Beloved Osho,
You have been telling us how easy it is to
drop our egos and become one
with the white cloud.
You have also told us that we have had
millions of lives and many of them
have been with Buddhas, Krishnas and Christs –
yet still we have not given up our egos.
Aren't you creating false hopes in us?

LL HOPES ARE FALSE. To hope is to be false. So it is not a question of creating false hopes: whatsoever you can hope will be false. Hope comes out of your falsity of being. If you are real there is no need for any hope. Then you never think about the future, about what is going to happen. You are so real, so authentic that the future disappears.

When you are unreal then the future becomes very significant, then you live in the future. Then your reality is not here and now, your reality is somewhere in your dreams, and you make those dreams look real because through those dreams you gain your reality. As you are, you are unreal. That's why so much hoping goes on. All hopes are false; *you* are real. My whole effort is how to throw you to yourself.

The ego is all false hopes combined together. Ego is not a reality, it is the collectivity of all your dreams, of all that is unreal, of all that is false. The ego cannot exist in the present. Look at this phenomenon. The ego exists either in the past or in the future, never here and now – never, never. That is impossible. Whenever you think of the past, the ego comes, the I comes. Whenever you think of the future, the I comes.

But when you are here, not thinking of past and future, where is your I? Sitting under a tree, not thinking of past and future, just being there, where are you? Where is the I? You cannot feel it. It is not there. The ego has never existed in the present. Past is no more, future is yet to be. Both are not. Past has disappeared, the future has not yet appeared. Both are not. Only the present is and in the present nothing like the ego has ever been found.

So when I say drop the ego, what do I mean? I am not giving you a new hope, I am taking all your hopes away. And that is the difficulty: you live through the hope, so you feel that if all hopes are taken away you will be dead. Then the question will arise: Why live? For what? Why move from one moment to another? For what? The goal has disappeared with the disappearance of the hope. So why go on and on if there is nowhere to reach? You cannot live without hope. That's why it is so difficult to drop the ego. Hope has become synonymous with life.

So whenever a man is hoping, he appears to be more vital, appears to be more alive, appears to be very strong. When he is not hoping he appears to be weak, depressed, thrown back to himself, not knowing what to do, where to go. And whenever there is no hope you feel meaninglessness come into you. Immediately you create another hope; a substitute is created. If one hope is frustrated, immediately another is substituted – because you cannot live in the gap, you cannot live hopelessly.

I tell you that that is the only way to live.

Without any hope, life is real, for the first time life is authentic.

So the second thing to be understood is: when I say it is easy to drop the ego, I don't mean that it will be easy for *you* to drop it. I mean it is easy to drop it because the very phenomenon of ego is so unreal. If the ego is false, how can it be difficult to drop it? If the dream is just a dream, how can it be difficult to come out of it? If it was real, then there would have been difficulty. If a dream is just a dream, where is the problem to come out of it? You can come out! The dream cannot catch hold of you, the dream cannot prevent you. The dream cannot become a barrier. The dream has no force – that's why we call it a dream. It is easy to come out of a dream. That's what I mean when I say it is easy to drop the ego. But I don't mean that it will be easy for *you*, because the dream is still a reality for you, it is not a dream. The ego is not false to you, it is the only reality. Everything else is false.

We are living around the ego. We are seeking more and more egotistical journeys – somebody through wealth, somebody through status, power, prestige, somebody through politics, somebody through religion, priesthood. There are millions of ways. But the end, the result, the goal is the same: seeking more and more the I, seeking more and more the ego.

To you it is a reality; to you, I say, it is the only reality. The false has become the real. The shadow has become the substance. That's why it is difficult – not difficult because ego is very power-ful, no; it is difficult because you still believe in it, in its power. If you believe in it, it is going to be difficult, because on the one hand you want to drop it, and on the other hand you go on clinging to it. It is going to be difficult. When I say to you it is a dream, you want to believe it because you have suffered so much through it – because you feel the truth of what I am saying. If you feel the truth of what I am saying you will drop it immediately. You will not ask how. There is no how to it. You see the point and you drop it!

You don't see the truth of what I am saying. When I say it is not realized that the ego is false and can be dropped, when I say that the ego can be dropped, you create a hope out of it. Because you have been suffering so much through it, you create a hope that if the ego *can* be dropped then all suffering will be dropped. You become happy with this hope.

I am not creating the hope, *you* are creating the hope. I am sim-ply stating a fact that this is the construction of the ego. This is how an ego is structured, this is how an ego is created and this is how it can be dropped! And because it is false, no effort is needed. Just seeing the point it disappears.

A man is running, scared, afraid to death, and running because of his own shadow. You stop him and tell him: You are foolish!

This is your own shadow – nobody is following you and nobody is going to murder you. There is nobody except you. You have become scared of your own shadow.

But once you start running the shadow also runs faster. The faster you run, the faster the shadow follows. Then the logical mind can say that you are in danger, and the logical mind will say: If you want to escape run faster and faster. But whatsoever you do the shadow will be following you. And if you cannot get rid of it, you will get more and more scared. You are creating the whole thing out of yourself.

But if I say to you: This is just a shadow, nobody is following you – and you realize the point, you look at the shadow and you feel the point – will you ask me how to drop this shadow? Will you ask about some technique, method, some yoga, how to drop it? You will simply laugh. You have dropped it! In the moment you see that this is just a shadow and nobody is following you, it has been dropped already. There is no question of how. You will have a good laugh. The whole thing was nonsense.

The same happens with the ego. If you can see the truth of what I am saying, the thing has happened. In the very seeing of it the thing has happened. There is no more how to it. If you still ask how, the thing has not happened and you have not seen the point – but you have created a hope out of it, because you have been suffering through this ego. You have always wanted to drop it, but this want has always been half of your mind.

All your suffering has come through the ego, but all your pleasures have also come through the ego. A crowd applauds you, appreciates you – you feel good. That is the only bliss you have known. Your ego rises high, reaches to a peak, becomes an Everest. You enjoy it! And then the crowd condemns you and you feel hurt. The crowd becomes indifferent; you are crushed by it. You fall into a valley, a depression. You have been gaining pleasure through the ego, you have been suffering through it. Because of suffering you want to drop it, but because of pleasures you cannot drop it.

So when I say that the ego can be dropped easily, hope is created in you. Not that I am creating it, your greed does that. It doesn't become a realization, it becomes a new greed, a new search for gratification. You feel that now there is a way, and there is a man who can help you to drop the ego and all the misery that ego creates. But are you ready to drop all the pleasures that the ego creates too? If you are ready it is such an easy thing – just like dropping a shadow. But you cannot half drop it, and you cannot half carry it. Either the whole will go or the whole will cling to you. This is the problem and this is the difficulty.

All your pleasures and all your sufferings are related to one phenomenon only: you want to preserve the pleasures and you want to drop the sufferings. You are asking the impossible. Then it is difficult – not only difficult, it is impossible. It is not going to happen to you. Whatsoever you do will be futile, no result will come of it.

You create hope out of it...a heaven, the intense blissfulness of a Buddha. Listening to me or listening to a Jesus or a Buddha, hope is created. But I am not creating it, you are creating it. You are projecting hope on it. And this is the problem, the complexity: every hope is food for the ego again. Even this hope of reaching a paradise, a heaven, becoming enlightened, is a hope. And every hope is food for the ego.

Who is trying to become enlightened? The one who is trying to become enlightened is the problem. Nobody ever becomes enlightened. Enlightenment happens, but nobody ever becomes enlightened. When the room is empty, enlightenment happens. When there is nobody to reach enlightenment, enlightenment is there. Because of our language, because of the duality of the language, whatsoever is said about such deep things becomes false.

We say: Gautam Buddha became enlightened. This is false. Gautam Buddha never became enlightened. Gautam Buddha was the unenlightenment. When he was not there, when he became absent, enlightenment happened. When suddenly one day he realized that he was following an absurd pattern, when he realized: I am the problem, so whatsoever I do will create more problems.... It is not a question of doing right or wrong, this or that. Whatsoever you do will strengthen the ego. Once Buddha realized this – but this realization took many years of effort – when he realized that: Whatsoever I do will help my ego more and more, he simply dropped doing. In that moment of realization he simply became a non-doer, absolutely inactive.

Remember, this is the problem: you can even create activity out of your inactivity, or you can create activity just to help inactivity come to you. But then you miss. You can stand still, you can sit silently, but if you are making an effort to stand still, your standing is false. You are not standing, you are moving. If you are sitting silently and there is effort, if you are trying to be silent, that silence is false. You are not silent.

When Buddha realized that he was the problem, and that every activity of his gave more substance to the ego, he simply dropped. Then he was not making any effort to create a non-active state. He was not doing at all. Whatsoever was happening was happening. The wind was blowing, and the tree must have been dancing; then came the full moon, and the whole existence was celebrating. And the breathing coming in, going out, and the blood circulating in the veins, and the heart beating, and the pulse – and everything was happening, but he was not doing anything. In this nondoing Gautam Siddhartha disappeared.

By the morning there was no one to receive enlightenment, but enlightenment was there. Under that bodhi tree a vacant vehicle was sitting – breathing of course, heart beating of course, better than ever. Everything functioning perfectly, but no doer there. Blood circulating, the whole existence around – alive, dancing. Every atom in Buddha's body dancing, alive. It had never been so alive, but now energy was moving of its own accord – nobody pushing it, nobody manipulating it. Buddha became a white cloud. Enlightenment happened.

It can happen to you also, but don't create any hope out of it. Rather, seeing the point, drop all hopes. Become hopeless, perfectly hopeless. It is difficult to become perfectly hopeless. Many times you reach hopelessness but it is never perfect. One hope drops, you feel hopelessness. But immediately to cover it up you create another hope, and hopelessness is gone.

People go on moving from one master to another; that is movement from one hope to another. They go to one master with hopes that he will give through his grace, that through his energy the thing will happen. Then they try, then they wait with a very strained mind, because a mind which hopes can never be at ease; with a very impatient mind, because a mind which is filled with hope cannot be patient. And then they start feeling uneasy because the thing is not happening. So this master is wrong, they must move to someone else. This is not movement from one master to another, this is movement from one hope to another. People move from one religion to another; there are conversions just because of hope. You can go on doing it for many, many lives. You have been doing that.

Now try to see the point. It is neither a question of a master nor a question of a right method. It is a question of a direct insight, an immediate penetration into the phenomenon of what is happening, of why you hope, of why you can't be without hope. And what have you gained out of all your hoping? See it. It drops by itself. You are not even required to drop it. That's why I say it is easy, and I know well it is very difficult. Difficult because of you, easy because of itself. The phenomenon is easy, you are difficult.

And this can happen any moment. When I say this can happen any moment, I mean the phenomenon of enlightenment, of egolessness, is not caused by anything. No cause is needed. It is not an outcome of many causes, it is not a by-product. It is simple insight. It can happen to a sinner; it may not happen to a saint. So no necessary condition is needed really. If he can see, it can happen even to a sinner. If he becomes hopeless, if he feels that there is nothing to be gained and achieved, if he comes to see that the whole thing is just an absurd game, it can happen. It may not happen to a saint, because the saint goes on trying to achieve. He is not yet hopeless. This world has become futile, but another world has become meaningful. He realizes that he has to leave this earth, but there are heavens beyond – he has to reach there.

And even people near a Jesus or Buddha go on asking things like this. Just on the last night, when Jesus was going to be caught and the next day killed, his disciples asked him: Master, tell us: in the kingdom of God, when you are sitting on the right side of God's throne, what will our positions be there? Where will we be sitting, in what order? God sitting on his throne, Jesus on his right side, the only begotten son, and then these twelve disciples: Where will we be sitting and what will be the order?

People around Jesus asking such a foolish question! But this is how human mind is. They don't ask anything of this world – they have become beggars, but they ask of the other world. They are not really beggars, they are hoping. They have staked this world, but it is a bargain: Where will we be there? Who will be sitting next to you?

There must have been competition among those twelve disciples. There must have been politics, ambition, somebody up, somebody down, somebody becoming the chief. There must have been much conflict, inner politics, undercurrents of violence and aggression. Even with Jesus one starts hoping. Hope is deep-rooted in you. Whatsoever is said, you convert it into a hope. You are a hope-creating mechanism, and this hope-creating mechanism is the ego.

So what is to be done? In fact, there is nothing to be done. You only need clearer eyes, more perceptive eyes, more penetrating eyes. All that is needed is to have a fresh look about you, your being, at whatsoever you have been doing, hoping – a fresh look.

And I say to you, in that fresh look, in that innocent look, ego drops by itself, of its own accord. It is the easiest phenomenon, and at the same time the most difficult. But remember well, I am not creating any hope in you.

Beloved Osho,
In relation to what you've just said,
Zen has a saying: Effortless effort.
Would you talk to us about that, and
how it applies to your Dynamic Meditation.

MEDITATION IS AN ENERGY PHENOMENON. One very basic thing has to be understood about all types of energies. This is the basic law: energy moves in a dual polarity. That is the only way it moves; there is no other way for its movement. It moves in a dual polarity. For any energy to become dynamic, the anti-pole is needed. It is just like electricity moving with negative and positive polarities. If there is only negative polarity, electricity will not happen; or if there is only positive polarity, electricity will not happen. Both the poles are needed. And when both the poles meet they create electricity. Then the spark comes up.

And this is so for all types of phenomena. Life goes on... between man and woman, the polarity. The woman is the negative life-energy; man is the positive pole. They are electrical, hence so much attraction. With man alone life would disappear; with woman alone there could be no life, only death. Between man and woman there exists a balance. Between man and woman – these two poles, these two banks – flows the river of life. Wherever you look you will find the same energy moving into polarities, balancing itself.

This polarity is very meaningful for meditation, because mind is logical and life is dialectical. When I say mind is logical, it means mind moves in a line. When I say life is dialectical, it means life moves with the opposite, not in a line. It zigzags from negative to positive, positive to negative, negative to positive. It zigzags. It uses the opposites.

Mind moves in a line, a simple, straight line. It never moves to the opposite. It denies the opposite. It believes in one and life believes in two. So whatsoever mind creates, it always chooses the one.

If mind chooses silence, if mind has become fed up with all the noise that is created in life and it decides to be silent, then the mind goes to the Himalayas. It wants to be silent. It doesn't want anything to do with any type of noise. Even the song of the birds will disturb it, a breeze blowing through the trees will be a disturbance. The mind wants silence. It has chosen the line; now the opposite has to be denied completely. But this man living in the Himalayas, seeking silence, avoiding the other, the opposite, will become dead, he will certainly become dull. And the more he chooses to be silent the duller he will become – because life needs the opposite, the challenge of the opposite.

There is a different type of silence which exists between two opposites. The first is a dead silence, the silence of the cemetery. A dead man is silent, but you would not like to be a dead man. A dead man is absolutely silent, nobody can disturb him. His concentration is perfect, you cannot do anything to distract his mind. His mind is absolutely fixed. Even if all around the whole world goes mad, he will remain in his concentration. But still you would not like to be a dead man. Silence, concentration, or whatever it is called, you would not like to be dead – because if you are silent when dead, the silence is meaningless.

Silence must happen while you are absolutely alive, vital, bubbling with life and energy. Then silence is meaningful. But then silence will have a different, altogether different quality to it. It will not be dull, it will be alive. It will be a subtle balance between two polarities.

Then such a type of man, who is seeking a live balance, a live silence, would like to move to the market and to the Himalayas both. He would like to go to the market to enjoy noise, and he would also like to go to the Himalayas to enjoy silence. He will create a balance between these two polar opposites, and he will remain in that balance. And that balance cannot be achieved through linear efforts.

That is what is meant by the Zen technique of effortless effort. It uses contradictory terms – effortless effort, or gateless gate, or

pathless path. Zen always uses the contradictory term immediately, just to give you the hint that the process is going to be
dialectical, not linear. The opposite is not to be denied but
absorbed. The opposite is not to be left aside, it has to be used.
Left aside it will always be a burden on you. Left aside it will hang
with you unused. You will miss much. The energy can be converted and used. And then, using it, you will be more vital, more
alive. The opposite has to be absorbed, then the process becomes
dialectical.

Effortlessness means not doing anything, inactivity – *akarma*.
Effort means doing much, activity – karma. Both have to be there.
Do much, but don't be a doer; then you achieve both. Move in
the world but don't be a part of it. Live in the world but don't let
the world live in you. Then the contradiction has been absorbed.
Then you are not rejecting anything, not denying anything. Then
the whole existence has been accepted.

And that's what I'm doing. Dynamic Meditation is a contradiction. The dynamic means effort, much effort, absolute effort, and
meditation means silence, no effort, no activity. You can call it a
dialectical meditation. Be so active that the whole energy becomes
a movement, no energy is left static in you. The whole energy has
been called forth, nothing is left behind. All the frozen parts of
energy are melting, flowing. You are not a frozen thing now, you
have become dynamic. You are not like substance now, you are
more like energy. You are not material, you have become electrical. Bring total energy to work, to be active, moving.

When everything is moving and you have become a cyclone, then
become alert. Remember, be mindful – and in this cyclone suddenly
you will find a center which is absolutely silent. This is the center of
the cyclone. This is you – you in your divinity, you as a god.

All around you is activity. Your body has become an active
cyclone – everything moving fast, faster. All the frozen parts have
melted, you are flowing. You have become a volcano, fire, electricity. But just in the center, amidst all this movement, there is a non-
moving point, the still point.

This still point is not to be created. It is there, you are not to do anything about it. It has always been there. It is your very being, the very ground of your being. This is what Hindus have been calling the *atman*, the soul. It is there, but unless your body, unless your material existence becomes totally active, you will not be aware of it. With total activity the totally inactive becomes apparent. The activity gives you a contrast. It becomes the blackboard, and on the blackboard is the white dot. On a white wall you cannot see a white dot; on a blackboard the white dot appears to you.

So when your body has become active, dynamic, a movement, suddenly you become aware of a point which is still, absolutely still – the unmoving center of the whole moving world. That is effortless. No effort is made for it. No effort is needed, it is simply revealed. Effort on the part of the periphery, no effort on the part of the center. Movement on the periphery, stillness at the center. Activity on the periphery, absolute inactivity at the center. And between these two....

This will be a little difficult, because you may get identified with the center Hindus have called atman, the soul. If you get identified with the center which is still, you have again chosen something between the two. You have again chosen something and rejected something.

There is a very subtle Eastern discovery, and that is: if you get identified with the still point you will never know God; you will know the self but you will never know God. And there are many traditions, particularly Jainas, who became too identified with the self – so they say there is no God, the self is the only God.

Hindus who have penetrated really deep, they say about this still point and this activity on the periphery that either you are both or you are none. Either you are both or you are none – both mean the same. These are the two poles. These are the two dialectical poles, the thesis and the antithesis. These are the two banks and you are somewhere between these two – neither moving nor non-moving. This is the ultimate transcendence. This is what Hindus call the Brahman.

Effort and effortlessness, movement and no movement, activity and no activity, matter and the soul – these are the banks. And between these two flows the invisible. These two are visibles. Between these two flows the invisible. That you are. *Tattwamasi Swetketu*, says the Upanishad. That which flows between these two banks, that which cannot be seen, that which is really a subtle balance, nothing else – between these two, that art thou. That has been called the Brahman, the supreme self.

A balance has to be achieved, and balance can be achieved only when you use both the polarities. If you use one you become dead. Many have done that; even whole societies have become dead. This has happened to India. If you choose one then imbalance, lopsidedness, happens. It happened in India, in the East, that the silent part, the still point, was chosen and the active part denied. So the whole East became dull. The sharpness was lost. The sharpness of intelligence, the sharpness of body vigor, everything was lost. The East became more and more dull, ugly, as if life was just a burden to be carried somehow and dropped, a duty to be fulfilled, a karma to be suffered – not an enjoyment, not a vigorous dance, but a dull, lethargic movement.

And it had its consequences. The East became weak, because with a still point you cannot remain strong forever, for long. Strength needs activity, strength needs movement. If you deny activity, strength disappears. The East lost its muscles completely; the body became flabby. So anybody who desired to could conquer the East. For thousands of years slavery was the only destiny for the East. Anyone who had just an idea to make anybody a slave would turn towards the East. The East was always ready to be conquered, because the Eastern mind had chosen a point against the polar opposite. The East became silent, but dead and dull also. This type of silence is not worth anything.

The opposite is happening in the West. It has happened in other societies also. They have chosen the active part, the periphery, and they think that there is no soul. They think this activity is all, and to be active and to enjoy, and to achieve and to be ambitious and to conquer, is all that life consists of. The ultimate result is going to be more and more madness in the West – because without that still point you cannot remain sane. You will become insane. With only the still point, you cannot remain alive, you become dead; with only the active, you become insane. People who are insane, what has happened to them? They have lost all contact with their still point. That's what their insanity is.

The West is turning into a big madhouse. More and more people are being psychoanalyzed, psychiatrically treated; more and more people are being put into madhouses. And those who are out, they are out not because they are sane, but only because so many people cannot be put in houses for the insane; otherwise the whole society would have to be put in a prison. They are normal, workably normal. But Western psychology says that now it is difficult to say that any man is normal, and they may be right. In the West it has happened: no man is normal. Activity alone creates madness; balance is impossible. Active civilizations become mad in the end, inactive civilizations become dead. This happens to societies, this happens to individuals.

To me, balance is all. Don't choose, don't reject. Accept both – and create an inner balance. Dynamic Meditation is an effort towards that balance. Active...enjoy it, be ecstatic, be fully with it. Then silent...enjoy it, be ecstatic about it. Move between these two as freely as possible and don't create any choice. Don't say: I am this or that. Don't get identified. Say: I am both. Don't be afraid of contradicting yourself. Contradict, be both, and move easily.

And when I say this, I say it unconditionally – not only for activity and inactivity. Whatsoever is called bad and good, that too is included; whatsoever is called the devil and the divine, that too is included.

Always remember: everywhere there are banks, and if you want to be a river use both the banks unconditionally. Don't say: Because I was active, how can I be inactive? Don't say: Because I was inactive, now how can I be active? Don't say: I am this, so how can I be that? You are both and there is no need to choose.

The only thing to remember is to be balanced between the two. Then you will transcend both. Then the devil and the divine will both be transcended. When both are transcended, that is Brahman. Brahman has no polarity against him, because he is just a balance between two polarities. There is no anti-pole to it.

Move in life as freely as possible, and use both the opposites, both the banks, as much as possible. Don't create any contradiction. They are not contradictory, they only appear to be contradictory. Deep down they are one. They are just like your legs, right and left. You use the right, you use the left. While you raise the right, the left is waiting on the earth, helping. Don't become addicted. Don't be a rightist or a leftist. Both legs are yours, and in both legs your energy flows – undivided. Have you ever felt that the right leg has one energy and the left leg some other energy? You are flowing in both. Close your eyes: left disappears, right disappears. They are both you, and while moving you can use them. Use both! If you become addicted to the right, as many people have become, then you will be crippled, you cannot use the left. Then you can stand, but you will be crippled, and by and by you will become dead.

Move and constantly remember the unmoving center. Do and constantly remember the non-doer. Make effort and remain effortless. Once you know this secret alchemy of using the opposite, the contradictory, you are free; otherwise you create inner imprisonments.

There are people who come to me and say: How can I do this? I have never done this. Just the other day there was somebody who said to me: How can I do active meditation, because for many years I have been sitting silently?

He has chosen, and he has reached nowhere; otherwise there was no need to come to me. But he cannot do the active meditation because he has become identified with an inactive posture. This is getting frozen.

Become more movement. Be moving and allow life to flow. Once you know that between the opposites balance is possible, once you have a glimpse of it, then you know the art. Then everywhere in life, in every dimension of life, you can attain that balance very easily. Really, to say that you can attain is not good. Once you know the knack of it, whatsoever you do the balance follows you like a shadow. This inner balance between the opposites is the most significant thing that can happen to a man.

Enough for today.

Dropping
the Ego
Now

CHAPTER FIVE

Beloved Osho,
You said the ego can be dropped this very moment.
Can the ego also be dropped progressively?

T HE DROPPING ALWAYS HAPPENS in the moment and always in *this* moment. There is no progressive, gradual process for it. There cannot be. The happening is instantaneous. You can't get ready for it, you can't prepare for it, because whatsoever you do – and I say *whatsoever* – will strengthen the ego. Any gradual process will be an effort, something done on your part. So you will be strengthened more and more through it. You will become stronger. Everything gradual helps the ego. Only something absolutely non-gradual, something like a jump, not like a process, something discontinuous with the past, not in continuity with it – only then the ego drops.

The problem arises because we cannot understand what this ego is. The ego is the past, the continuity, all that you have done, all that you have accumulated, all the karmas, all the conditionings, all the desires, all the dreams of the past. That whole past is the ego. And if you think in terms of gradual process you bring the past in. The dropping is non-gradual, sudden; it is a discontinuity. The past is no more, the future is no more. You are left alone here and now. Then the ego cannot exist.

The ego can exist only through the memory: who you are, from where you come, to whom you belong, the country, the race, the religion, the family, the tradition, and all the hurts, wounds, pleasures – all that has happened in the past. All that has happened is the ego. And you are that to whom all this has happened. This distinction has to be understood: you are that to whom all has happened, and the ego is that which has happened. The ego is around you; you are in the center, egoless.

A child is born absolutely fresh and young – no past, no ego. That's why children are so beautiful. They don't have any past; they are young and fresh. They cannot say I, because from where will they bring the I? The I has to develop gradually. They will get educated, they will get awards, punishments, they will be appreciated, condemned – then the I will gather.

A child is beautiful because the ego is not there. An old man becomes ugly, not because of old age but because of too much past, too much of the ego. An old man can also become again beautiful, even more beautiful than a child, if he can drop the ego. Then there is a second childhood, then a rebirth.

This is the meaning of the resurrection of Jesus. It is not an historical fact, it is a parable. Jesus is crucified and then he resurrects. The man who was crucified is no more; that was the son of the carpenter, Jesus. Now Jesus is dead, crucified. A new entity arises out of that. Out of this death a new life is born. This is Christ – not the son of a particular carpenter in Bethlehem, not a Jew, not even a man. This is Christ, something new, egoless.

And the same will happen to you whenever your ego is on the cross. Whenever your ego is crucified there is a resurrection, a rebirth. You are born again. And this childhood is eternal, because this is a rebirth of the spirit, not of the body. Now you will never become old. Always and always you will be fresh and young – as fresh as the dewdrop in the morning, as fresh as the first star in the night. You will always remain fresh, young, a child, innocent – because this is a resurrection of the spirit. This always happens in a moment.

Ego is time – the more time, the more ego. Ego needs time. If you penetrate deeply you may even be able to conceive that time exists only because of the ego. Time is not part of the physical world around you, it is part of the psychic world within you, the mind-world. Time exists just as a space for the ego to evolve and to grow. Room is needed; time gives the room.

If it is said to you that this is the last moment of your life, next moment you are going to be shot dead, suddenly time disappears. You feel very uneasy. You are still alive, but suddenly you feel as if you are dying, and you can't think what to do. Even to think becomes difficult, because even for thinking time is needed, future is needed. There is no tomorrow – then where to think, how to desire, how to hope? There is no time. Time is finished.

The greatest agony that can happen to a man happens when his death is fixed and he cannot avoid it, it is certain. A person who is sentenced, imprisoned, waiting for his death – he cannot do anything about it, death is fixed. After a certain period he will die; beyond that time there is no tomorrow for him. Now he cannot desire, he cannot think, he cannot project, he cannot even dream. The barrier is always there. Then much agony follows. That agony is for the ego. Because ego cannot exist without time – ego breathes in time, time is breath for the ego – the more time, the more possibility for the ego.

In the East much has been worked out, much has been done to understand the ego, much probing has been done. And one of the findings is that unless time drops from you, ego will not drop. If tomorrow exists the ego will exist. If there is no tomorrow how can you pull on the ego? It will be just like pulling a boat without the river. That will become a burden. A river is needed, then the boat can function.

The river of time is needed for the ego. That's why the ego always thinks in terms of the gradual, in terms of degrees. The ego says: Okay, enlightenment is possible – but time is needed, because you will have to work for it, prepare, get ready. This is a very logical thing. For everything time is needed. If you sow a seed, time is needed for the tree to grow. If a child is to be born, if a child is to be created, time is needed. The womb will need time. The child will have to grow. Everything grows around you. For growth time is needed, so it seems logical that spiritual growth will also need time.

But this is the point to be understood: spiritual growth is not really a growth like a seed. The seed has to grow to become a tree.

Between the seed and the tree there is a gap. That gap has to be traveled, there is distance. You don't grow like a seed; you are already the growth. It is just a revelation. There is no distance between you as you are and you as you will be. There is no distance! The ideal, the perfect, is already there.

So it is not really a question of growth, but just a question of unveiling. It is a discovery. Something is hidden – you pull away the screen and it is there. It is just as if you are sitting with closed eyes: the sun is there on the horizon, but you are in darkness. Suddenly you open the eyes and it is day, it is light.

The spiritual growth is not really a growth. The word is erroneous. Spiritual growth is a revelation. Something that was hidden becomes unhidden. Something that was already there, you realize that it is there; something that you had never missed, simply forgotten, you remember. That's why mystics go on using the word remembrance. They say the divine is not an achievement, it is simply a remembrance. Something you have forgotten, you remember.

Really, no time is needed. But the mind says, the ego says, for everything time is needed, for everything to grow time is needed. And if you become a victim of this logical thought, then you will never achieve it. Then you will go on postponing. You will say tomorrow and tomorrow and tomorrow, and it will never come because tomorrow never comes.

If you can understand what I am saying, that the ego can be dropped this very moment, and if it is true, then the question arises: Why is it not dropping? Why can't you drop it? If there is no question of gradual growth, then why are you not dropping it? Because you don't *want* to drop it. This will shock you, because you go on thinking that you want to drop it. Reconsider it, think again. You don't want to drop it, hence it continues. It is not a question of time. Because you don't want to drop it, nothing can be done.

Mysterious are the ways of the mind. You think that you want to drop it, and deep down you know you don't want to drop it. You may want to polish it a little more, you may want it to be more refined, but you don't really want to drop it. If you want to drop it there is no one who is preventing you. No barrier exists. Just for the wanting it can be dropped. But if you don't want to drop it nothing can be done. Even a thousand buddhas working on you will fail, because nothing can be done from the outside.

Have you really thought about it, have you ever meditated on it, whether you want to drop it? Do you really want to become a non-being, a nothing? Even in your religious projections you want to be something, you want to achieve something, reach somewhere, be something. Even when you think of being humble, your humility, your humbleness is just a secret hiding-place for the ego and nothing else.

Look at so-called humble people. They say they are humble and they will try to prove that they are the most humble in their town, in their city, in their locality – the most humble. And if you argue and if you say: No, somebody else is more humble than you, they will feel hurt. Who is feeling hurt?

I was just reading about one Christian saint. He says every day to his god in his prayer: I am the most wicked person on this earth, the greatest sinner. Apparently he is a very humble man, but he is not. He says he is the greatest sinner on the earth, and if even God is going to dispute it he will argue. The interest, the deep interest, is in being the greatest, not in being the sinner. You can be a sinner if you are allowed to be the greatest sinner. You can enjoy it. The greatest sinner – then you become a peak. Virtue or sin is immaterial; you must be someone. Whatsoever the reason for it, your ego must be at the top.

George Bernard Shaw is reported to have said: I would rather be first in hell than second in heaven. Hell is not a bad place if you are the first and foremost. Even heaven will look dull if you are just standing somewhere in a queue, a nobody. And Bernard Shaw is right. This is how the human mind functions.

Nobody wants to drop the ego. Otherwise, there is no problem – you can simply drop it right now. And if you feel that time is needed, then time is needed only for your understanding that you are clinging to it. And the moment you can understand that it is your clinging, the thing will happen.

You may take many lives to understand this simple fact. You have already taken many lives and you have not yet understood. This looks very weird. There is something which is a burden to you, which gives you hell, a continuous hell, but still you cling to it. There must be some deep reason for it, a very deep-rooted cause. I would like to talk about it a little. You may become aware.

The way the human mind is it will always choose occupation rather than being unoccupied. Even if the occupation is painful, even if it is a suffering, the mind will choose to be occupied rather than to be unoccupied – because unoccupied you start feeling that you are dissolving.

Psychologists say that when people retire from their work, their job, their service or business, they die soon. Their life is reduced immediately by almost ten years. Before their death they start dying. There is no more occupation, they are unoccupied. When you are unoccupied you start feeling meaningless, futile. You start feeling that you are not needed, that without you the world can go on easily. When you are occupied you feel that the world cannot continue without you, that you are a very essential part of it, very significant – without you everything will stop.

If you are unoccupied, suddenly you become aware that without you the world goes on beautifully. Nothing is changing. You have been discarded. You are thrown on the junk pile. You are not needed. The moment you feel you are not needed the ego becomes uneasy – because it exists only when you are needed. So all around the ego goes on forcing this attitude on everybody: you are a must, you are needed; without you nothing can happen, without you the world will dissolve.

Unoccupied, you come to realize that the game continues. You are not an essential part. You can be discarded easily. Nobody will bother about you, nobody will think about you. Rather, they may even feel relieved. That shatters the ego. So people want occupation

– something or other, but they have to remain occupied. They must continue the illusion that they are needed.

Meditation is an unoccupied state of mind. It is a deep retirement. It is not just a superficial retirement like going to the Himalayas. That may not be a retirement at all, because again you can become occupied in the Himalayas. You can create fantasies there that you are saving the world. Sitting in the Himalayas meditating, you are saving the world from a third war; or because you are creating such vibrations the world is reaching towards a utopia, a peaceful state of society. And you can enjoy this occupation there. Nobody is going to argue because you are alone. Nobody is going to dispute the fact that you are in illusion or a hallucinatory state. You can get really involved with it. The ego will assert itself again in a subtle new way.

Meditation is not a superficial retirement. It is a deep, intimate, real retirement, a withdrawal – a withdrawal from occupation. It is not that you will not be occupied; you can continue whatsoever you are doing, but you withdraw yourself and your investment in occupation. Now you start feeling that this constant hankering after being needed is foolish, stupid. The world can continue quite well without you. And there is no depression in it. It is good. So far, so good...the world can continue without you. This can become a freedom if you understand. If you don't understand then you feel you are being shattered.

So people continue to be occupied, and the ego gives them the greatest occupation possible. Twenty-four hours the ego gives them occupation. They are thinking how to become a member of parliament, they are thinking how to become a deputy minister and a minister and a prime minister, and how to become a president. The ego goes on and on and on. It gives you a constant occupation – how to achieve more riches, how to create a kingdom. The ego gives you dreams, continuous inner occupation, and you feel much is going on. Unoccupied, suddenly you become aware of inner emptiness. These dreams fill the inner emptiness.

Now psychologists say that a man can live without food for at least ninety days, but he cannot live without dreaming for ninety days. He will go mad. If dreaming is not allowed within three weeks you will go mad. Without food, three weeks will not harm you – it may even be good for your health. Three weeks without food, a good fast will rejuvenate your whole system, you will be more alive and young. But three weeks of non-dreaming...you will go mad.

Dreaming must fulfill some deep-rooted need. The need is that it gives you occupation; without real occupation it gives you occupation. You can sit and dream and do whatsoever you like, and the whole world moves according to you – in your dreams at least. Nobody creates a problem. You can kill anybody, you can murder. You can change as you like. You are the master there.

The ego feels most vital while dreaming, because there is nobody who can antagonize you, who can say: No, this is wrong. You are whole and sole. Whatsoever you want you create. Whatsoever you don't want you destroy. You are absolutely powerful. You are omnipotent in your dreams.

Dreams stop only when ego drops. So this is the sign, really; in old yoga scriptures this is the sign of a man who has become enlightened. He cannot dream. Dreaming stops because there is no need. It was an ego-need. You want to be occupied. That's why you cannot drop the ego.

Unless you are ready to be empty, unoccupied, unless you are ready to be nobody, unless you are ready to enjoy and celebrate life even if you are not needed, ego cannot be dropped. You have a need to be needed. Somebody must need you – then you feel good. If more and more people need you, you feel better and better. That's why leadership is so much enjoyed, because so many people need you. A leader can become very humble. There is no need to assert his ego; his ego is already so deeply fulfilled because so many people need him, so many people depend on him. He has become the life of so many people, so he can be humble, he can afford to be humble.

You must remember this fact, that people who assert their egos too much are always people who cannot influence others. Then they become assertive because that is their only way to say: I am somebody. If they can influence people, if they can persuade, they will never be assertive. They will be very humble, apparently at least. They will not look egoistic, because in a very subtle way so many people depend on them – they have become significant, their life appears meaningful to them. If your ego is your meaning, if your ego is your significance, how can you drop it?

Listening to me you start thinking to drop it. But just by thinking you cannot drop the ego. You have to come to understand the roots – where it is, where it exists, why it exists. These are the unconscious forces working within you without your knowledge. They have to be made conscious. You have to bring all the roots of your ego out of the soil and earth so you can look and see.

If you can remain unoccupied, if you can remain satisfied without being needed, the ego can drop this very moment. But these ifs are big. Meditation will prepare you for these big ifs. The happening will happen in a moment, but the understanding will take time. It is just like when you heat water. It becomes hotter and hotter and hotter; then, at a particular degree, at one hundred degrees, it starts evaporating. Evaporation happens in a single moment. It is not gradual, it is sudden. From water to vapor there is a jump. Suddenly the water disappears, but time is involved because the water has to be heated up to boiling point. Evaporation happens suddenly, but heating takes time. Understanding is just like heating. It takes time. Dropping of the ego happens like evaporation. It happens suddenly.

So don't try to drop the ego. Rather, try to deepen your understanding. Don't try to make water change into vapor. Heat it. The second thing will follow automatically, it will happen.

Grow in understanding. Make it more intense, more focused. Bring all your energy to understand the phenomenon of your being, your ego, your mind, your unconscious. Become more and more alert, and whatsoever happens, make it a point to try to understand it also. Somebody insults you and you feel anger.

Don't miss this opportunity; try to understand why, why this anger. And don't make it a philosophical thing. Don't go to the library to consult about anger. Anger is happening to you – it is an experience, a live experience. Focus your whole attention on it and try to understand why it is happening to you. It is not a philosophical problem; no Freud is to be consulted about it. There is no need! It is just foolish to consult somebody else while anger is happening to you. You can touch it, you can taste it. You will be burned by it.

Try to understand why it is happening, from where it is coming, where the roots are, how it happens, how it functions, how it overpowers you, how in anger you become mad. Anger has happened before, it is happening now; but now add a new element to it, the element of understanding – and then the quality will change. Then, by and by, you will see that the more you understand anger, the less it happens. And when you understand it perfectly it disappears. Understanding is like heat. When the heat comes to a particular point – one hundred degrees – the water disappears. Sex is there – try to understand it. The more there is understanding, the less you will be sexual. And a moment will come when understanding is perfect – and sex disappears.

This is my criterion: whatsoever the phenomenon of inner energy, if it disappears through understanding it is sin; if through understanding it deepens it is virtue. The more you understand, the wrong will disappear and the right will become more rooted. Sex will disappear and love will deepen. Anger will disappear and compassion will deepen. Greed will disappear, sharing will deepen.

So whatsoever disappears through understanding is wrong; whatsoever becomes more rooted is right. And this is how I define good and evil, virtue and sin – *punya* and *paap*. A holy man is a man of understanding, nothing else. A sinner is a man of no understanding, that's all. Between a holy man and a sinner the distinction is not of sin and holiness, it is of understanding.

Understanding works as a heating process. A moment comes, a right moment, when the heating has come to the boiling point.

Suddenly the ego drops. You cannot drop it directly – you can prepare the situation in which it happens. That situation will take time.

Two schools have always existed. One school is of sudden enlightenment which says enlightenment happens suddenly; it is non-temporal. The other school, just contradicting the first, is of gradual enlightenment. It says that enlightenment comes gradually, nothing happens suddenly. And both are right, because both have chosen one part of the phenomenon.

The gradual school has chosen the first part, the understanding part. They say it has to be through time, understanding will come through time – and they are right. They say you need not worry about the sudden; you simply follow the process, and if the water is heated rightly it will evaporate. You need not bother about evaporation; you simply leave it completely out of your mind. You simply heat the water.

The other school, quite the opposite, which says enlightenment is sudden, has taken the end part. It says the first thing is not very essential: the real thing is that that explosion happens in a no-time gap. The first thing is just the periphery. The real, the second thing, is the center.

But I tell you both are right. Enlightenment happens suddenly, it has always happened suddenly, but understanding takes time. Both are right and both can be interpreted wrongly also. You can play tricks with yourself, you can deceive yourself. If you don't want to do anything, it is beautiful to believe in sudden enlightenment. Then you say: There is no need to do anything. If it happens suddenly it will happen suddenly – what can I do? I can simply wait. That may be a self-deception. Because of this, in Japan particularly, religion simply disappeared.

Japan has a long tradition of sudden enlightenment. Zen says enlightenment is sudden. Because of this, the whole country became irreligious. By and by, people came to believe that sudden enlightenment is the only possibility. Nothing can be done about it – whenever it is going to happen it will happen. If it is going to happen it will happen. If it is not going to happen it will not happen, and we cannot do anything, so why bother?

In the East, Japan is the most materialistic country. In the East, Japan exists as a part of the West. This is strange, because Japan has one of the most beautiful traditions of *dhyana, ch'an* – Zen. Why did it disappear? It disappeared because of this concept of sudden enlightenment. People started deceiving themselves. In India another phenomenon has happened...and that's why I go on saying again and again that the human mind is so deceptive and cunning. You have to be constantly alert, otherwise you will be deceived.

In India we have another tradition, that of gradual enlightenment. That's what yoga means. You have to work for it, work hard through many lives. Discipline is needed, work is needed, and unless you work hard you will not achieve it. So it is a long process, a very long process – so long that India says one life is not enough, you will need many lives. Nothing is wrong with this. As far as understanding is concerned, it is true. But then India believed that if it is going to be so long there is no hurry: then why be in such a hurry? Enjoy the world...there is no hurry and there is enough time. It is such a long process that you cannot achieve it today. And if you cannot achieve it today then the interest is lost. Nobody is so keen that he can wait for many lives. He will simply forget it. The gradual concept has destroyed India; the sudden concept has destroyed Japan.

To me, both are true, because both are half parts of a whole process. And you have to be constantly alert so that you are not deceiving yourself. It will look contradictory, but this is what I would like to say to you: It can happen this very moment, but this very moment may take many lives to come. It can happen this very moment, but you may have to wait for many lives for this moment to come.

So work hard, as if it is going to happen this very moment. And wait patiently, because it is not predictable. Nobody can say when this will happen – this may not happen for many lives. So wait patiently as if the whole process is a long gradual development, and work hard, as hard as possible, as if this can happen this very moment.

Beloved Osho,
Would you talk to us about
using our sexual energy for growth,
as it seems to be one of
our main preoccupations in the West.

SEX IS *THE* ENERGY. So I will not say sexual energy – because there is no other energy. Sex is the only energy you have got. The energy can be transformed – it can become a higher energy. The higher it moves, the less and less sexuality remains in it. And there is an end peak where it becomes simply love and compassion. The ultimate flowering we can call divine energy, but the base, the seat, remains sex. So sex is the first, bottom layer of energy – and God is the top layer. But the same energy moves.

The first thing to be understood is that I don't divide energies. Once you divide, then a dualism is created. Once you divide, then conflict and struggle are created. Once you divide energies *you* are divided; then you will be for or against sex. I am neither for nor against, because I don't divide. I say sex is the energy, the name of the energy; call that energy *x*. Sex is the name of that *x* energy, the unknown energy, when you are using it only as a biological reproduction force. It becomes divine once it is freed from biological bondage, once it becomes non-physical – then it is the love of Jesus or the compassion of Buddha.

The West is much obsessed today because of Christianity. Two thousand years of Christian suppression of sex energy has made the Western mind so much obsessed with it. First, for two thousand years the obsession was how to kill it. You cannot kill it – no energy can be killed, energy can only be transformed. There is no way to destroy energy. Nothing can be destroyed in this world, it can only be transformed, changed, moved into a new realm and dimension. Destruction is impossible. You cannot create a new energy and you cannot destroy an old energy. Creation and destruction are both beyond you. They cannot be done. Now, scientists agree to this – not even a single atom can be destroyed.

For two thousand years Christianity was trying to destroy sex energy. Religion consisted of becoming absolutely without sex. That created a madness. The more you fight, the more you suppress, the more sexual you become. And then sex moves deeper into the unconscious, it poisons your whole being. So if you read the lives of Christian saints you will see they are obsessed with sex. They cannot pray, they cannot meditate. Whatsoever they do, sex comes in. And they think that the devil is playing tricks. Nobody is playing tricks. If you suppress *you* are the devil.

After two thousand years of continuous sex repression, the West became fed up with it. It was too much. The whole wheel turned. Now, instead of repression, indulgence, indulging in it became the new obsession. From one pole the mind moved to the other pole. The disease remained the same. Once it was repression, now it is how to indulge more and more in it. Both are sick attitudes.

Sex has to be transformed – neither repressed nor madly indulged. And the only possible way to transform sex is to be sexual with deep meditative awareness. It is just the same as I was saying about anger. Move into sex, but with an alert, conscious, mindful being. Don't allow it to become an unconscious force. Don't be pulled and pushed by it. Move knowingly, understandingly, lovingly. But make sexual experience a meditative experience. Meditate in it. This is what the East has done through Tantra.

Once you are meditative in sexual experience, the quality of it starts changing. The same energy which is moving into sexual experience starts moving towards consciousness. You can become as alert in a peak sexual orgasm as you can otherwise never become – because no other experience is so deep, no other experience is so absorbing, no other experience is so total. In a sexual orgasm you are totally absorbed, root and all – your whole being vibrating, your whole being in it. Body, mind – both are in it, and thinking stops completely. Even for a single second, when the orgasm reaches its peak, thinking stops completely, because you are so total you cannot think.

In a sexual orgasm you *are*. Being is there without any thinking. In this moment, if you can become alert, conscious, then sex can become the door towards the divine. And if in this moment you can become alert, that alertness can be carried in other moments also, in other experiences also. It can become a part of you. Then eating, walking, doing some work, you can carry that alertness. Through sex the alertness has touched your deepest core. It has penetrated you. Now you can carry it. And if you become meditative you will come to realize a new fact. That fact is that it is not sex that gives you bliss, it is not sex that gives you the ecstasy. Rather, it is a thoughtless state of the mind and total involvement in the act that gives you a blissful feeling.

Once you understand this then sex will be needed less and less, because that thoughtless state of mind can be created without it. That's what meditation means. And that totality of being can be created without sex. Once you know that the same phenomenon can happen without sex, sex will be needed less and less. A moment will come when sex will not be needed at all.

Remember, sex is always dependent on the other. So in sex a bondage, a slavery remains. Once you can create this total orgasmic phenomenon without any dependence on anybody else, when it has become an inner source, you are independent, you are free. That's what is meant when in India we say only a *brahmachari*, an absolutely celibate person, can be free – because now he is not dependent on anybody else, his ecstasy is his own.

Sex disappears through meditation, but this is not destroying the energy. Energy is never destroyed; only the form of the energy changes. Now it is no longer sexual. And when the form is no longer sexual then you become loving.

So really, a person who is sexual cannot love. His love can only be a show. His love is just a means towards sex. A person who is sexual uses love just as a technique towards sex. It is a means. A sexual person cannot really love, he can only exploit the other, and love becomes just a way to approach the other.

A person who has become non-sexual, and the energy is moving within, has become auto-ecstatic. His ecstasy is his own. Such a person will be loving for the first time. His love will be a constant showering, a constant sharing, a constant giving. But to achieve this you are not required to be anti-sex. To achieve this you have to accept sex as part of life, of natural life. Move with it – only move with more consciousness. Consciousness is the bridge, the golden bridge, from this world to the other, from hell to heaven, from the ego to the divine.

Enough for today.

Are You
Still
Carrying
Her?

CHAPTER SIX

Beloved Osho,
There is a Zen story about two monks
who were returning to their monastery.
While walking ahead, the older monk came to a river.
On the bank there was a beautiful young girl.
She was afraid to cross alone. The old monk
quickly looked away from her and crossed the river.
When he was on the other side he looked back,
and to his horror he saw the younger monk carrying
the girl across the river on his shoulders.
The two monks continued their journey side by side.
When they were just outside the monastery gates
the older monk said to the younger:
That was not good, that was against the rules;
we monks are not supposed to touch women.
The younger monk replied:
I left her on the bank of the river.
Are you still carrying her?

Would you talk to us about the alternative
to suppressing or expressing our emotions.

 AN IS THE ONLY BEING who can suppress his energies – or who can transform them. No other being can do either. Suppression and transformation, they exist as two aspects of one phenomenon, which is that man can do something about himself.

The trees exist, the animals exist, the birds exist, but they cannot do anything about their existence – they are part of it, they cannot stand out of it. They cannot be the doers. They are so merged with their energy, they cannot separate themselves. Man can do. He can do something about himself. He can observe himself from a distance – he can look at his own energies as if they are separate from him. And then either he can suppress them or he can transform them. Suppression means only trying to hide certain energies which are there – not allowing them to have their being, not allowing them to have their manifestation. Transformation means transforming, changing energies towards a new dimension.

For example, sex is there. There is something in sex which makes you feel embarrassed about it. This embarrassment is not only because society has taught it to you. All over the world many types of societies exist, have existed, but no society, no human society, has taken sex easily. There is something in the very phenomenon of sex that makes you embarrassed, guilty, self-conscious. What is that? Even if nobody teaches you anything about sex, nobody moralizes to you about it, nobody creates any conceptions about it, still there is something in the very phenomenon that you are not at ease with. What is that?

First, sex shows your deepest dependence. It shows that somebody else is needed for your pleasure. Without somebody else that pleasure is not possible. So you depend, your independence is lost. This hurts the ego. So the more a person is an egoist, the more he will be against sex. Your so-called saints are against sex – not because sex is bad, but because of their egos. They cannot conceive of themselves being dependent on somebody, begging for something from somebody. Sex hurts the ego most.

Secondly, in the very phenomenon of sex the possibility of rejection is there – the other can reject you. It is not certain whether you will be accepted or rejected; the other can say no. And this is the deepest rejection possible, when you approach somebody for love and the other rejects you. This rejection creates fear. The ego says it is better not to try than to be rejected.

Dependence, rejection, the possibility of rejection...and still deeper, in sex you become just like animals. That hurts the human ego very much, because then there is no difference between a dog making love and you making love. What is the difference? Suddenly you become like animals, and all the preachers, moralists, they go on saying to man: Don't be an animal! Don't be like animals! That is the greatest condemnation possible.

In no other thing are you so animal-like as in sex, because in no other thing are you natural – in everything else you can be unnatural. You are eating food. We have created so much sophistication about eating that you are not like animals. The basic thing is like the animal; but your tables, your table manners, the whole culture, the etiquette you have created around food is just to make it distinct from animals.

Animals like to eat alone. So every society creates in the mind of every individual that to eat alone is not good. Share, eat with the family, eat with friends, invite guests. No animal is interested in guests, in friends, in family. Whenever an animal is eating he wants nobody to come near; he goes into aloneness. If a man wants to eat alone you will say he is animal-like, he doesn't want to share. His habit of eating is natural, not sophisticated. Around food we have created so much sophistication that hunger has become less important, taste has become more important. No animal bothers about the taste. Hunger is a basic necessity – hunger is fulfilled, the animal is satisfied. But not man – as if hunger is not the point; something else is the point. More important is taste, more important are manners, more important is *how* you eat, not what you eat.

In everything else man has created his own artificial world around him. Animals are naked – that's why we don't want to be nude. And if somebody is nude suddenly he hits our civilization totally, he cuts the very roots. That's why there is so much antagonism against naked people all over the world.

If you go and move naked in the street, you are not hurting anybody, you are not doing any violence to anybody; you are absolutely innocent. But immediately the police will come, the whole neighborhood will become agitated. You will be caught and beaten and put into jail. But you have not done anything at all! A crime happens when you *do* something. You have not been doing anything – simply walking naked! But why does the society get so angry? The society is not so angry even against a murderer. This is strange. But a naked man...and society is absolutely angry. It is because murder is still human. No animal murders. They kill for eating, but they don't murder. And no animal murders his own species, only man. So it is human, the society can accept it. But nudity the society cannot accept – because suddenly the naked man makes you aware that you are all animals. Howsoever hidden behind clothes, the animal is there, the nude, the naked animal is there, the naked ape is there.

You are against the nude man not because he is nude but because he makes you aware of your nudity, and the ego is hurt. Clothed, man is not an animal. With eating habits, manners, man is not an animal. With language, morality, philosophy, religion, man is not an animal. The most religious thing is to go to a church, to a temple, to pray. Why is it so religious? – because no animal goes to a church and no animal prays; it is absolutely human. Going to a temple to pray, this makes the distinction absolute, that you are not animals.

But sex is animal activity. Whatsoever you do, howsoever you hide it, whatsoever you create around it, the basic fact remains animal. And when you move into it you become like animals. Because of this fact many people cannot enjoy sex. They cannot become totally animal, their egos won't allow it.

So ego and sex, this is the conflict – sex versus ego. The more egoistic a person is, the more he is against sex. The less egoistic a person is, the more involved he is in sex. But even the lesser egoist feels a guilt – feels less, but still feels something is wrong. When one moves deeply into sex the ego is lost, and as the moment comes nearer when the ego is disappearing, fear grips you.

So people make love, go into sex, not deeply, not really. They just make a superficial show that they are making love, because if you really make love all civilization will have to be dropped. Your mind will have to be put aside – your religion, philosophy, everything. Suddenly you will feel a wild animal is born within you. A roar will come to you. You may start actually roaring like a wild animal – screaming, groaning. And if you allow it, language will disappear. Sounds will be there, just like birds or animals making sounds. Suddenly the whole civilization of a million years is dropped. You are again standing like an animal, in a wild world.

There is fear, and because of that fear love has become almost impossible. And the fear is real – because when you lose the ego you are almost insane; you become wild, and then anything can happen. And you *know* that anything can happen. You may even kill, murder your beloved, you may start eating her body, because then controls are removed. Suppression seems to be the easiest way to avoid all this. Suppress, or allow only as much as will not lead you into danger – just a part of it which can be controlled always – and you remain in control. You manipulate. You allow up to an extent and then you don't allow. Then you close yourself and shut yourself.

Suppression exists as a protection, as a safeguard, as a security measure, and religions have used this security measure. They have exploited this fear of sex and they have made you more afraid. They have created an inner trembling. They have made sex the basic sin, and they say: Unless sex disappears you will not be able to enter into the kingdom of God. They are right in a sense, and still wrong. I also say unless sex disappears you will not be able to enter into the kingdom of God. But sex disappears only when you have accepted it totally – not suppressed but transformed it.

Religions have exploited human fear and the human tendency to be egoistic. They have created many techniques to suppress. It is not very difficult to suppress but it is very costly – because your whole energy becomes divided against itself, fighting, and then the whole life is dissipated.

Sex is the most vital energy, the only energy, I say, which you have. Don't fight with it – it will be a waste of life and time – rather, transform it. But how to do it? How to transform it? What can we do? If you have understood the fear, then you can understand the clue, what can be done.

The fear is there because you feel that the control will be lost, and once the control is lost you cannot do anything. I teach you a new control: the control of the witnessing self, not the control of a manipulating mind but the control of a witnessing self. And I tell you that that control is the highest possible, and that control is so natural that you never feel you are controlling. The control happens spontaneously with witnessing.

Move into sex but be a witness. The only thing to remember is: I must encounter the whole process, I must see through it, I must remain a witness, I should not become unconscious – that's all. Become wild but don't become unconscious. Then there is no danger in wildness; then wildness is beautiful. Really, only a wild man can be beautiful. A woman who is not wild cannot be beautiful – because the more wild, the more alive. Then you are just like a wild tiger, or a wild deer running in the forest...and the beauty of it!

But the problem is, not to become unconscious. If you become unconscious then you are under unconscious forces, then you are under the forces of karma. Whatsoever you have done in the past is accumulated there. That accumulated conditioning can take grip of you and move you in certain directions which will be dangerous for you and for others. But if you remain a witness that past conditioning cannot interfere.

So the whole method, or the whole process of becoming a witness, is the process of transforming the sex energy. Moving into sex, remain alert. Whatsoever is happening, observe it, see through it; don't miss a single point. Whatsoever is happening in your body, in your mind, in your inner energy, the new circuit is being made, the body electricity is moving in a new way, in a new circular way; now the body electricity has become one with the partner, with the wife, with the consort. And now an inner circle is created – and you can feel it. If you are alert you can feel it. You will feel that you have become a vehicle of a vital energy moving.

Remain alert. Soon you will become aware that the more the circuit is created, the more thoughts are dropping; they are dropping like yellow leaves from a tree. Thoughts are dropping...the mind is becoming more and more empty. Remain alert and soon you will see that you are but there is no ego. You cannot say I. Something greater than you has happened to you. You and your partner both have dissolved into that greater energy.

But this merger should not become unconscious; otherwise you miss the point. Then it is a beautiful sex act, but not trans-formation. It is beautiful, nothing is wrong in it, but it is not transformation. And if it is unconscious then you will always be moving in a rut. Again and again you will want to have this experience. The experience is beautiful as far as it goes but it will become a routine. And each time you have it, again more desire is created. The more you have it the more you desire it, and you move in a vicious circle. You don't grow, you just rotate.

Rotation is bad, because then growth is not happening. Then energy is simply wasted. Even if the experience is good the energy is wasted because much more was possible. It was just at the cor-ner – just a turn and much more was possible. With the same energy the divine could have been achieved. With the same energy the ultimate ecstasy is possible, and you are wasting that energy in momentary experiences. And by and by those experiences will become boring, because repeated again and again everything becomes boring. When the newness is lost, boredom is created.

If you remain alert you will see: first, changes of energy in the body; second, dropping of the thoughts from the mind; and third, dropping of the ego from the heart. These three things have to be observed, watched carefully. And when the third has happened sex energy has become meditative energy. Now you are no longer in sex. You may be lying with your beloved, bodies together, but you are no more there – you are transplanted into a new world.

This is what Shiva goes on talking about in Vigyan Bhairav Tantra and in other tantra books. He goes on talking about this phenomenon: you are transmuted, a mutation has happened. This will happen through witnessing.

If you follow suppression you can become so-called human beings – bogus, superficial, hollow within; just dummies, not authentic, not real. If you don't follow suppression but follow indulgence you will become like an animal – beautiful, more beautiful than so-called civilized man, but just animals – not alert, not aware, not conscious of the possibility of growth, of the human potential.

If you transform the energy then you become divine. And remember, when I say divine both things are implied in it. The wild animal with its total beauty of being is there. That wild animal is not rejected and denied. He is there – richer, because he is more alert. So all the wildness is there and the beauty of it, and all that civilization has been trying to force is there, but spontaneous, not forced. Once the energy is transformed, nature and God meet in you – nature with its beauty, God with total grace.

This is what a sage means. A sage means a meeting of nature and the divine, a meeting of the created and the creator, a meeting of body and soul, a meeting of that which is below and of that which is above, a meeting of the earth and the sky.

Says Lao Tzu: Tao happens when earth and heaven meet. This is the meeting.

Witnessing is the basic source. But it will be difficult to become a witness in the sex act if you are not trying to become a witness in other acts of your life. So try it the whole day, otherwise you will be in self-deception. If you cannot become a witness while walking on the road, don't try to deceive yourself, you cannot become a witness while making love. If just walking on the road, such a simple process and you cannot become a witness, you become unconscious in it, how can you become a witness while making love? The process is so deep, you will fall unconscious.

You fall unconscious while walking on the road. Try it – even for a few seconds you will not be able to remember. Try it – walking on the road just try: I will remember I am walking, I am walking, I am walking. After a few seconds you have forgotten. Something else has popped into the mind, you have followed some other direction, you have completely forgotten. And suddenly you remember: I have forgotten. So if such a small act like walking cannot be made conscious, it is going to be difficult to make love a conscious meditation.

So try with simple things, simple activities. While eating, try it. While walking, try it. While talking, listening, try it. Try from everywhere. Make it a constant hammering inside; let your whole body and mind know that you are making an effort to be alert. Only then some day in love the witnessing will happen. And when it happens ecstasy has happened to you – the first glimpse of the divine has descended upon you. From that moment onwards sex will not be sex at all. Sooner or later sex will disappear. This disappearance gives you brahmacharya – then you become a celibate.

Monks in the Catholic monasteries, or monks following traditional Jainism, or other types of monks, are only celibates for the name's sake, because their mind goes on making love – more so than your mind. For them sex becomes cerebral, which is the worst possible thing that can happen, because it is a perversion. If you think about sex it is a perversion. Making love is natural; thinking about it, constantly being involved inside in the mind, is a perversion. The so-called monks are perverted beings, not because they are monks but because they have chosen the path of suppression, which is a wrong path, which leads nowhere.

Jesus, Mahavira and Buddha, are following the path of witnessing. Then brahmacharya happens. This word brahmacharya is very beautiful. The very word means: the way the divine behaves. The way the divine behaves – brahmacharya. It has nothing to say against sex; it is not against sex at all, the word. The word simply says this is how the divine acts, behaves, moves, walks. Once you have known the satori that is possible by witnessing the sex act your whole life will be transformed, you will start behaving like a god.

What are the characteristics of the behavior of a god? How does the divine behave? One thing: he is not dependent, he is absolutely independent. He gives his love to you, but this is not a need. He gives out of his abundance, he has too much. You simply unburden him if you take it, but this is not a need. And the god is a creator: whenever sex has become a transformed force your life becomes creative. Sex is creative force. Right now it moves into biology; it creates new beings, it gives birth. When there is no sex and the energy is transforming it moves into a new world of creativity. Then many new dimensions of creativity become open to you.

It is not that you will start painting or making poetry or doing something else – not that. It may happen, it may not happen, but whatsoever you do will become a creative act, whatsoever you do will become artistic. Even Buddha, sitting under his bodhi tree not doing anything, is creative. The way he is sitting, the very way he is sitting there, he is creating a force, an energy, vibrations all around him.

Much research has been done recently on Egyptian pyramids, and they have come to know many mysterious facts. One of the facts is that the shape of the pyramid, the very shape, is mysterious. Suddenly scientists became aware that if you put a dead body in a pyramid it will be preserved without any chemicals; just the shape helps preservation.

Then one scientist in Germany thought: If the shape can do so much that the body is preserved automatically – just by the shape, just the pressure of the shape.... So he tried it on his razor blade. He made a small pyramid, a cardboard pyramid, and tried it with his used razor blade. Within hours the razor blade was again ready to be used. The shape had given sharpness again to the blade. Then he patented it. One razor blade can be used for your whole life; you just put it in the pyramid. Nothing is to be done; just the shape gives sharpness again – again and again. Now scientists say that every shape creates a particular milieu.

A Buddha is sitting under a bodhi tree: the way he sits, the posture, the gesture, the very phenomenon of his being there without any ego is creating millions of vibrations around. They will go on spreading. Even when this Buddha has disappeared from this tree those vibrations will go on and on and on – they will touch other planets and other stars. Wherever a buddha vibration touches it is creative, it gives you a thrill, it gives you a new breeze.

When sex energy is transformed your whole life becomes creative – independent, free, creative. Whatsoever you do, you create through it. Even if you do not do anything, nondoing becomes creative. Just your very being creates much that is beautiful, that is true, that is good.

Now the story. The old monk who says to the younger: This is against the rules, you should not have touched the girl, is not only saying so because of the rules. Many things are implied. He is rationalizing; he is feeling jealous. And this is how the human mind works – you cannot say directly that you are feeling jealous.

The girl, a beautiful girl, was standing near the river. The sun was setting, down and down, and the girl was afraid. Then came this old monk who was going to his monastery. He looked at the girl...because it is very difficult for a monk to miss a girl and not to look at her. Very difficult for a monk, he is so obsessed with women! He is fighting hard. He is constantly aware that the enemy is there in the woman. You can miss a friend but you cannot miss an enemy – you *have* to see him. If you pass down the street and the enemy is there, it is impossible not to see him. Friends can be passed without even becoming aware that they are there. But enemies, no – because with the enemy is fear. And a beautiful girl, standing alone, nobody else! The girl wanted somebody to help her – the river was unknown and she was afraid to cross it.

This old man must have tried to close his eyes, must have tried to close his heart, must have tried to close his sex center, because that is the only protection against the enemy. He must have hurried, he must have avoided looking back. But when you avoid, you look; when you try not to look, you are looking. His whole mind was filled with the girl. His whole being was around the girl. He was passing the river, but he was not aware of the river now – he could not be. He was going to the monastery but he was not interested in the monastery now; the whole interest was left behind.

Then suddenly he remembers that his colleague, another young monk, is coming. They had been on a begging tour. He looks back, and not only is the young monk there, but the young monk is carrying the girl on his shoulders! This must have created a deep jealousy in the old man. This is what *he* would like to have done. Because of the rules he couldn't do it. But he must take revenge! They walked in silence for miles, and at the monastery gate the old man suddenly said: This was not good – this is against the rules.

That silence was false. For all those miles the old man was thinking how to take revenge, how to condemn this young man. He was continuously obsessed; otherwise nothing happens so suddenly. Mind is a continuity. For these two or three miles he was continuously thinking what to do, and only now he speaks. It is not sudden. Inside there has been a current, a running current. And he says: This is not good, it is against the rules, and I will have to report it to the abbot, to the chief of the monastery, to the master. You have broken a rule, a very basic rule, that no monk should touch a woman. You have not only touched her, you have carried her on your shoulders.

The young monk must have felt amazed. So sudden...because there was no girl now, no river, nobody carrying her. The whole thing has happened in the past. For three miles they have been completely silent. And the young monk said: I left that girl on the bank of the river but you are still carrying her.

This is a deep insight. You can carry things which you are not carrying; you may be burdened by things which are not there; you may be crushed by things which don't exist. The old monk is on the path of repression. The young monk is a symbol of an effort towards transformation, because transformation accepts the woman, the man, the other. Because transformation has to happen through the other, the other will participate in it. Suppression, repression, rejects the other, is against the other. The other has to be destroyed.

This story is beautiful. The new monk is the way. Don't become the old monk, become the new. Accept life as it is and try to be alert. This young monk must have remained alert while carrying the girl on his shoulders. And if you are alert, what can the girl do?

There is a small anecdote: One monk is leaving Buddha. He is going on a tour to spread the message. So he asks Buddha: What should I do about women? That is always the problem with monks.

Buddha says: Don't look at them. This is the simplest way: just close yourself. Don't look at them means just close yourself, forget that they are. Alas, the problem is not so easy. Had it been so easy then all those who know how to close themselves would have been transformed.

One of Buddha's disciples, Ananda, knows the problem is not so easy…. For Buddha it may look easy. This is a problem. You come with a problem to me; it may be easy for me, but that is not going to help. Ananda knows Buddha has replied casually: Don't look at them. So easy for Buddha! Ananda says: But it is not so easy. And he asks: If there is a situation where we have to look, if we cannot avoid looking, then what is to be done?

Buddha says: Don't touch. A look is also a touch – through the eyes. You reach through the eyes and touch. That's why if you stare at a woman for more than three seconds, she will become uneasy. Three seconds is the maximum limit allowed. It is allowed because in life we have to look at each other. But more than three seconds and the woman will become uneasy because you are touching her. Now you are using your eyes as hands. So Buddha says: Don't touch.

But Ananda is persistent. Ananda has done such great work for the whole of humanity because he would always persist. He said: Sometimes there are even situations when we have to touch. What do you say then? If the woman is ill or the woman has fallen in the street and there is nobody else to help and we have to touch. If the situation is such, then what should we do?

Buddha laughs and he says: Then be alert!

The last thing Buddha says is the first. Closing the eyes won't help, non-touching won't help – because you can touch in imagination, you can see in imagination. A real woman is not needed, a real man is not needed. Just close your eyes and you can have an imaginary world of women and men, and you can touch and you can see.

Finally, only one thing can help: Be alert.

This old monk cannot have heard the whole story, all Buddha's three answers. He remained with the first two. The young monk has understood the thing – be alert. He must have come near the girl...desire arises...be alert that the desire has arisen. The problem is not the girl, because how can the girl be your problem? She is her problem, not your problem. The desire arises in you, the desire for woman – that is the problem. The girl is not at all the question. Any girl, any woman would do the same. She is just a point of reference. Seeing the girl, the desire has arisen. To be alert means to be alert to this desire, that: Desire has come to me.

Now, a man who is on the path of repression will suppress this desire, close his eyes towards the object and run away. That is a run-away method. But where can you run? – because you are running from yourself. You can run from the woman who is standing on the riverbank, but you cannot run from the desire that is arising within you. Wherever you go the desire will be there. Be alert that the desire has arisen. Don't really do anything with the woman. If she asks: Help me! – help her. If she says: I am afraid and I cannot cross this river, carry me on your shoulders – carry her! She is giving you a golden opportunity to be alert. And be thankful towards her. Just be alert, feel what is arising in you. What is happening in you? You are carrying the girl, what is happening in you?

If you are alert, then there is no woman – only a little weight on your shoulders, that's all. If you are not alert, then there is a woman. If you are alert, then it is just bones, pressing, weight. If you are not alert, then it is all that desire can create, the fantasy, the maya, the illusion. Carrying a girl on your shoulders, both are possible. If you lose alertness for a single moment, suddenly the maya is sitting on your shoulders. If you are alert, just a little weight, that's all...carrying a weight.

This young man crossing the river was passing through a great discipline. Not avoiding the situation that is life – not avoiding life; passing through it with an alert mind. Many times he may have missed. Many times he may have completely forgotten. Then the whole illusion and the maya was there. Many times he may have recaptured his alertness again when suddenly there is light and darkness disappears. But it must have been beautiful to experience this alertness.

Then he dropped the girl on the other bank and started walking towards his monastery, still alert – because it is not a question of whether the woman is there or not: the memory can follow. He may not have enjoyed the woman, her touch, while crossing the river – but he may enjoy it now in the memory.

He must have remained alert. He was silent, his silence was true. True silence always comes through alertness. That's why he says: I have left the girl there, back at the river. I am not carrying her at all. You are still carrying her. In the old monk's mind things are continuing – and he has not done anything, he has not even touched the girl.

So doing is not the question; it is mind, how your mind is functioning. Be alert and by and by energies are transformed. The old dies and the new is born.

Enough for today.

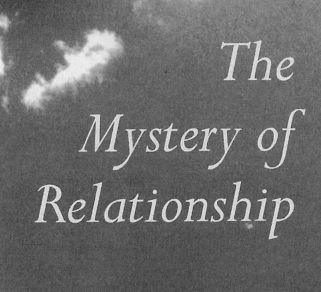

The
Mystery of
Relationship

CHAPTER SEVEN

Beloved Osho,
Would you talk to us about
our living partners –
our wives, husbands and lovers.
When should we persevere with a partner,
and when should we abandon a relationship
as hopeless – or even destructive?
And are our relationships influenced
by previous lives?

ELATIONSHIP IS ONE OF THE MYSTERIES. And because it exists between two persons, it depends on both. Whenever two persons meet a new world is created. Just by their meeting a new phenomenon comes into existence which was not before, which never existed before. And through that new phenomenon both persons are changed and transformed.

Unrelated, you are one thing; related, immediately you become something else. A new thing has happened. A woman when she becomes a lover is no longer the same woman. A man when he becomes a father is no longer the same man. A child is born, but we miss one point completely: the moment the child is born the mother is also born. This never existed before. The woman existed, but the mother never. And a mother is something absolutely new.

Relationship is created by you, but then, in its turn, relationship creates you. Two persons meet, that means two worlds meet. It is not a simple thing but very complex, the most complex. Each person is a world unto himself or herself, a complex mystery with a long past and an eternal future.

In the beginning only peripheries meet. But if the relationship grows intimate, becomes closer, becomes deeper, then by and by centers start meeting. When centers meet it is called love. When peripheries meet it is acquaintance. You touch the person from the without, just from the boundary, then it is acquaintance. Many times you start calling your acquaintance your love. Then you are in a fallacy. Acquaintance is not love.

Love is very rare. To meet a person at his center is to pass through a revolution yourself, because if you want to meet a person at his center you will have to allow that person to reach to your center also. You will have to become vulnerable, absolutely vulnerable, open. It is risky. To allow somebody to reach your center is risky, dangerous, because you never know what that person will do to you. And once all your secrets are known, once your hiddenness has become unhidden, once you are exposed completely, you never know what that other person will do. The fear is there, that's why we never open.

Just acquaintance and we think that love has happened. Peripheries meet and we think we have met. You are not your periphery. Really, the periphery is the boundary where you end, just the fencing around you; it is not you. The periphery is the place where you end and the world begins. Even husbands and wives who may have lived together for many years may be just acquaintances. They may not have known each other. And the more you live with someone, the more you forget completely that the centers have remained unknown.

So the first thing to be understood is: don't take acquaintance as love. You may be making love, you may be sexually related, but sex is also peripheral. Unless centers meet sex is just a meeting of two bodies, and a meeting of two bodies is not *your* meeting. Sex also remains acquaintance – physical, bodily, but still acquaintance. You can allow somebody to enter to your center only when you are not afraid, when you are not fearful.

So I say to you that there are two types of living. One, fear-oriented; one, love-oriented. Fear-oriented living can never lead you into deep relationship. You remain afraid, and the other cannot be allowed – cannot be allowed to penetrate you to your very core. To an extent you allow the other and then the wall comes and everything stops.

The love-oriented person is the religious person. The love-oriented person means one who is not afraid of the future, one who is not afraid of the result and the consequence, who lives here and now.

That's what Krishna says to Arjuna in the Gita: Don't be bothered about the result. That is the fear-oriented mind. Don't think about what will happen out of it. Just be here, and act totally. Don't calculate. A fear-oriented man is always calculating, planning, arranging, safeguarding. His whole life is lost in this way.

I have heard about an old Zen monk. He was on his deathbed. The last day had come, and he declared that that evening he would be no more. So followers, disciples, friends started coming. He had many lovers; they all started coming. From far and wide people gathered.

One of his old disciples, when he heard that the master was going to die, ran to the market. Somebody asked: The master is dying in his hut, why are you going to the market?

The old disciple said: I know that my master loves a particular type of cake, so I am going to purchase the cake.

It was difficult to find the cake, because now it had gone out of fashion, but by the evening somehow he managed. He came running with the cake. And everybody was worried – it was as if the master was waiting for someone. He would open his eyes and look, and close his eyes again. And when this disciple came, he said: Okay, so you have come. Where is the cake?

The disciple produced the cake – and he was very happy that the master asked about the cake. Dying, the master took the cake in his hand, but his hand was not trembling. He was very old, but his hand was not trembling. So somebody asked: You are so old and just on the verge of dying. The last breath is soon to leave you, but your hand is not trembling...?

The master said: I never tremble, because there is no fear.

My body has become old but I am still young, and I will remain young even when the body is gone.

Then he took a bite, started munching the cake. And then somebody asked: What is your last message, Master? You will be leaving us soon. What do you want us to remember?

The master smiled and said: Ah, this cake is delicious.

This is a man who lives in the here and now: This cake is delicious. Even death is irrelevant. The next moment is meaningless. This moment this cake is delicious.

If you can be in this moment, this present moment, this presentness, the plenitude, then only can you love. Love is a rare flowering. It happens only sometimes. Millions and millions of people live in the false attitude that they are lovers. They believe that they love, but that is their belief only.

Love is a rare flowering. Sometimes it happens. It is rare because it can happen only when there is no fear, never before. That means love can happen only to a very deeply spiritual, religious person. Sex is possible for all, acquaintance is possible for all, not love.

When you are not afraid then there is nothing to hide; then you can be open, then you can withdraw all boundaries, and then you can invite the other to penetrate you to the very core. And remember, if you allow somebody to penetrate you deeply, the other will allow you to penetrate into himself or herself, because when you allow somebody to penetrate you, trust is created. When you are not afraid the other becomes fearless.

In your love, fear is always there. The husband is afraid of the wife, the wife is afraid of the husband. Lovers are always afraid. Then it is not love, then it is just an arrangement of two fearful persons depending on each other, fighting, exploiting, manipulating, controlling, dominating, possessing – but it is not love. If you can allow love to happen there is no need for prayer, there is no need for meditation, there is no need for any church, any temple. You can completely forget God if you can love, because through love everything will have happened to you: meditation, prayer, God, everything will have happened to you.

That's what Jesus means when he says: Love is God.

But love is difficult. Fear has to be dropped. And this is the strange thing, that you are so afraid and you have nothing to lose. Kabir has said somewhere: I look into people. They are so much afraid, but I can't see why – because they have nothing to lose. Says Kabir: They are like a person who is naked but never goes to take a bath in the river because he is afraid – where will he dry his clothes? This is the situation you are in – naked, with no clothes, but always afraid about the clothes.

What have you got to lose? Nothing. This body will be taken by death. Before it is taken by death, give it to love. Whatsoever you have will be taken away. Before it is taken away why not share it? That is the only way of possessing it. If you can share and give you are the master. It is going to be taken away. There is nothing which you can retain forever. Death will destroy everything.

So if you follow me rightly, the struggle is between death and love. If you can give there will be no death. Before anything can be taken away from you, you will have already given it, you will have made it a gift.

There can be no death. For a lover there is no death.

For a non-lover every moment is a death, because every moment something is being snatched away from him. The body is disappearing, he is losing every moment. And then there will be death, and everything will be annihilated.

What is the fear? Why are you so afraid? Even if everything is known about you and you are an open book, why fear? How can it harm you? Just false conceptions, just conditionings given by the society...that you have to hide, that you have to protect yourself, that you have to be constantly in a fighting mood, that everybody is an enemy, that everybody is against you.

Nobody is against you! Even if you feel somebody is against you, he too is not against you – because everybody is concerned with himself, not with you. There is nothing to fear. This has to be realized before a real relationship can happen. There is nothing to fear.

Meditate on it. And then allow the other to enter you, invite the other to enter you. Don't create any barrier anywhere; become a passage always open, no locks, no doors on you, no closed doors on you. Then love is possible.

When two centers meet there is love. And love is an alchemical phenomenon – just like hydrogen and oxygen meet and a new thing, water, is created. You can have hydrogen, you can have oxygen, but if you are thirsty they will be useless. You can have as much oxygen as you want, as much hydrogen as you like, but the thirst will not go.

When two centers meet a new thing is created. That new thing is love. It is just like water. The thirst of many, many lives is satisfied. Suddenly you become content. That is the visible sign of love; you become content, as if you have achieved everything. There is nothing to achieve now; you have reached the goal. There is no further goal, destiny is fulfilled. The seed has become a flower – has come to its total flowering.

Deep contentment is the visible sign of love. Whenever a person is in love he is in deep contentment. Love cannot be seen but contentment, the deep satisfaction around him...his every breath, his every movement, his very being – content.

You may be surprised when I say to you that love makes you desireless, but desire is with discontent. You desire because you don't have. You desire because you think if you have something it will give you contentment. Desire is out of discontent. When there is love, and two centers have met and dissolved and merged and a new alchemical quality is born, contentment is there. It is as if the whole existence has stopped – no movement. Then the present moment is the only moment. And then you can say: Ah, this cake is delicious. Even death doesn't mean anything to a man who is in love.

So I say to you, love will make you desireless. Be fearless, drop fears, be open. Allow some center to meet the center within you. You will be reborn through it, a new quality of being will be created. This quality of being says: This is God. God is not an argument, it is a fulfillment, a feeling of fulfillment. You may have observed that whenever you are discontent you want to deny God.

Whenever you are dissatisfied your whole being wants to say: There is no God.

Atheism is not out of logic, it is out of discontent. You may rationalize it – that's another thing. You may not say you are an atheist because you are discontent. You may say: There is no God and I have got proofs. But that is not the true thing. If you are satisfied, suddenly your whole being says: There *is* God. Suddenly you feel it. The whole existence becomes divine. If love is there you will be really for the first time in the feeling that existence is divine and everything is a blessing. But much has to be done before this can happen. Much has to be destroyed before this can happen. You have to destroy all that creates barriers in you.

Make love a *sadhana*, an inner discipline. Don't allow it just to be a frivolous thing. Don't allow it just to be an occupation of the mind. Don't allow it just to be a bodily satisfaction. Make it an inner search, and take the other as a help, as a friend.

If you have heard anything about Tantra you will know that Tantra says: If you can find a consort, a friend, a woman or a man, who is ready to move with you towards the inner center, who is ready to move with you to the highest peak of relationship, then this relationship will become meditative. Then through this relationship you will achieve the ultimate relationship. Then the other becomes just a door.

Let me explain it: if you love a person, by and by first the periphery of the person disappears, the form of the person disappears. You come more and more in contact with the formless, the inner. The form becomes, by and by, vague and disappears. And if you go deeper, then even this formless individual starts disappearing and melting. Then the beyond opens. Then that particular individual was just a door, an opening. And through your lover you find the divine.

Because we cannot love, we need so many religious rituals. They are substitutes, and very poor substitutes. A Meera needs no temple to go to. The whole existence is her temple. She can dance before a tree and the tree becomes Krishna. She can sing before a bird and the bird becomes Krishna. She creates her Krishna around her everywhere. Her love is such that wherever she looks the door opens and the Krishna is revealed, the beloved is revealed.

But the first glimpse will always come through an individual. It is difficult to be in contact with the universal. It is so big, so vast, so beginningless, endless – from where to start? From where to move into it? The individual is the door. Fall in love.

And don't make it a struggle. Make it a deep allowance for the other, just an invitation. Allow the other to penetrate you without any conditions, and suddenly the other disappears and God is there. If your lover or beloved cannot become divine, then nothing in this world can become divine. Then all your religious talk is just nonsense. This can happen with a child. This can happen with an animal, your dog. If you can be in deep relationship with a dog, it can happen – the dog becomes divine!

So it is not a question of man and woman only. That is one of the deepest sources of the divine and it reaches you naturally, but it can happen from anywhere. The basic key is this: you should allow the other to penetrate you to your very deepest core, to the very ground of your being.

But we go on deceiving ourselves. We think we love. And if you think that you love, then there is no possibility for love to happen – because if this is love, then everything is closed. Make fresh efforts. Try to find in the other the real being that is hidden. Don't take anybody for granted. Every individual is such a mystery that if you go on and on into him it is endless.

But we get bored with the other – because just the periphery, and always the periphery....

I was reading a story. A man was very ill and he tried all types of 'pathies', but nothing would help. Then he went to a hypnotist and the hypnotist gave him a mantra to repeat continuously: I am not ill. For at least fifteen minutes in the morning and fifteen minutes at night: I am not ill, I am healthy. And the whole day, whenever you remember, repeat it.

Within a few days he started getting better. And within weeks he was absolutely okay. Then he told his wife: This has been a miracle! Should I go to this hypnotist for another miracle also?...because lately I am feeling no sexual appetite and the sexual relationship has almost stopped. There is no desire.

The wife was happy. She said: You go – because she was feeling very frustrated.

The man went to the hypnotist. He came back, and his wife asked: What mantra, what suggestion has he given now? The man wouldn't tell her. But within weeks his sexual appetite started returning. He started feeling desire again.

So the wife was very puzzled. She continuously persisted in asking, but the man would laugh and would not say anything. So one day she tried – when he was in the bathroom in the morning doing his meditation, that fifteen-minute mantra, she tried to hear what he was saying.

He was saying: She is not my wife, she is not my wife, she is not my wife.

We take people for granted. Somebody is your wife – relationship is finished. Somebody is your husband – relationship is finished. Now there is no adventure. The other has become a thing, a commodity. The other is not now a mystery to be searched, the other is no longer new.

Remember, everything goes dead with age. The periphery is always old, and the center is always new. The periphery cannot remain new, because every moment it is getting old, stale. The center is always fresh and young. Your soul is neither a child, nor a young man, nor an old man. Your soul is simply eternally fresh. It has no age.

You can experiment with it: you may be young, you may be old, just close your eyes and find out. Try to feel how your center is – old? young? You will feel that the center is neither. It is always new, it never gets old. Why? – because the center doesn't belong to time.

In the process of time everything becomes old. A man is born – the body has started becoming old already. When we say that a child is one week old, it means one week of oldness has penetrated into the child. The child has already passed seven days towards death, he has completed seven days of dying. He is moving towards death – sooner or later he will be dead.

Whatsoever comes in time becomes old. The moment it enters time it is already becoming old. Your body is old, your periphery is old. You cannot be eternally in love with it. But your center is always fresh, it is eternally young. Once you are in contact with it, love is an every-moment discovery. And then the honeymoon never ends. If it ends it was not a honeymoon at all – it was just an acquaintance.

And the last thing to remember is: in the relationship of love you always blame the other if something goes wrong. If something is not happening as it should, the other is responsible. This will destroy the whole possibility of future growth. Remember you are always responsible, and change yourself. Drop those qualities which create trouble. Make love a self-transformation.

As they say in salesmen's courses: The customer is always right. I would like to say to you: In the world of relationship and love, you are always in the wrong, the other is always right. And this is how lovers always feel. If there is love, they always feel: Something is wrong with me if things are not happening as they should. And both feel the same way! Then things grow, then centers open, then boundaries merge.

But if you think that the other is wrong, you are closing yourself and the other. And the other also thinks that *you* are wrong. Thoughts are infectious. If you think the other is wrong even if you have not said it, even if you are smiling and showing that you don't think the other is wrong – the other has got the point through your eyes, through your gestures, through your face. Even if you are an actor, a great actor, and you can just arrange your face, your gestures as you like, then too the unconscious is continuously sending signals: You are wrong. And when you say that the other is wrong, the other starts feeling that you are wrong.

Relationship is destroyed on this rock and then people become closed. If you say somebody is wrong, somebody starts protecting, safeguarding. Then closure happens. Remember always: in love you are always wrong. And then the possibility will open and the other will also feel the same. We create the feeling in the other. When lovers are close, immediately thoughts go jumping from one to the other. Even if they are not saying anything, they are silent, they communicate. Language is for non-lovers, those who are not in love. For lovers silence is enough language. Without saying anything they go on speaking.

If you take love as sadhana, then don't say the other is wrong. Just try to find out: somewhere something must be wrong in you, and drop that wrongness. It is going to be difficult because it is going to be against the ego. It is going to be difficult because it will hurt your pride. It is going to be difficult because this will not be dominating, possessing. You will not be more powerful through possessing the other. This will destroy your ego – that's why it is going to be difficult.

But destruction of the ego is the point, the goal. From wherever you like to approach the inner world – from love, from meditation, from yoga, from prayer – whatsoever the path you choose, the goal is the same: the destruction of the ego, throwing the ego away.

Through love it can be done very easily. And it is so natural! Love is the natural religion. Anything else is going to be more and more unnatural. If you cannot work through love, it will be difficult for you to work through anything else. Don't think much about past lives, and don't think much about the future. The present is enough. Don't think that relationship is coming from the past – it *is* coming from the past, but don't think about it because then you will get more complicated. Make things easier.

It *is* going on – from your past lives things have a continuity, so I don't deny the fact, but don't get burdened by it. It will continue in the future, but don't think about it. The present is more than enough. Munch the cake and say: This cake is delicious. Don't think of the past and don't think of the future; they will take care of themselves. Nothing is discontinuous. You have been in relationships in the past. You have loved, you have hated, you have made friends and you have made enemies. That continues; known, unknown to you, it is always there. But if you start brooding about it, you will miss the present moment.

So think as if there is no past, and think as if there is no future. This moment is all that is given to you. Work it out, as if this moment is all. Behave as if this moment is all and work out how you can transform your energies into a loving phenomenon – this very moment.

People come to me and they want to know about their past lives. They had past lives, but it is irrelevant. Why this inquiry? What are you going to do about the past? Nothing can be done now. The past is past and it cannot be undone. You cannot change it. You cannot go back. That's why nature, in its wisdom, doesn't allow you to remember past lives; otherwise you would go mad.

You may be in love with a girl. If you suddenly become aware that that girl was your mother in your past life, things will become very complicated. Then what to do? And when that girl has been your mother in a past life, making love to her now will create guilt. Not making love to her will also create guilt, because you love her.

That's why I say nature in its wisdom never allows you to remember your past lives – unless you come to a point where it can be allowed. When you become so meditative that nothing disturbs you, then the gates open and all your past lives are before you. It is an automatic mechanism, though sometimes the mechanism doesn't work. Through accidents some children are born who can remember, but their lives are destroyed.

One girl was brought to me a few years ago. She remembered her past two lives. She was only thirteen at that time, but if you looked in her eyes they looked nearabout seventy – because she remembered seventy years, two past lives. Her body was thirteen years old, but her mind was seventy years old. She couldn't play with other children, because how can an old woman of seventy play with children? She would talk and behave like an old woman.

And she was burdened, the worries of all those years in her mind. She remembered so accurately that her two past families could be found. One was in Assam, the other in Madhya Pradesh. When she came in contact with her old families, she became so much attached to them that it became a problem: where should she live now?

I told the parents: Leave the girl with me for at least three weeks. I will make an effort to help her forget, because this girl's life will be a perversion. She cannot fall in love with somebody – she is too old. Your oldness is concerned with your memory. If the memory span is of seventy years, then you feel like seventy. And she seemed so tortured – her face, the features, all tortured. She seemed so ill at her center – uneasy, uncomfortable. Everything seemed to be wrong.

But the parents were enjoying the whole thing, because people started coming and the newspapers started giving the report. They were enjoying the whole thing. They wouldn't listen to me and I told them: This girl will go mad.

They never brought the girl to me again. But after seven years they came – the girl had gone mad. They said: Now do something. I said: It is now impossible to do anything. Now only death will be a help to her.

You don't remember because it would be difficult for you to manage. Even in this life you are making such a mess – many lives remembered, you would simply go mad. Don't think about it. It is irrelevant also.

The relevant point is: be here and now and work out your way. If you can work it out through relationship, beautiful. If you cannot work it out through relationship, then work it out in your loneliness. These are the two paths. Love means working out your path through relationship. And meditation: working it out in your loneliness. Love and meditation – these are the two paths. Feel which will suit you. Then bring your total energies to it, and move on that path.

Beloved Osho,
Your words are so beautiful,
yet we feel there is also another
communication happening
when you are talking to us.
Would you talk to us
about silent communication,
and how we can become more open to it.

T IS ALWAYS THERE. While I am talking to you, I am also 'being' to you. Talking is relating to you through the intellect, and being is relating to you with my totality. While you are listening to me, if you are really listening, then it is not only a listening to the words. Listening to me your mind stops. Listening to me you are not thinking. When you are not thinking you are open. And when you are not thinking and your mind is not functioning you start feeling. Then I can overwhelm you, I can move and fill you. Words are used only as a device.

I myself am not interested much in words. But I have to speak, because this has been my feeling: while I am speaking you become silent. If I am not speaking, then you are speaking within and you are not silent. If you are silent without my speaking, then there will be no need to speak. I am waiting for that moment when you can just sit by my side, just sit near me, not thinking. Then there is no need to talk – because talk is partial. Then I can come in my totality to you, directly, no need for any mediating words.

But if I tell you to sit silently near me, you will not be able to sit silently. You will go on chattering, you will go on talking within. An inner talk will continue. To stop your inner talk I have to talk to you, so while I am talking you are engaged. My talking is just like a toy given to a child. He goes and plays with the toy and becomes silent, absorbed. I give you my words as toys. You play with them, and while you are playing with them you are so absorbed that you become silent. Whenever silence happens I can flow into you.

Words can be beautiful but they can never be true. Beauty is an aesthetic value. You can enjoy it, just like a beautiful painting, but nothing much will happen out of that enjoyment. It is good as far as it goes. But words are never true – they cannot be by their very nature. Truth can be communicated only in silence. But this is the paradox: those who have insisted that truth can be communicated only in silence have all used words. This is a shame, but nothing can be done about it. Words have to be used to make you silent. While listening to me you become silent. That silence is significant, and that silence will give you glimpses of truth.

Even if you have glimpses of truth through my words, that glimpse comes through your silence, not through my words. Even if you feel absolutely certain that whatsoever I am saying is true, that feeling of absolute certainty comes through your silence, not through my words. Whenever you are silent truth is there. Whenever you are chattering inside, the monkey-chatter goes on inside, you miss the truth which is always present.

Whatsoever I do – talk to you, help you to meditate with me, force you into a catharsis, or persuade you to dance, to celebrate – whatsoever I do, there is only one aim: somehow to help you to become silent, because whenever you are silent doors are open; you are in the temple. How you become silent is not relevant. You become silent and then I am within you, you are within me. Silence knows no boundaries. In silence love is happening. I have become a lover to you; you have become a lover to me. In silence all that is significant happens. But to bring silence is a problem, arduous.

So I am not much interested in what I say to you. I am interested in what happens to you while I am saying anything – x, y, z. Sometimes I go on contradicting myself. Today I say something, tomorrow I will say something else, because what I say is not the point. My talking is just like poetry. I am not a philosopher. I may be a poet but I am not a philosopher. Tomorrow I will say something else, the day after tomorrow something else. That is not the point. My sayings may contradict, but *I* am not contradictory – because today I say something and you become silent; tomorrow I say something absolutely contradictory and you become silent; the day after tomorrow I again say something absolutely contradictory – all that I have said contradicts it – but you become silent.

Your silence is my consistency. I am consistent, constantly consistent – contradicting on the surface, but the inner current remains the same.

And remember, if I say the same thing every day to you, you will not be silent. Then you will get bored and your inner talk will start. If I go on saying the same thing it will become old. When it is old you need not listen to it, or even without listening you know what I am saying, so you can continue your inner talk. I have to be inventive saying things, shocking you sometimes. But one inner consistency remains: that is to create silence in you – because then I can be with you and you can be with me. The love, the truth, can flower there.

Whenever there is silence, truth flowers.

Truth is a flowering of silence.

Enough for today.

*Only a
Ripe Fruit
Falls*

CHAPTER EIGHT

Beloved Osho,
I feel that through developing an attitude
of endurance towards difficulties,
I have become resigned to much of life.
This resignation feels like a weight pushing against
my effort to become more alive in meditation.
Does this mean that I have suppressed my ego,
and that I must find it again
before I can really lose it?

NE OF THE GREATEST PROBLEMS. It will appear very paradoxical, but this is true: before you can lose your ego, you must attain it. Only a ripe fruit falls to the ground. Ripeness is all. An unripe ego cannot be thrown, cannot be destroyed. And if you struggle with an unripe ego to destroy and dissolve it, the whole effort is going to be a failure. Rather than destroying it, you will find it more strengthened in new, subtle ways.

This is something basic to be understood: the ego must come to a peak, it must be strong, it must have attained an integrity – only then can you dissolve it. A weak ego cannot be dissolved. And this becomes a problem.

In the East all the religions preach egolessness, so in the East everybody is against the ego from the very beginning. Because of this 'anti' attitude, ego never becomes strong, never comes to a point of integration from where it can be thrown. It is never ripe. So in the East it is very difficult to dissolve the ego, almost impossible.

In the West...the whole Western tradition of religion and psychology propounds, preaches, persuades people to have strong egos – because unless you have a strong ego, how can you survive?

Life is a struggle; if you are egoless you will be destroyed. Then who will resist? Who will fight? Who will compete? And life is a continuous competition. Western psychology says: Attain to the ego, be strong in it.

But in the West it is very easy to dissolve the ego. So whenever a Western seeker reaches an understanding that ego is the problem he can easily dissolve it, more easily than any Eastern seeker. This is the paradox: in the West ego is taught, in the East egolessness is taught. But in the West it is easy to dissolve the ego, in the East it is very difficult.

This is going to be a hard task for you, first to attain and then to lose – because you can lose only something which you possess. If you don't possess it, how can you lose it? You can be poor only if you are rich. If you are not rich your poverty cannot have that beauty which Jesus goes on preaching: Be poor in spirit. Your poverty cannot have that significance which Gautam Buddha has when he becomes a beggar. Only a rich man can become poor, because you can lose only that which you have. If you have never been rich, how can you be poor? Your poverty will be just on the surface, it can never be in the spirit. On the surface you will be poor, and deep down you will be hankering after riches. Your spirit will hanker towards riches, it will be an ambition, it will be a constant desire to attain riches. Only on the surface will you be poor. And you may even console yourself by saying that poverty is good.

But you cannot be poor – only a rich man, a really rich man, can be poor. Just to have riches is not enough to be really rich. You may still be poor. If the ambition is still there, you are poor. What you have is not the point. If you have enough then the desire disappears. When you have enough riches the desire disappears. Disappearance of the desire is the criterion of enoughness. Then you are rich – you can drop it, you can become poor, you can become a beggar like Buddha. And then your poverty is rich; then your poverty has a kingdom of its own.

And the same happens with everything. Upanishads or Lao Tzu or Jesus or Buddha – they all teach that knowledge is useless. Just getting more and more knowledgeable is not much help. Not only is it not much help, it can become a barrier. Knowledge is not needed. But that doesn't mean you should remain ignorant. Your ignorance will not be real. When you have gathered enough knowledge and you throw it, then ignorance is attained. Then you really become ignorant – like Socrates who can say: I know only one thing, that I don't know anything. This knowledge, or this ignorance – you can call it whatever you like – is totally different, the quality is different, the dimension has changed.

If you are simply ignorant because you never attained to any knowledge your ignorance cannot be wise, it cannot be wisdom – it is simply absence of knowledge. And the hankering will be inside: How to gain more knowledge? How to gain more information?

When you know too much – you have known the scriptures, you have known the past, the tradition, you have known all that can be known – then suddenly you become aware of the futility of it all, suddenly you become aware that this is not knowledge, this is borrowed! This is not your own existential experience, this is not what you have come to know. Others may have known it, you have simply gathered it. Your gathering is mechanical; it has not arisen out of you, it is not a growth. It is just rubbish gathered from other doors, borrowed, dead.

Remember, knowing is alive only when *you* know, when it is your immediate, direct experience. But when you know from others it is just memory, not knowledge. Memory is dead. When you gather much – the riches of knowledge, scriptures, all around you, libraries condensed in your mind, and suddenly you become aware that you are just carrying the burden of others, nothing belongs to you, you have not known – then you can drop it, you can drop all this knowledge. In that dropping a new type of ignorance arises within you. This ignorance is not the ignorance of the ignorant; this is how a wise man is, how wisdom is.

Only a wise man can say: I don't know. But in saying: I don't know, he is not hankering after knowledge, he is simply stating a fact. And when you can say with your total heart: I don't know, in that very moment your eyes become open, the doors of knowing are open. In that very moment when you can say with your totality: I don't know, you have become capable of knowledge. This ignorance is beautiful, but it is attained through knowledge. It is poverty attained through richness. And the same happens with ego – you can lose it if you have it.

When Buddha comes down from his throne, becomes a beggar...what is the necessity for Buddha? He was a king, enthroned, at the peak of his ego – why this extreme, moving down from his palace to the streets, becoming a beggar? But Buddha has a beauty in his begging. The earth has never known such a beautiful beggar, such a rich beggar, such a kingly beggar, such an emperor.

What happened when he stepped down from his throne? He stepped down from his ego. Thrones are nothing but symbols, symbols of the ego, of power, prestige, status. He stepped down and then egolessness happened. This egolessness is not humbleness; this egolessness is not humility. You may find many humble people, but under their humility subtle egos are functioning.

It is said that once Diogenes came to visit Socrates. Diogenes lived like a beggar; he always wore dirty clothes with many patches and holes. Even if you presented him with a new dress he would not use it – first he would make it dirty, old, torn, and then he would use it. He came to visit Socrates, and he started talking about egolessness. But Socrates' penetrating eyes must have come to realize that this man was not an egoless man. The way he was talking about humility was very egoistic. Socrates is reported to have said: Through your dirty clothes, through the holes in your clothes, I cannot see anything else but the ego. You talk of humility, but that talk comes from a deep center of the ego.

This will happen, this is how hypocrisy happens. You have the ego, you hide it through the opposite; you become humble on the surface. This surface humbleness cannot deceive anyone. It may deceive you, but it cannot deceive anyone else. From the holes of the dirty dresses your ego goes on peeping. It is always there. This is a self-deception and nothing more. Nobody else is deceived.

This happens if you start throwing the unripe ego.

What I teach will look contradictory but it is true to life. Contradiction is inherent in life. I teach you to be egoists so that you can become egoless. I teach you to be perfect egoists. Don't hide it, otherwise hypocrisy will be born. And don't struggle with the unripe phenomenon. Let it ripen – and help it, bring it to a peak! Don't be afraid – there is nothing to be afraid of. This is how you will come to realize the agony of the ego. When it comes to its peak, then you will not need a Buddha or me to tell you that the ego is hell. You will know it, because the peak of the ego will be the peak of your hellish experiences, it will be a nightmare. And then there is no need for anybody to tell you: Drop it! It will be difficult to carry it on.

One reaches to knowledge only through suffering. You cannot throw anything just by logical argument. You can throw something only when it has become so painful that it cannot be carried any further. Your ego has not become that painful yet – hence you carry it. It is natural. I cannot persuade you to drop it. Even if you feel persuaded you will hide it, that's all.

Nothing unripe can be thrown. Unripe fruit clings to the tree and the tree clings to the unripe fruit. If you force it to separate, a wound is left behind. That scar will continue, the wound will always remain green and you will always feel hurt. Remember, everything has a time to grow, to be ripe, to fall down into the earth and dissolve. Your ego also has a time. It needs maturity.

So don't be afraid of being egoists. You are, otherwise you would have disappeared long ago. This is the mechanism of life: you have to be egoists, you have to fight your way, you have to fight with so many millions of desires around you, you have to struggle, you have to survive.

Ego is a survival measure. If a child is born without the ego he will die. He cannot survive, it is impossible, because if he feels hunger he will not feel: I am hungry. He will feel there is hunger, but not related to him. The moment hunger is felt, the child feels: I am hungry. He starts crying and making efforts to be fed. The child grows through the growth of his ego.

So to me, ego is part of natural growth. But that doesn't mean that you have to remain with it forever. It is a natural growth, and then there is a second step when it has to be dropped. That too is natural. But the second step can be taken only when the first has come to its crescendo, its climax, when the first has reached its peak. So I teach both: I teach ego-ness and I teach egolessness.

First be egoists, perfect egoists, absolute egoists, as if the whole of existence exists for you and you are the center; all the stars revolve around you and the sun rises for you; everything exists for you, just to help you to be here. Be the center, and don't be afraid, because if you are afraid then you will never be ripe. Accept it. It is part of growth. Enjoy it and bring it to a peak.

When it comes to a peak, suddenly you will become aware that you are not the center. This has been a fallacy, this has been a childish attitude. But you were a child, so nothing is wrong in it. Now you have become mature, and now you see that you are not the center.

Really, when you see that you are not the center, you also see there is no center in existence, or everywhere is the center. Either there is no center and existence exists as a totality, a wholeness without any center as a control point, or every single atom is a center.

Jakob Böhme has said that the whole world is filled with centers, every atom is a center, and there is no circumference – centers everywhere and circumference nowhere. These two are the possibilities. Both mean the same; only the wording is different and contradictory. But first become a center.

It is like this: you are in a dream; if the dream comes to a peak it will be broken. Always it happens – whenever a dream comes to a climax it is broken. And what is the climax of a dream? The climax of a dream is the feeling that this is real. You feel this is real, not a dream, and you go on and on and on and on to a higher peak and the dream becomes almost real. It can never become real; it becomes *almost* real. It comes so close to reality that now you cannot go further, because one step more and the dream will become real – and it cannot become real because it is a dream! When it comes so close to reality sleep is broken, the dream is shattered, you are fully awake.

The same happens with all types of fallacies. Ego is the greatest dream. It has its beauty, its agony. It has its ecstasy, its agony. It has its heavens and hells, both are there. Dreams sometimes are beautiful and sometimes nightmares, but both are dreams.

So I don't tell you to come out of your dream before the time has come. No, never do anything before the time. Allow things to grow, allow things to have their time so that everything happens naturally. Ego will drop. It can drop of its own accord also. If you simply allow it to grow and help it to grow, there will be no need to drop it.

This is very deep. If *you* drop it, ego has remained inside. Who will drop it? If you think *you* will drop it you are the ego, so whatsoever you drop will not be the real thing. The real thing will be preserved and you will have thrown something else. You cannot make yourself egoless. Who will do it? It happens, it is not a doing. You grow into ego and a point comes when the whole thing becomes so hellish that the dream is broken. Suddenly you see the goose is out – it has never been in the bottle. You have never been an ego. It was just a dream around you. A necessary dream, I say, so I don't condemn it – a necessary part of growth.

In life everything is necessary. Nothing is unnecessary, nothing can be unnecessary. Whatsoever has happened had to happen. Whatsoever is happening is happening because of certain deep causes. You need it so you can remain in the fallacy. It is just a cocoon that helps you, protects you, helps you to survive. One need not be in the cocoon forever. When you are ready, break the cocoon, come out. The ego is the shell of the egg, it protects you. But when you are ready, break the shell, come out of the egg. The ego is the shell. But wait. Hurry will not be of much help; haste will not help – it may hinder. Allow time, and don't condemn it...because who will condemn it?

Go to the so-called saints; they talk of humbleness, humility. Look into their eyes: you will not find such refined egos anywhere else. Now their egos have taken the garb of religion, yoga, saint-hood – but the ego is there. They may not be collecting riches, they may be collecting followers; the coins have changed and they go on counting how many followers....

They may not be after the things of this world, they are after the things of that world, but this or that, both are worlds. And they may be even more greedy, because they say these temporary things, momentary things of this world, consist of momentary pleasures – and they want eternal pleasures. Their greed is supreme. They cannot be satisfied by momentary pleasures, they want eternal pleasures. Unless something is eternal they are not gratified. Their greed is deep, their greed is absolute, and greed belongs to the ego. Greed is the hunger of the ego.

So it happens sometimes that saints are more egoistic than sinners, and then they are far away from the divine. And some-times sinners can attain to God more easily than those so-called saints, because ego is the barrier. This has been my experience, that sinners can drop their egos more easily than saints, because sinners have never been against the ego. They have been feeding it, they have been enjoying it, they have lived with it totally. And saints have always been fighting the ego, so they never allowed it to become ripe.

So this is my attitude: ego has to be dropped, but it may take a long waiting; and you can drop it only if you cultivate it. This is the arduousness of the whole phenomenon, because the mind says: If we have to drop it, then why cultivate it? The mind says: When we have to destroy it, then why create it? If you listen to the mind you will be in trouble. Mind is always logical and life is always illogical, so they never meet. This is simple logic, ordinary mathe-matics, that if you are to destroy this house, then why build it? Why this whole trouble? Why this effort and waste of time and energy? The house is not there, so why build it and then destroy it?

The house is not the point really – you are the point. Building the house you will change, and then destroying the house you will change completely, you will not be the same – because creating the house, the whole process of it will prove a growth to you. Then when the house is ready you pull it down. That will be a mutation.

Mind is logical and life is dialectical. Mind moves in a simple line and life moves always jumping from one pole to another, from one thing to the very opposite. Life is dialectical. Create, and then life says: Destroy! Be born, and then life says: Die! Attain, and then life says: Lose! Be rich, and then life says: Become poor! Be a peak, an Everest of the ego, and then become an abyss of egoless-ness. Then you have known both – the illusory and the real, the maya and the Brahman.

Almost every day it happens, somebody comes to be initiated into sannyas and then his mind starts functioning and he says to me: Wearing orange will make me more egoistic because then I will feel that I am somebody different, distinct – I am a sannyasin, one who has renounced. So wearing orange will make me more egoistic, he says, and I say to him: Become! Become egoistic, but consciously.

Ego is a disease if you are unconscious about it, if you hide it in the unconscious. Ego is a game if you are conscious about it. You can enjoy it. You can play it. Be conscious, mindful, and play the game. A game is not bad, but when you forget that it is a game and become too serious then problems arise.

So I say sannyas is not serious; it is a game – a religious game, of course. It has its own rules, because every game must have rules; without rules no game can be played. Life can be without rules, but games cannot be.

If somebody says: I am not going to follow this rule – then you cannot play the game. You play cards, then you follow rules. And you never say: These rules are just arbitrary, artificial, why can't we change them? You *can* change them, but then the game will be difficult. And if every individual follows his own rules, then the game is impossible.

Life is possible! You can play as you like because life never believes in rules – it is beyond rules. But games have rules. Remember, wherever you see rules, know immediately this is a game. This is the criterion: wherever you see rules, immediately know this is a game, because games exist through rules.

So if I say: Wear orange, have the mala – this is a game, obviously. Play it as well as you can – and don't be serious about it, otherwise you miss the point. Be egoists – perfect, cultivated, refined. Go on working on your ego and make it a beautiful statue, because before you give it back to existence it must be something worth giving, it must be a present.

Beloved Osho,
You have said that much energy is needed
to achieve the inner alchemy.
Would you talk to us about energy:
how can we build it up, and how can we retain it?
In what ways do we lose it, and
can we gain it from outside sources?

THE FIRST THING: you are part of an infinite energy, a wave in an infinite ocean. If you can remember this you never lose energy, because an infinite source is always available. You are just a wave, and deep down the ocean is hidden.

You are born – who gives you birth? Who gives energy to you to move into the body? Who gives energy to the body to become an automatic, delicate mechanism, an organism? For seventy years or eighty years, or even a hundred years, the body continues being alive. And now scientists say that death is an accident, the body can continue infinitely. Scientists say there is no necessity for death to exist. It exists because we have not been able to use the infinite energy that is around us.

So the first thing to remember is: you are part of an infinite energy. Continuously remember it and feel it. Moving, walking, eating, sleeping – feel you are infinite. This is what the Upanishads say: always feel you are the Brahman, the eternal. If you can feel this more and more, you will become aware that you are not losing any energy. The source becomes available. You become a vehicle. Then do whatsoever you want to do. By doing, nobody loses energy.

This is one of the fallacies of the human mind, that if you do something you lose energy. No. If you have this idea that doing something I am losing energy, you lose energy, not by doing but by having the idea. Otherwise, through doing you can gain energy – if you have the idea. If you don't have any idea, then also no energy is lost.

When people are retired they start thinking that now they have less energy so they must rest and relax more; they should not do anything, otherwise their energy is lost. And then they die sooner than they would have died. Statistics say that the life span is reduced by ten years: a person who is working may have lived to seventy; retired, he will die at sixty.

Your body is a dynamo. The more you use it, the more energy from the infinite source is supplied. If you don't use it there is no need for any new supply. Then by and by the supply stops. Be more active and you will have more energy. Be less active and you will lose much energy. Through activity energy is not lost, through activity you renew it. You use the energy, then from the source more energy becomes available.

Look at the trees. The sun rises and from the leaves of the trees water starts evaporating. The moment a leaf starts evaporating water, new water circulates from the roots. It is a long process. The leaf releases water, then just near the leaf dryness is created. That dryness immediately sucks water from the twig; then the twig is dry, the twig sucks water from its branch. This goes on down to the roots; then the roots suck water from the earth. If the leaves think: If we evaporate water then we will die, we will feel thirsty – then this tree is going to die, because then new sources will not be available, then the roots will not be able to function.

You also have roots in the infinite. When you use energy you suck energy from the infinite. Your roots start working. A very fallacious idea is in the human mind, that through activity we lose energy. No. The more active, the more energy you will have; the less active, the less energy. And this is true of activity in all directions of life. Love more and you will have more love to give. Become a miser and think: If I love more, then my love will be dissipated, and sooner or later I will not have any love any more, so it is better to preserve it. Then your love will die and you will not be able to love.

Love, and more love becomes available; use more, and you have more. This is the law of life. You can eat the cake and have it also. Compassion, love, activity, whatsoever the dimension, the same rule applies. Whatsoever you want more of, do the same. If you want to become an infinite source of love, then go on sharing love as much as you can. Don't be a miser; only misers lose energy. And we are all misers, that's why we always feel dissipated.

But the idea can be dangerous, poisonous. If you have an idea, that idea works. Mind works through hypnosis. For example, just a few decades ago all over the world it was taught that you have a limited quota of sexual energy. You make love, energy is lost. That idea created sexual misers all over the world. The whole idea is fallacious. But if you have the idea in your mind, then whenever you make love you are continuously hypnotizing yourself that you are losing energy. Then energy is wasted. This idea becomes imprinted in your mind. And when you make love you are so vulnerable, so receptive, you are so soft, so to speak, that whatsoever you are thinking goes deep into you. And then the consequences follow: you feel dissipated, you feel your energy is lost. And when you feel dissipated and energy is lost, the old idea is strengthened still more. This becomes a vicious circle.

Now scientists, biologists say that sex is infinite energy. You cannot lose it, because every day it is being created by your food, by your breathing, by your activity. It is created. It is not a stored thing so that when you take a particular quantity out that much is lost, you now have less. It is not that way. It is not something stored there, it is being created every moment. If you don't use it, it goes stale and dead. If you don't use it, it will make you stale and dead. Then the flow has stopped. But if you go on flowing, more and more becomes available to you.

Jesus says somewhere – one of the most foundational things he says: If you try to cling to life, you will lose it; and if you are ready to lose it, you will have it in abundance.

All over the world up to this century children were taught that any leakage of semen in any way is very destructive: You may go mad, you may become crippled; at least your intelligence will be less, and the possibility of becoming crazy and eccentric and weak will be more. This is absolutely false! But the teaching did make many people crazy, many people weak, many people stupid, mediocre, because the idea.... And this is such a dangerous idea. When a child has grown up and become mature, at the age of fourteen or fifteen, he starts losing semen. He cannot do anything about it. He will masturbate, or if morality is too much he will not masturbate but nocturnal ejaculations will be there, in the night he will lose semen. And all around the propaganda is going on: If you lose semen, everything is lost.

In India they used to say – if you go to old saints and their followers, they still say – that one drop of semen means forty days of work for the body. So for forty days the body has to work, then one drop of semen is created. So if one drop is lost, forty days of life is wasted.

Small children don't know anything, and they are very receptive. When the whole society teaches this, they become hypnotized by it. Then they cannot do anything because the semen flows; when the body is ready, the semen is bound to go out. This teaching is all around and they cannot tell anybody that they are losing semen.

They hide it. They suffer inside, they go through a constant torture. And they think they are the exceptions, because they can't know that everybody else is going through the same thing, because nobody talks about it, nobody speaks about it. And whosoever talks about it, talks against it.

Many people go on writing letters to me saying that their lives are wasted because they have lost so much semen, they have lost so much sex energy. That idea is very dangerous, and if an idea is there, the thing will happen. It happens through hypnosis.

Any idea can become a help or a hindrance. It is difficult to live in the no-idea. So before you can reach to a mind which is thoughtless, when everything becomes available spontaneously – before that, it is better to have this idea in the mind: that you are part of an infinite energy, and by doing you are gaining, not losing. By giving you are attaining, not losing.

Love, sex, activity – whatsoever, always remember and be filled with the idea that whenever you give something, from the roots more becomes available to you, more is given to you. God is the giver, the unconditional giver.

If you are also a giver, your hands will always be empty and God can give you more. If you are a miser, your relationship with the divine is cut. Then you live as a small wave, always afraid of losing.

Live as the ocean. Be oceanic! Never think of losing, about anything. Nothing is lost, nothing can be lost. And you are not an individual, you only appear as an individual. The whole is joined to you; you are just a face of the whole, just a way the whole has happened. Don't be worried about it. It is never going to end. This existence is beginningless and endless.

Enjoy, celebrate, be active, and always be a giver. To be a giver so totally that you never think of retaining or holding anything is the only real prayer. To give is to pray. To give is to love. And those who can give, they are always given more.

Enough for today.

Surrender and I Will Do the Rest

CHAPTER NINE

Beloved Osho,
You have said: Not in thousands and
thousands of years has such
an opportunity come to this earth.
And you have also said: This age is like any other.
You have said: Surrender to a stone
and it will happen.
And you have said: It is essential to tread
this dangerous path only with
the guidance of a true master.
You have said: Surrender and I will do the rest.
And you've said: I do nothing.
For us here and now, and for those in the West
who will read these words, would you talk to us some more
about the master/disciple phenomenon.

I CONTRADICT MYSELF and do it knowingly. Truth is so infinite, so great, that no partial statement can contain it; the opposite has to be included immediately. The whole will always be contradictory, only the part can be consistent – because the whole has to consider the opposite also. The opposite is there. It exists.

Philosophers can be consistent because their understanding is partial. They can be neat and clean, they can afford to be logical. I cannot afford it, because if I try to be consistent immediately the whole thing becomes untrue. The opposite has to be involved, the opposite has to be absorbed.

For example, when I say: Surrender and I will do the rest, this is one part. And why am I saying it? I am saying it so that you can surrender totally. If you can feel this and trust this, that the remaining shall be done, your surrender can be complete.

If you have a fear, a distrust, then even after surrender you will have to do something, the surrender cannot be complete. If after surrender you have also to do something, then you have to retain yourself, you have to hold back – surrender cannot be total. And when surrender is not total it is not surrender at all. Surrender can only be total, you cannot surrender in part. You cannot say: I surrender half – because the half that has been retained will be against the surrender. It can only be retained against it.

So surrender can only be total. It is just like a circle, a geometric circle. It cannot be half; you cannot draw a half circle. If you draw it you cannot call it a circle. A circle must be complete. Half, then it is something else, not a circle at all. Surrender can only be total. It is also a circle, a spiritual circle. You surrender from end to end. Nothing is left behind.

To help this, I say: You surrender, and the remaining will be done by me. The emphasis that *I* shall do – you simply surrender – is to make your surrender total. But *I* know that if you have surrendered, there is no need for anything to be done, not even on my part. Surrender itself is the thing, nothing else is needed. The very phenomenon of surrendering is enough. No further help is needed. Everything will be done by surrender itself. Surrendering means you are no more, surrendering means the ego has been dropped. Surrendering means now the center has been dispersed; you exist but without a center. If there is no center there is nothing to protect; the walls drop by themselves. If there is no one, your whole structure of defense disappears by and by; it becomes futile. You become an open space.

This open space will do everything, this openness will do everything. God will pass through you unhindered. God can move through you, in and out – there is nobody to create any barrier. Surrendered, you become open to the divine forces. Everything happens spontaneously after that.

The problem is surrendering. After surrendering there is no problem. So I am not needed to help you. Nothing is needed.

That's why I go on contradicting myself and I say I don't do anything. There is no need! Now you can look at the whole.

If I say I will not do, I cannot do anything, there is no need – if I say only this, your surrendering will be impossible. You will be afraid – alone, moving into the unknown, nobody to help, nobody to guide, and this man says: I'm not going to do anything – how can you surrender totally? It will be difficult for you. If I say only that I will do everything without contradicting it, that will not be true, because, really, I am not going to do anything. So what to do now? How to say this whole? There is only one way, to contradict consistently.

The relationship between a master and a disciple is a very complex phenomenon – in a way very simple, otherwise very complex. It is simple because the relationship exists only on the part of the disciple. On the part of the master there is no relationship, because the master doesn't exist. He is no longer there. He is a nobody. It appears to you that he is. This appearance will persist unless you surrender. Once you surrender, once you become a non-being, suddenly you will see that the master has never been there.

The master is an absence. But the absence can be seen only when you have also become an absence. Only two absences meet. If you are present, you go on projecting on the master also that he is. It is your projection, because your ego cannot see non-ego. Only the similar can respond to the similar. Your ego can only see egos everywhere. That is a way to protect your own self. Wherever you look, immediately you project an ego. So even the master will look like somebody, some ego. And you will find ways and means to prove to yourself that he is also an ego. Your rationalizations may be perfectly logical, but I say they are absurd, because you cannot see the phenomenon of non-ego as you are. Surrendered, suddenly you will see that the master is not there. If you are surrendered right this moment you will see this chair is empty. This man who is talking to you is not here. This man is just an emptiness. But only absent will you be able to see this absence.

Relationship cannot exist on the part of the master. If it exists he is not a master at all – he is still there. He cannot guide you, he can only misguide you. The teaching may be beautiful but he will misguide you, because whatsoever he does – I say whatsoever, unconditionally – will be wrong. It is not a question of this thing being wrong and that thing being right. Whatsoever comes out of the ego is wrong. It may be virtue, it may be nonviolence, it may be love – but whatsoever comes out of the ego is wrong. The ego perverts everything. The ego is the greatest perverter.

If the master loves you and the ego is there, his love will become possessive. He will destroy you, he will kill you. The relationship will be poisonous. The ordinary relationship of love will be there. He won't allow you to move to another master. He will fight, he will create barriers so that you cannot move from him – because he depends on you, his ego depends on you.

The master, if with the ego, cannot exist without the followers. The followers are needed to feed. The greater the crowd the better he will feel. If everybody leaves him he will simply be dead. Then the ego will be hurt. So so-called masters go on fighting, competing with other so-called masters. It becomes a market. The whole competition of the market comes in.

If the master has an ego that means he is not really a master – just pretending. Then his compassion will be only compassion in name. He will be cruel, he will torture you – of course, in such a way that you will feel this torturing is a discipline. He will force you to do things which are painful and unnecessary, but he will enjoy that pain. He will rationalize it. He will say: Fast, because without fasting you cannot reach. And when you fast and you are tortured, he will be happy. His compassion is just a hidden cruelty. In the name of compassion he is a sadist. Torturing, he will feel happy. Looking at you, seeing that you are sad, tortured, depressed, he will say: *Vairagya* has been won – you have become non-attached.

The more you are sad, the happier he will be. If he sees a smile on your face, he will condemn it immediately. If he feels you are blissful, immediately he will find that something has gone wrong, because how can you be blissful in this world, in this wrong world? How can you be happy? Life is misery. How can you be ecstatic? Then you must be enjoying the senses somewhere, somehow. If you look young and fresh and alive, then you are too much attached to the body.

He will start destroying your body. He is a sadist and a very subtle sadist, more subtle than a Hitler or Mussolini – because they kill immediately, their murdering is simple. This man will also murder you, but in installments – slowly, slowly. Go around this country: you will find many who have been murdering others.

And remember: he can kill you only if he is also suicidal, otherwise not. If he enjoys good food he cannot force fasting on you – impossible. If he lives in a beautiful house he cannot tell you to live in a hut, in a cottage. So this is absolutely logical: if he wants to destroy you, he will have to destroy himself. The more he tortures himself the more he gets control to torture you. He will fast, he will destroy his body. And the more he destroys his body, the more he has got you around your neck. Now he can crush you completely and crush you with a good conscience.

This is the phenomenon. With a wrong master, with an egoistic master, whatsoever happens goes wrong; his discipline becomes a sadism, his own life becomes masochistic, his whole being becomes destructive. Ego is destructive. Then relationship can exist. With a wrong master relationship can exist, because on the part of the master also there is ego, and the ego wants to relate. The ego cannot exist without relating.

But if there is a real master, relationship exists only on the part of the disciple. You love him. You obey him. He is not concerned with your obedience. He is not concerned with your love. That doesn't mean that he doesn't care. He cares infinitely, but there is no one who can be related. His care is natural – just as water flows downward his care flows towards you. Even if you are not there his care goes on flowing.

Whatsoever I am here with you, when you are not here I am the same, my being goes on flowing in the same way. When nobody is there I remain the same. When you are there I am the same. If I change then the ego is there, because the ego exists in relationship. When you come there, the ego comes in, becomes active and alive. When you go the ego becomes lazy, falls asleep. Then there is a change.

With you or without you my emptiness remains the same. The care goes on flowing. The love goes on flowing. There is no lover. I cannot choose to love or not to love. If I can choose, then I am there. Relationship exists on your part, and it will continue to exist until you surrender.

So surrender is the greatest and deepest relationship – and the end of relationship also. If you surrender you have come to the deepest relationship that is possible. Beyond that, relationship disappears. Surrendered, you are no more; and the master has never been there. Two empty spaces cannot be two. You cannot draw a line between two empty spaces. You cannot make boundaries around emptiness. Two emptinesses become one, and relationship cannot exist – because for relationship two are needed.

So at the last moment of surrender – try to understand this – at the last moment of surrender, the greatest relationship that is possible exists. The deepest, the most intimate relationship exists – of course, on your part. The next moment, when you have surrendered, everything has disappeared. Now there is neither master nor disciple. And now the master and disciple both can laugh. They can have a belly laugh. They can have an uproarious laugh about the whole nonsense that was there just a moment before.

The effort to help, the effort to get the help, the surrender, the constant struggle of the ego not to surrender, all the explanations, all the teachings – the whole thing becomes absurd. Your many, many lives become just like dreams. And now you can laugh, because you could have awakened any moment. You could have become enlightened, you could have come out of your dreaming at any moment in any life.

Once you attain this enlightenment...because surrender is one aspect, enlightenment is the other side of the coin. It is the same door. When you enter, on the door is written: Surrender. When you have entered and you look back, on the door is written: Enlightenment. It is the same door! From one side it is the entrance; from the other side it is the exit. That's why there is so much insistence on surrender – *samarpan*.

The relationship is very complex, because only one exists. The other relater is not there. So all the games with a master are really your games. You are playing, it is a game of patience. The other is simply watching you play. You change tactics, you try this way and that way. You try in many ways, but unnecessarily, because the only effort which will be helpful is surrender. All else is just to prepare you to come to a moment of realization when you see the whole absurdity of all effort and simply drop it.

Many techniques are used. Those techniques are not really going to help. They are only going to help you to realize that you have to surrender. They will simply prove the futility of all effort. But you play a game. You go on changing your tactics. The ego employs every type of strategy – for the ego it is a life-and-death problem. It will deceive you, it will deceive you continuously. And the ego is a perfect rationalist. When it deceives it gives you reasons. You cannot argue with it, and if you try to argue you will be defeated. Hence the supremacy of trust and faith. Only a faithful one can surrender, and only a faithful one can reach to the very peak of existence, to the climax of bliss.

In the West one of the deepest psychologists of this century was Abraham Maslow. His whole life he worked around the phenomenon of peak experience. His whole life he devoted to the phenomenon of certain experiences which he called the peak, the ultimate, the final – the enlightenment of Buddha, or the luminous unconsciousness of Ramakrishna, or the ecstasy of Meera, Böhme, Eckhart – the peak, the highest that can happen to human consciousness.

Trying to probe into this phenomenon, Maslow became aware that there are two types of people. One he calls peakers; the other he calls non-peakers. Peakers are those who are ready and open and receptive; non-peakers are those who are convinced that no peak experience is possible. In the non-peakers he includes scientists, rationalists, logicians, materialists, businessmen, politicians – practical types, so-called practical people, for whom the end is meaningless; they are means-oriented. These people create walls around them, and because of those walls they cannot have any ecstasy. When they cannot have any ecstasy, their original standpoint is confirmed. Then they create more walls, and that becomes a vicious circle.

There are peakers.... Poets, dancers, musicians, madmen, impractical adventurers – these are peakers. They don't bother, they don't argue with their mind – they simply allow things to happen. And then even in ordinary life sometimes certain peaks are achieved.

I have heard about one psychoanalyst who was being analyzed by another psychoanalyst. This first psychoanalyst who was being analyzed went for a holiday. From the holiday spot he telegrammed the other, saying: I am feeling very happy – why?

This type of person cannot accept even happiness. They will ask: Why? Why am I feeling happy? There must be something wrong. They have a notion that happiness is not possible.

The great psychologist Freud says that happiness is impossible for human beings. He says the very structure of the human mind is such that happiness is not possible; at the most you can be tolerably unhappy. If this is the attitude – and Freud has convinced himself, he has fortified himself with all types of arguments – if this is the concept, the notion, the idea, that happiness is impossible, then you are closed. Then happiness will not be possible for you. And when it is not possible, your original concept is strengthened, that you were right. Then there is less possibility for happiness. Then your original concept is strengthened still more, and there is even less possibility. Finally a moment will come when you say that unhappiness is the only possibility.

A disciple should be a peaker...and the greatest openness comes with surrender. But what should a peaker have? How should he structure his mind so he is open? Less reason, more trust; less practicality, more adventure; less prose, more poetry. Be illogical; otherwise happiness is not for you.

Logic is the enemy. Logic will prove that life is misery. Logic will prove that there is no meaning. Logic will prove that there is no God. Logic will prove that there is no possibility of any ecstasy. Logic will prove that life is just an accident, and in this accident there is no possibility. Between birth and death, if you can at the most manage somehow to exist, that's enough.

Logic is suicidal. If you go with it, finally it will give you the key to get out of life. Finally it will say that suicide is the most logical step to be taken, because life is meaningless. What are you doing here, repeating the same routine? In the morning getting out of bed – unnecessarily, because you have been getting up every day and nothing has happened. So why get up today again? And then taking your breakfast – you have been taking it your whole life, and nothing has happened out of it. Then reading your newspaper, going to the office, coming back again, and doing the same nonsensical things! And then eating your food, then going to sleep, then the morning again...a repetitious circle, leading nowhere, moving in a rut. If you are really logical your mind will say: Commit suicide! Why prolong this whole nonsense?

Logic leads to suicide; faith leads to supreme life. And faith is illogical – it doesn't ask, it doesn't argue, it simply enters into the unknown, it tries to experience. Experience is the only argument for a man who has faith. He will try to taste it, he will try to experience it. Without experiencing he will not say anything. He will not decide, he will remain open.

By one step, then another step, then another, faith leads to surrender – because the more you try with faith the more you know, the more you experience. Your life becomes intense. Every step says to you: Go beyond it, much more is hidden beyond. Beyond becomes the goal. Transcend everything and go beyond. And life becomes an adventure, a continuous discovery of the unknown. Then more trust is created.

When every step taken into the unknown gives you a blissful glimpse, when every step taken into madness gives you a higher form of ecstasy, when every step taken into the unknown helps you realize that life doesn't consist of the mind, it is a total organic phenomenon, your whole being is needed and called – then by and by your inner being becomes convinced. And it is not a logical conviction, it is your experience, it is experiential; or you can say it is existential, not intellectual – it is total. Then a moment comes when you can surrender.

Surrender is the greatest gamble. Surrender means putting the mind aside completely. Surrender means going mad. I say surrender means going mad, because all those who live in their logic and in their minds will think you have gone mad. To me it is not madness. To me madness, this type of madness, is the only courageous way of life. To me this madness is the deepest jump. To me this madness is all that a man is called to be. But to the logicians your trust will look like madness. This is one of the phenomena that has to be penetrated very deeply.

All the great religions are born around some madman. A Jesus is a madman, perfectly insane. A Buddha is a madman. But the people who gather around are not all mad. Many come who are not peakers, who are intellectuals. They are attracted to Jesus and to Buddha also. The very being of Buddha is so magnetic now, filled with so much infinite energy, that they are attracted. Their mind reasons that something has been attained by this man – but they are not peakers, they are non-peakers. Intellectually they become attracted. The very phenomenon of a Buddha and his being becomes a logical argument to them. They listen to Buddha, they rationalize his sayings, they create metaphysics around them, then a religion is born. At the base is a madman, but in the structure are logicians. They are the contradictory people, absolutely contradictory, opposite to Buddha. They create the organization. They create Buddhism and the philosophies.

Jesus is a madman, Saint Paul is not. He is a perfect logician. The church is created by Saint Paul, not by Jesus. The whole of

Christianity is created by Saint Paul, not by Jesus. And this is one of the dangerous things that has been happening. There is no way to prevent it. It is in the nature of things.

If Jesus is born now, the church will deny him immediately. The church will not allow any madmen. Eckhart or Böhme, the church will deny them – they are madmen. They will be expelled from the organization. They will not be allowed because they can prove destructive. They say such things that, if people listen to them and believe in them, they will destroy the whole structure, the whole organization.

Religion is born. At the base is a madman, and then it is taken over by the logicians who are the opposite. They create all organizations. Peakers give birth, and then the child is adopted by the non-peakers. So every religion at its birth source is beautiful – but never again. Then it becomes ugly. Then, really, it becomes anti-religious.

Whatsoever I am saying to you, you are fortunate – you are at the source, that's why I say you are fortunate. And it happens only after thousands of years that you are near the source. It will not be so again. Even with my ideas it will not be so again. Sooner or later the logician will enter, the non-peaker will come. They are bound to come – they are already on the way. They will systematize everything, they will destroy everything. And then the opportunity will be missed. Then it will be a dead thing. Right now it is alive and you are near the source. That's why I say you are fortunate.

In your mind also both possibilities are there – the peaker and the non-peaker. If you allow your peaker, then you will surrender. If you allow your non-peaker, then you will listen to me, argue about it, rationalize about it, philosophize about it. Then either you are convinced by me, or not convinced by me. If you are convinced, you hang around me. If you are not convinced you leave. But in both cases you miss. Whether you hang around me or leave is irrelevant.

If you are trying to be convinced intellectually you have missed. This can be done when I am dead. Right now something else is possible and can be done – and that is: allow your peaker, allow your trusting soul to adventure. Don't make it a reasoning within you. Make it a jump. The source happens rarely, and very few people can take advantage. This has always been so; this will always be so. Around Jesus there were only a few people; around Buddha only a few people. And then for centuries they weep and they cry.

When Buddha was dying many were crying and weeping. Only a few were blissfully sitting around – only a few. Those were the peakers who were sitting blissfully; they had become one with the source. They had become one with the Buddha; the disciple and the master had disappeared long ago and now there is going to be no death. Only a few – a Mahakashyapa, a Sariputta, were sitting silently, enjoying. Even Ananda, Buddha's chief disciple, was crying and weeping.

Buddha opened his eyes and said: Why are you weeping, Ananda?

Ananda said: For many, many years I was with you and I missed the chance, and now you will be no more. What will happen to me now? You were here and I couldn't attain. Now you will not be here. What will happen to me? Now how many lives will I have to wander?

Even if the source is available to you, you can miss. You can miss by not surrendering. Surrender, and the remaining I will do.

Beloved Osho,
Before you start talking, you smile.
When you start talking, your smile disappears
and you don't smile again until
you've finished. Can you tell us about that.

I T IS RELEVANT, because to speak is such a torture and such a useless activity. It has to be done because there is no other way to bring you towards the silence that exists in me. You won't listen to it; you can listen only to words. So I am smiling when I start talking, but while I am talking it is difficult to smile. It is such a torture and such a futile effort to say something which cannot be said, to talk about something which cannot be talked about, to go on continuously pointing with the finger to a moon which cannot be indicated. But there is no other way, so I have to continue it.

By and by you will become able to listen to the nonverbal, to the wordless. By and by you will become able to listen when I am not talking. Then there will be no need...then I will be smiling continuously. So when I finish, I smile again – the torture is no more!

Enough for today.

You
Are
the Way

CHAPTER TEN

Beloved Osho,
The old Zen custom was that a monk
should stay with his master for ten years
before he went out on his own teaching.
There is a Zen story about a monk
who had completed his ten years in the monastery.
One rainy day the monk visited his master, Nan-in.
After Nan-in had greeted him, he said to the monk:
No doubt you have left your shoes in the vestibule.
On which side of your umbrella did you leave your shoes?
For a moment the monk hesitated,
and through that hesitation realized that
he was not in every-minute Zen.
You have told us that life has a pulsation –
in and out, yin and yang.
Do we have to keep trying for every-minute awareness,
or can we too pulsate with life,
and at times let go our trying?

HE FIRST THING to be understood: awareness should be moment to moment, but it can be only when it has become effortless. With effort you will lose contact again and again, with effort you will have to rest. Effort cannot be continuous, it is impossible. How can you make an effort continuously? You will get tired and then you will have to relax.

Every effort needs relaxation. So if awareness is through effort, then awareness cannot be a constant, continuous flow. There will be moments when you will have to lose awareness. Those will be the moments of relaxation from the effort.

Life pulsates. Life always moves to the opposite. Effort, then you have to rest. Again you make the effort, then you have to rest. But there is an awareness which goes beyond life – the transcendental. Then there is no pulsation; it is effortless, it is spontaneous.

What happened to this monk, this disciple of Nan-in? The master asked: Where have you left your shoes – on the right or on the left? He hesitated. And he realized that in the moment of leaving the shoes he was not aware – otherwise he must have known where he had left them, on the left or on the right. His consciousness is not yet continuous. That shows only that his consciousness is not yet effortless. He has still to remember, consciously make effort. His mindfulness is still with a tension. He has not yet become mindful. So sometimes he succeeds, sometimes he fails.

Nan-in is asking only: Is your awareness now natural? You need not manipulate it? You need not do anything about it? It is there – is it there whatsoever you do, or do you have to make an effort for it to be there? If the effort is there it is a strained thing, and a strained thing is bound to be unnatural. An unnatural awareness is not really awareness – it exists only on the periphery, not in you. If it exists in you there is no need to make any effort.

What I am trying to say is: Effort is always on the periphery. You cannot touch the center through effort. You can do something on the periphery – you can change your behavior, you can change your so-called character. On the periphery, with effort, you can become a good man from being bad, you can become virtuous from being a sinner; you can even become a saint – on the periphery, with effort.

But the center can never be touched and penetrated through effort – because no action can lead to *you*. You are already there! There is no need to do anything. You have to be simply silent, spontaneous, and then the center arises. It comes out of the clouds. There is a break, a gap. You suddenly realize your spontaneous awareness. You are awareness. It is nothing you do, it is nothing which has to be done – your very nature is awareness.

Hindus have called you *satchitananda*. They have used three words – *sat, chit, ananda*. Sat means the existential, that which can never go into nonexistence. Sat means the true, which can never become untrue. Sat means the eternal – that which was, which is, which will be. Chit means awareness, consciousness. That is your nature. You have always been conscious, you are conscious, you will be conscious. That consciousness cannot be taken from you, but it exists at the very core of your being, not on the periphery. It is you, but you are not in contact with yourself. And ananda means bliss, ecstasy. It is not that you have to achieve bliss – it is you. You have always been blissful, you cannot be otherwise; there is no possibility. You cannot change it.

You will say this seems absolutely absurd – because we are in misery. You are in misery because you have become so much obsessed with the periphery. You have forgotten completely the center. You have become so much engaged with others, so much occupied with others, that the whole attention is focused on the other, and you have fallen into the shade, into the darkness.

You *are* satchitananda.

The Zen master Nan-in is asking the disciple: Have you now become alert to who you are? Are you now rooted in your nature?

If the disciple was really rooted in his nature, what would have been the case?

The story is very difficult to understand. It is not a question of leaving the shoes on the left or on the right; that is not the point of the story. That seems to be the point, but it is not. The real point is: when Nan-in asked this the disciple hesitated. That is the real point. And in that moment of hesitation he was not aware that he was hesitating. If he had been aware that there was hesitation, he would have been accepted. But at that very moment he lost awareness.

And you cannot deceive Nan-in. If you go to see Nan-in you can remember very well where you have left your shoes, that is not difficult. If Nan-in asks you: Where have you left your shoes, on the left or on the right? you can immediately answer: On the right. And still you will lose. That is not the point, that is just a deception.

Nan-in is diverting the mind just to see right now what is happening in the disciple.

In the very moment when Nan-in asked: Where are your shoes, on the right or on the left? the disciple missed. In that very moment he hesitated – and he was not aware of the hesitation. He started thinking. In that very moment that he became unaware, Nan-in looked into him. That question was just to divert the mind, it was just a deception.

The disciple failed, so he cannot be sent to teach others. He is not yet ready, he is not yet aware. How can one who is not aware teach others? Whatsoever he is going to teach will be false. There are many teachers who are not aware of their own selves. They can be good teachers, efficient, artful, but that is not the point. They cannot be of any help.

I was traveling in a train once. One small boy was a great nuisance. All the passengers in the carriage were troubled. He was running from this corner to that, toppling glasses, falling on people, and the father was very embarrassed. He tried many times to stop the boy, but the boy wouldn't listen.

Finally the father said: Willy, if you don't listen to me and if you don't stop, I am going to spank you.

The boy still continued running. He went to the other end of the carriage and he said: Okay, you spank me – but then I am going to tell the ticket collector how old I really am.

This father cannot be a teacher. Even a child is not going to listen to him. A teacher who is unaware of his own self cannot be a teacher. He cannot teach others what he has not himself attained.

Awareness is something like an infectious disease. When a master is alert, aware, you become infected with his awareness. Sometimes, just sitting by the side of the master, you suddenly become aware – as if the clouds have gone and you can see the open sky. Even for a moment...but that becomes a deep change in the very quality of your being.

Even not making any effort on your part, just being near a master who is a pool of silent awareness, suddenly you become silent.

He touches you. The closed doors open, or it is as if in a dark night suddenly there is lightning and you see the whole. It disappears because it cannot be retained by you. If it is not attained by you, you will lose it – but you will never be the same again. You have known something, something that was previously unknown. And now this knowing will remain a part of you. There will arise a desire, there will arise a new ambition: to attain this, to make this permanent – because even for a moment it was so blissful, it showered so much happiness on you, so much joy.

But if the master, if the teacher, is not himself aware, he can teach about awareness but he cannot teach awareness. And teaching *about* awareness is useless – it is verbal, it is a theory. You can learn the theory from him, but you cannot learn the fact. Hence, before this disciple leaves Nan-in, Nan-in must look into him – and this is a very different phenomenon.

In the world of education a student is examined, but only his memory is examined, never he himself. Always his memory is examined – never he. Nan-in is not examining the memory of the disciple. He is not asking: Where have you left your shoes, on the right or on the left? He is not asking for a perfect memory, because where he left the shoes is now past. He is trying to see into the being of the disciple right now. He is not examining the memory but trying to look into the consciousness this very moment. The past is not the question. The present, the present-ness is the question.

Just imagine that disciple sitting before Nan-in. Nan-in asks, and the disciple is lost in the past. He tries to think where he has left the shoes. He tries to think whether he can remember or not. He tries to think whether he has missed awareness or not. Right now he has become a confusion. His whole consciousness has become cloudy. He is no longer here. He is not in the presence of Nan-in, he has gone into the past, he has gone into thinking – he is not meditative. The hesitation, the thinking, the effort to try....

You cannot escape Nan-in. He will see through you; he will see all the clouds, he will see you are not here and now. Then you cannot be allowed to teach. You cannot be sent out, because what will you teach? That which you have not got you cannot teach. You can pretend but that pretension will be dangerous, because if you pretend that you are aware and you are not, that pretension will become infectious. A pseudo-master creates pseudo-disciples, and then like ripples that pseudo-ness goes on spreading.

The most dangerous sin that a man can commit is to pretend awareness. Even if you murder a man it is not such a great sin, because, really, you cannot murder. You can only destroy the body; the soul moves into another. You only destroy one game, another starts immediately. A murderer is not such a great sinner. But if you pretend that you are aware and you are not, if you pretend that you are a master and you are not, you are doing such harm, such infinite harm, that no sin can be compared to it – because others will get the pretension. They start pretending, and then it will go on and on – just like when you throw a stone into a silent lake, ripples arise and they go on and on. One ripple creates another, pushes another, and it goes on and on to the very boundaries of the lake.

The lake of consciousness has no boundaries. Once a ripple is created it will go forever; forever it will continue. You will not be here, but your pretensions, your falsity, will continue and many will be deluded by it.

A false master is the greatest sinner in the world. That's why Nan-in won't allow anybody to go and teach unless he has become enlightened himself. Then the very light that burns within you helps others to be lit. The very fire that burns within you makes others warm. The very life that has happened to you helps others to come out of their deadness.

But remember: alertness, awareness or consciousness can be continuous only when it has become effortless. In the beginning effort is bound to be there, because otherwise how are you going to start? You will make an effort, you will try to be mindful, you will try in every way to be conscious, but the effort will create a tension. And the more you make the effort, the more tense you will be. There will be tiny glimpses, but because of the tension the ecstasy will be missed. You have to pass through this state also, of making effort.

One thing you will become aware of sooner or later: that whenever you make effort, awareness comes to you but it is a very tortured awareness, nightmarish. It is very heavy, it sits just like a rock on your head. It is not joyful, it is not weightless, it is not dancing. But while making this effort, sometimes suddenly you will become aware – when you were not making the effort. And that awareness will be light, joyful, dancing, ecstatic.

This will happen only to those who are making efforts. While making efforts, sometimes, when you are not making effort, this glimpse will happen to you. Then you will become aware that through effort you cannot achieve that ultimate – only through non-effort it happens.

To many meditators around me it happens. They come to tell me that while meditating in the morning, in the evening, nothing much is happening. But suddenly in the night or suddenly in the afternoon they are sitting and something starts – and they were not doing anything. This will happen. Just as when you forget a name and you feel it is just on the tip of the tongue, you become very much strained, you make every effort to bring it to consciousness. It does not come, and the more you make an effort, the more you feel lost. You know that you know, continuously you know that you can remember. It is just around the corner but some barrier, something like a block is there, and the name is not coming to you – it may be the name of a cherished friend! And then the whole effort becomes so futile you leave it. You start reading a newspaper or go for a smoke, or you go in the garden for a walk, or you just start digging in the garden, and suddenly it pops up. Suddenly the name is there, the friend is standing there, the face is there.

What happened? When you were making the effort you were so tense that that very tenseness became the block; the very tenseness narrowed down the passage. The name wanted to come, the memory was knocking on the door, but the very tenseness became the closedness. That's why you were feeling it was just on the tip of the tongue. It was! But because you were so tense, so worried about it, so anxious to bring it out, your anxiety became a block. When a mind is very anxious it becomes closed.

All that is beautiful and true happens only when you are not anxious about it. All that is lovely happens only when you are not even waiting for it – not asking, not demanding. Then the mind has no blocks. That's why it happens when you have forgotten it. Effort *is* needed, in the beginning effort is a must – futile, but still a must. The futility will be realized by and by. When you have glimpses, sudden glimpses, with the feeling that you were not making any effort and those glimpses have showered upon you, gifts from the divine, then you can leave the effort – and leaving the efforts, more and more gifts will come.

In the East we have always believed, and believed rightly, that enlightenment is nothing like an achievement. It is like a grace, it is a gift, it is *prasad*. God gives it to you, you cannot snatch it away from his hand.

For a Western seeker this is very difficult to realize, because in the West in the last few centuries the whole human mind has been converted into a snatching thing. You have snatched everything from nature. Whatsoever secrets science knows are not given, they have been snatched. You have forced nature violently to open her doors of mysteries. Because you have succeeded with matter you think that the same can happen with the divine also. That cannot happen, that is impossible. You cannot attack heaven and you cannot go there with bayonets. You cannot force the divine to open its heart to you because whenever you are forcing you are closed. That is the problem: whenever you are forcing you are closed, and if you are closed the divine cannot be revealed to you.

When you are not forcing but floating like a white cloud, just roaming, not making any effort to reach anywhere; when there is no goal and no effort; when you don't want to achieve anything and there is no straining for it; when you are happy as you are, when you are happy as the world is; when you accept things as they are and you don't want to change anything – suddenly you are transported into a different dimension of being. You realize the doors have always been open. They were never closed, they cannot be closed. The divine mystery has always been near you. It was never very far. It cannot be, because you are part of the divine. Wherever you go the mystery moves with you.

It is not a question of searching and seeking; it is a question of remaining silent and allowing. When you seek you miss, because a seeker is always violent. When you search it will not come to you, because the mind that is searching is too preoccupied, it is not available. It is never here and now, it is always somewhere in the future – when the discovery will be made, when the research will be completed, when the seeking will come to an end. It is always somewhere in the end, it is not here. The divine is here, so you never meet. A seeker never reaches.

That doesn't mean you shouldn't be a seeker. You will have to be in the beginning, there is no other way. In the beginning you have to be a seeker, you will have to seek and make all the efforts. Just by making all the efforts and becoming a mad seeker, you will realize that it happens only when you are in a non-seeking mind.

Sometimes resting, it will come to you. Sometimes sleeping, it will descend on you. Sometimes just walking on the road it will be there. Sometimes just looking at the sun rising in the morning – not doing anything, just a passive awareness – looking at the sun rising or the moon shimmering on a cold night in a lake, or a flower opening its petals, and you are just a passive awareness.... Nothing is needed on your part. When a flower is opening, no help is needed from you.

There are foolish people who will try to help. They will destroy the whole beauty of the flower, and then the flower will never really open. Even if you force it to open it will be a closed flower. The flowering has not happened, it is a forced thing. Anything forced never flowers. You are not needed to help the sun to rise. There are people who think that their help is needed. There are people who create much mischief, *much* mischief, because they think their help is needed everywhere.

In real life, wherever reality is happening, nobody's help is needed. But it is very difficult to resist the temptation because when you help you feel you are doing something. When you do something you create the ego. When you don't do anything the ego cannot exist. In a non-doing moment the ego disappears. Looking at the sun rising, looking at a flower opening, looking at the moon shimmering in a cold lake, not doing anything – suddenly it will descend on you. You will find the whole existence is filled with the divine, your every breath is divine.

With effort, reach to effortlessness.

With seeking, reach to a state of no-seeking.

With mind, arrive at no-mind.

There are two types of people. To one type if I say to make an effort, they make an effort, but then they don't allow effortlessness. To the other type if I say it will happen only in effortlessness, they leave all effort. Both have gone wrong. Both have gone off the way.

This is the rhythm of life: make effort so you can be effortless also. Strain to the very end so that you can achieve moments of non-strained consciousness. Run as fast as you can so that when you sit, you really sit. Be exhausted in effort so when you rest, it is a real rest.

You can rest with restlessness inside you. You can lie down on the ground, but the restlessness goes on inside. So you are simply lying down, but it is not a rest. You may sit like a buddha and inside the child is running – the mind is working and functioning. Inside you are going mad, outside you are sitting in a buddha posture. You can be totally static outside, not moving, no activity, and inside the turmoil goes on. This won't help. Finish the turmoil in effort. Run as fast as you can. Be exhausted! Hence, my emphasis on Dynamic Meditation. It is both effort and effortlessness. It is both activity and inactivity. It is both running and then zazen – just sitting.

Nan-in is looking into the disciple. Has he transcended effort? Has he come to effortlessness? Has consciousness become a natural, spontaneous thing to him? Is he unconfused? Is he clear like a clear blue sky? Then he can be a master, he can be allowed to go and teach others.

Remember this whenever the temptation comes to you to teach someone. If you want to say something to somebody, just say that it is *about* – about God, about awareness. Make the other aware that you have not achieved – you have heard. You have heard such beautiful things that you would like to share, but you have not achieved. Then you can be a help without any poisoning, without poisoning the other.

Always remember: if you don't know, you don't know. Never pretend, not even negatively. Because you can simply remain silent, not saying that you have not attained. Even that is not good, because in silence the other may carry the feeling that you have known. Make it clear that you have not known it, but you have known persons who do know, you have heard about it.

In India there exist two types of scripture. One is called *shruti*, the other is called *smriti*. Smriti means memory and shruti means that which has been heard. The literature that is called smriti belongs to those who have known themselves. It is their own. They have related their own memory, they have related their own experiences. Shruti is the second type of literature; it is from those who have been fortunate to be near those who have known – they have heard.

Remember this always: if you have heard, then say that it is something you have heard, and it is so beautiful that even hearing it has become a treasure for you. Even hearing it has touched your heart and you would like to share. But this is just friendliness; you are not becoming a master. It is just a loving gesture, just sharing your happiness, but you are not sharing awareness. Unless you attain, unless you realize, unless it becomes your own, don't try to guide anyone. That is violent. And when you have attained, your very being will become a guidance.

The disciple who came to the master Nan-in was from the very beginning taking a wrong step, because if he had been ready Nan-in would have called him. It was not his part to decide: Ten years are now complete and I should go and teach. The whole thing was wrong. The master would know before the disciple when he was ready, because of course the master can observe more than you ever can of your own self.

The master follows you even in your nights and in your dreams. He is like a shadow constantly watching what is happening, whether you are aware of his watching or not. And you will not be aware, because it is such a subtle thing.

Whenever a disciple is ready the master will call him and tell him: Now you go! The disciple need not announce, and if the disciple decides to announce, that means he is not ready – the ego is there.

This disciple wanted to be a master – every disciple does – and the very wanting becomes the barrier. Ten years were completed; he must have been calculating. He must have been a very cunning fellow; otherwise, who will remember? What is the use of living with a master if you cannot forget time? What else are you going to forget? What is the hurry? This disciple is not surrendered. He is just waiting, calculating. Arithmetic is there, logic is there, and a fixed attitude towards things. He knows the history of the monastery, that in ten years' time a disciple is ready and then he goes.

But it depends. Every disciple will not be ready in ten years, some disciples will not be ready in ten lives, and some disciples will be ready in ten seconds. It is not a mechanical thing. It depends on the quality, the intensity of the consciousness of the disciple. Sometimes it has happened: just a look from the master and the disciple is ready. If he is open, if there is no barrier, if he is surrendered, then a single moment is enough. Even that is not needed, the thing happens timelessly.

But if you are calculating, thinking: When is it going to happen? I have waited enough. One year is lost, two years are lost, ten years are gone, and I am waiting and nothing is happening – you are calculating inside – then you are wasting time. A disciple must drop time-consciousness. Time belongs to the ego. Time belongs to the mind. Meditation is timeless.

This disciple comes to the master just to announce: Ten years are complete now. Where am I supposed to go and where am I supposed to teach now? I am ready...because ten years have passed. Nobody ever gets ready that way. That's why the master had to ask a question, just to make the disciple appear foolish to himself.

Zen masters are difficult people – very straight, penetrating, embarrassing. What a question to ask a great seeker who has been waiting for ten years: Where have you left your shoes, on the right or on the left? What type of question and what type of man is this who asks such a question of a great seeker? This is not metaphysical at all. You cannot find a more trivial question. A more profane question you cannot find – asking about the shoes. He should have asked about God, and the disciple would have been ready. He should have asked about heaven and hell, and the disciple would have been ready. The disciple must have crammed everything, every answer. That's why he has wasted ten years reading, studying. All the scriptures were with him, and he was ready...the master can ask any question!

Remember: if you are near an enlightened man, he is never going to ask a question which you can answer. It is not a question of answering, it is a question of responding with the whole being.

The master asks such a futile question: Where have you left your shoes? The whole metaphysics of the disciple must have been shattered, and he must have thought: What type of man...? Here I am, ready, bubbling with answers. Any type of question you raise and I will answer. Even questions which Buddha has not answered I will answer. I know all the books, all the scriptures. I have read everything; all the sutras are studied and memorized.

He was ready and this man asks about shoes! But really he asks a question which cannot be answered, because you cannot be ready for it beforehand. It was absolutely unpredictable. The disciple feels hesitation, and the hesitation is the response. Hesitation says everything about the disciple; he is still not aware, otherwise there can be no hesitation. You act. He would have done something if he had been alert. He would have responded in a total way, but he became a mind, puzzled...hesitation, confusion.

The story is beautiful. When for the first time Zen became known in the West they couldn't believe what these masters were doing and asking – questioning absurd things. You ask a master a question and he responds. No Zen master will give you the answer, he will respond.

One seeker, a philosophical seeker of course, came to a Zen master, Bokuju, and asked: What is the way?

Bokuju looked at the nearby hills and he said: The hills are very beautiful.

Seems absurd! He asks: What is the way? and Bokuju says: The hills are beautiful. Frustrated, the seeker left immediately. Then Bokuju had a beautiful laugh.

One disciple said: Master, that man must have thought you are mad.

Bokuju said: One of us is certainly mad. Either he is mad... because you cannot ask about the way, you have to travel it. Through traveling, the way is discovered. It is not there, ready-made, so I cannot say where it is. It is not like a super-highway, ready-made, waiting for you: Come and travel! There is no way like that, otherwise all would have reached long ago. If the way were ready-made, everyone would have traveled it. The way is created through your traveling, it is not there waiting for you. The moment you start traveling it is created. It comes out of you just like a spider's web. It comes through you. You create it, then you travel it. As you travel it you create more of it. And remember, the way disappears with you. Nobody else can travel on it; it cannot be borrowed.

So the master says: It cannot be asked, only foolish people ask such questions as, What is the way? *You* are the way!

Then the disciple said: I understand that, but why did you talk about the hills?

The master said: A master has to talk about the hills because unless you cross the hills there is no way to be found. The way is beyond the hills, and the hills are so beautiful that nobody wants to cross them. They are so enchanting, so hypnotizing, that everybody is lost in the hills – and the way exists beyond.

A master responds. He hits your real necessity. He is not worried about your question. Your question may be relevant or irrelevant – you are always relevant. He looks in you. He hits you. But intellectual people will always miss that type of answer.

Enough for today.

Renunciation
Is Not
Needed

CHAPTER ELEVEN

Beloved Osho,
When we're sitting in front of you,
hearing your words and feeling your presence,
everything feels possible.
But when we return to our daily living conditions,
things do not seem so clear and we feel cut off from you.
You have told us that we should not renounce the world,
but be meditative within it.
You have also said that we should
be spontaneous and mad.
How can we integrate the two without alienating
our families and friends and the society around us?

O NCE YOU START THINKING in terms of two contradictions and how to make them meet, you will always
be in difficulty. Then everything will be a compromise, and with compromise no one ever feels ful-
filled. Something is always lacking, missing. If you do this, then on
the other pole something has to be lost. If you do that, then on this
pole something has to be lost, and whatsoever you lose goes on
hovering in the mind. It will never allow you to be blissful.

So the first thing is: never think in terms of compromise. If you
think in terms of contradictions and how to make them meet,
you are bound to think in terms of compromise. So what am I to
suggest to you?

The first thing is: always be integrated within, and don't think
of any integration without – because you are the meeting point.
Alone you sit silently. In life you have to be active, involved.
Silence and involvement are contradictions, but they both meet in
you. You are silent and you are involved.

If you are integrated your silence and your involvement will be integrated. Your being alone, and your being with your wife or your husband or friends, are two things, contradictory, but you are in both. If you are integrated you will be happy alone. If you are integrated you will be happy with others. Happiness will be your quality. Happiness doesn't depend on being alone or with others. If it does depend there will be problems. If you feel that when you are alone you are happy and your happiness depends on being alone, then there will be difficulty. Then aloneness is a must. Then when with others you will feel unhappy and you will start thinking how to make these two opposites meet. The problem arises because you are dependent on your loneliness for your happiness.

Don't be dependent. Be happy when alone. Let happiness be your quality, and when you move from aloneness into involvement, into communication, relationship, carry that quality of happiness which was in aloneness – carry that. In the beginning it will be difficult, because you will almost always forget. It will be difficult because of forgetfulness, because of not being constantly aware, but by and by you can carry the quality. When living with somebody you can still be as alone as you were in your loneliness. You remain an integrated soul. While not doing anything you feel happy, at ease. This at-easeness should become a quality of *you*, not of inactivity.

Carry this quality in activity and there will be no problem. In the beginning there is going to be difficulty, but the point is to remember that your happiness, your bliss, your ecstasy, should not be dependent on any condition without. If it is, then there is contradiction because it will be dependent. People feel that they are happy when they are with their friends; then when they are alone they are bored, miserable – somebody is needed. These people are extroverts. The other type is the introvert. Whenever he is alone he feels happy; whenever he moves with someone, unhappiness enters. Both are in the bondage of their type. Type is a bondage. You should be free of the type. You should neither be extrovert, nor introvert, but both. Then you are free of the type.

So what is to be done? Never get fixed with a situation; always move to the opposite and carry the quality with you. Move as much as possible from one opposite to the other and carry the quality. Soon you will become aware that the quality can be carried anywhere. Then you cannot be sent to hell, because even if you are sent you will carry your happiness there. Then you will never be afraid.

Religious people are afraid of hell, and they seek and hanker for heaven. These people are not religious at all, because heaven and hell are both conditions without – they are not your own qualities. These are the worldly people. That's what worldly people are doing. They say: If this condition is fulfilled, then I will be happy. So happiness depends on the condition. If a palace is there, then I will be happy; so much money in the bank, then I will be happy; such a beautiful wife, then I will be happy, or such a good, loving husband, then I will be happy. You are happy only when something is fulfilled outside, and you say: If this is not fulfilled, I am unhappy. This is what an unreligious man is. And the so-called religious men also go on seeking heaven, avoiding hell. They are doing the same.

For you, this is going to be the *sadhana* – the discipline: move in opposites as much as possible and try to carry your inner integrity. Sitting silent, feel what the inner quality is. Then go into activity with that quality being retained inside. It will be lost many times, but don't be worried. If even once you can carry it into the opposite pole, you have become master of it. Then you know the knack of it.

Sometimes move to the hills; they are beautiful. Then come back to the world; that too is beautiful. If hills are beautiful, why not people? They are also hills in their own right. Sometimes be alone, sometimes be with others. And if you are alert, not only will there be no contradiction, help will be coming from the opposite.

If you can carry the quality of happiness from loneliness to society, suddenly you will become aware of a new phenomenon, a new happening within you – that society helps you to be alone, and aloneness helps you to be deeply related with people. A man who has never lived in loneliness cannot know the beauty of relationship; cannot know, I say, because he has never been alone. He has never been a person – how can he know the beauty of relationship? A person who has never lived in society cannot know the ecstasy of aloneness. A person who is born in a lonely place, is brought up in a lonely place, do you think he will be ecstatic? You think he will enjoy the loneliness? He will simply go dull and stupid.

Go to the hills, go to the Himalayas. People are living there – they have lived there for thousands of years, they are born there – but however much you feel the beauty of the Himalayas, they can't feel it. However much you enjoy the silence there, they cannot enjoy it. They are not even aware that the silence exists. When they come to the cities they feel a thrill – the same thrill as you feel when you go to the hills. People living in Bombay, London and New York feel the thrill when they go to the Himalayas. When they can come to Bombay, New York or London, then people living in the Himalayas feel how beautiful the world is. The opposite is needed to feel – it becomes a contrast. The day is beautiful because there is night. Life has such joy because there is death. Love becomes an inner dance because there is hate.

Love leads you to a high peak of consciousness, because love can be lost. It is nothing that you can rely on. This moment it is there and the next moment it is not. The possibility of its absence gives depth to its presence. Silence becomes more silent when in the background there is noise. An airplane passed just a few moments ago. You can look at it in two ways: if you are a disturbed man inside you will feel it as a disturbance of the silence; if you are integrated within, the noise of the airplane will deepen the silence here. The noise becomes a background; it gives shape, form to the silence. It gives a sharpness. The silence when the plane has passed is more than it was before. It depends on you.

Always remember: don't get dependent on things, situations, conditions. Then you can move. Don't avoid movement, otherwise you will get fixed. Everybody is afraid of movement because you are dependent. You cannot come out of your hills, your solitariness, to the world of the market, because you know you will be disturbed. What type of silence is this which can be disturbed by the market? What value does it carry? Of what worth is it? If the market can destroy it, if the world, the humdrum world, can destroy it, then your silence is very impotent. If your silence is really potent, if you have attained it, nothing can destroy it.

It is not very difficult to understand what I am saying about silence, but that is my attitude in every sphere of life. If you are a real *brahmachari*, a real celibate, you can move into sex and it will not destroy your celibacy. This will be very difficult to follow. If sex disturbs your celibacy, it was nothing worthwhile. You carry the quality within.

If you are really alive, full of energy, you can die happily. Only weaklings die unhappily – because they have never lived. They have never tasted the cup of life. They have always been hoping and hoping and hoping, and life never happened to them. That's why they are scared of death.

One who has lived is always ready to die. One who has really lived is ready every moment to accept death. The word accept is not good – it would be better if we say to *welcome* death, to receive it happily, joyfully. Then death is an adventure. It should be if you have really lived. Then death is not the enemy, death is the friend. A deeper life allows death, a shallow life avoids it. This is so in every sphere of life.

If you have known what friendship is, you will not be scared of enemies. You will not be! Then enmity has its own beauty. It is a sort of friendship – on the opposite pole. It is a love affair on the opposite pole. It is involvement, it is commitment. If you have known friendship, you will love the enemy.

That's what Jesus means when he says: Love your enemies. Not what Christians have been interpreting all these centuries. You cannot love your enemy – how can you love your enemy?

But I say to you: If you have loved friends, you will love your enemies – because once you know the beauty of friendship you also come to know the beauty of enmity. It is a friendship in reverse order. Both give, both enrich your life.

Opposites are not really opposites, deep down they have a great harmony. They are parts of one whole. This is what the Chinese say: yin and yang, they are part of one movement, part of one wheel – they are not two. They appear as two because we have not looked deep down. It is because of our shallow eyes, non-penetrating minds, superficial consciousnesses – that's why they look like opposites, otherwise they are not.

Life and death are friends. They exist through each other, they contribute to the other. Without the other they would not be there at all. Can life exist without death? Man has been dreaming for ever and ever how to destroy death. This is the attitude of the mind, the linear mind, the logical mind – how to destroy death. The logical mind says: If there is no death, there will be life in abundance. Simple logic! Even a child can understand the arithmetic: if there is no death, there will be more life. But I say to you: If there is no death, there will be no life.

That's why simple logic is always fallacious. Apparently it looks so right: if there is no enemy the whole world will be your friend. You are wrong. If there is no enemy there will be no possibility of friendship. Logic says: If there is no hatred, love and love and more love will be there. So logicians have been trying to destroy the opposite. They cannot destroy it, because life is greater than any logic. It is fortunate that they cannot destroy the opposite, because they don't know what they are doing. If the opposite is not there, then don't go on believing that life will be more, love will be more, friendship will be more, happiness will be more – no. There will be no possibility, because the very ground has been destroyed.

Dialectics says something quite the contrary, and dialectics is truer to life. Dialectics says: If you want more life, then be more ready for death.

You may not be aware but this happens. When you are driving

a car and you gain more and more speed, you get involved in the speed. A point comes when any moment death can happen. Then you are alive, then the flame of life burns fast, sharp. That's why speed is so attractive and magnetic – because speed brings you nearer death. When you are nearer death, life is more; it grows in proportion. That's why there is so much attraction for war – because in war death is at close quarters, always near you.

You may think that soldiers fighting in the field must be very miserable. You are wrong; otherwise no one would fight. They are not miserable. The real thing is quite the opposite: when they come back to the ordinary world they are miserable. When they are in the field, fighting on the front, they are not miserable. All misery disappears. They are so near death that they feel for the first time alive, and their aliveness becomes more and more the nearer death comes. When all around there is bombardment, shells are passing from here to there and any moment they can drop dead, at that moment they feel an ecstasy. They are in touch, in deepest touch with life. When death kisses you it is also a kiss of life. That's why there is so much attraction to adventure, courage. If you are afraid you will not gain life.

I tell you that meditation is the greatest courage and the greatest adventure, because even on a battlefield you are not so near death. Even if you feel you are near death, it is only physical death. Physical death means a superficial death – of the shell, of the body. Your house is near death, not you; your shelter is going to be destroyed, not you. But in meditation you are going to be destroyed – not only the shelter, but the host, not only the house, but the host. The ego is to be destroyed. So the greatest warriors are always interested in meditation.

I would like to tell you about one phenomenon that has happened in India, that has happened in Japan, and that will happen to any country which gives birth to warriors. All the great meditators in India were *kshatriyas*, warriors, not brahmins. This looks strange. Brahmins should be the great meditators. They have been writing commentaries on the Upanishads, the Gita, the Vedas.

They have been creating metaphysics, and they are the greatest metaphysicians the world has ever known. Nobody, anywhere in the world, can compare with brahmins as far as verbal expression is concerned, logic is concerned. They are very subtle, but they are not the great meditators.

Buddha is a great meditator; he is a kshatriya, a warrior. Mahavira is a great meditator; he is a kshatriya – a warrior – not a brahmin. All the twenty-four *tirthankaras* of the Jainas are warriors. This seems strange. Why? In Japan, samurais have existed – warriors – the greatest warriors the world has ever known. The samurai is the peak, the ultimate possibility of being a warrior. In every moment, the samurai is ready to die. For such trivial things he is ready to die, you cannot imagine.

I have heard about one historical fact that happened three hundred years ago. One samurai, one great warrior, was very, very drunk. Suddenly he was called by the king for some purpose, so he went there. He tried to be alert but he was too drunk. He forgot some trivial mannerism in how you have to bow to the king, how much. He bowed, of course, but it was not as exact as it should have been.

The next morning when he became sober he immediately killed himself. Hara-kiri is a word you must have heard. Hara-kiri belongs to samurais, warriors. The moment they feel something has gone wrong – just an ordinary mannerism, and the king had not said anything.... The warrior was so great that the king would not have mentioned it at all – but he killed himself. The next day, when the king became aware that the warrior had killed himself, he wept. The warrior had three hundred disciples. They immediately killed themselves, because if a master has committed a wrong the disciples should follow.

And you will be surprised, it seems unbelievable, that for one hundred years continuously it continued, this small thing – more disciples, and disciples' disciples, because once a master.... And it is never heard of: a samurai going to the king drunk and doing something wrong. For trivial things, death seems so easy and at hand! These samurais created Zen, the greatest *dhyan* tradition in the world. These samurais meditated deeply.

This is my feeling, that unless you are ready to die you cannot be ready to meditate. War and meditation are synonymous in a deep sense. Wherever there is the possibility of your being destroyed, in that moment your flame of life burns in its totality. The full intensity comes to you.

Opposites are already meeting. You need not try for any meeting, any synthesis of them; they are already meeting, they are in deep harmony. You are not in a harmony, that is the problem.

So when you are healthy and you feel a wellbeing, carry that wellbeing when you are unhealthy and ill. I tell you that the feeling of wellbeing is not dependent on health. The feeling of wellbeing is an inner feeling; it is not dependent on the body. You can carry it even while ill.

Ramana Maharshi was dying. He had cancer, throat cancer, and it was almost impossible for him to talk, almost impossible for him to eat anything. But all those who surrounded him on his last day were surprised – he was so happy. His eyes were filled with a subtle wellbeing. The condition of the body was just a ruin, the whole body was a ruin – but not Ramana; he was as healthy as ever.

Once a master was dying. He was very old, almost a hundred. Disciples were there – they couldn't weep because he was laughing. They couldn't cry because it looked so absurd. The man was so happy, bubbling with happiness just like a child – enjoying his last breath. They could weep only when he was dead.

And somebody asked: When he was alive, why were you not weeping?

They said: It seemed so absurd. Looking at his face, looking at his eyes, it appeared as if he was going to a higher realm of being, as if death was just a door to the divine, as if he was not going to die, rather as if he was being reborn. And he was not an old man; if you looked in his eyes, he was a child – his body was old.

The wellbeing can be carried. Even when you are seriously ill you can remain in the inner wellbeing. You know the other thing: even when perfectly healthy you remain in the non-wellbeing. You know it, so the other is possible: perfectly healthy and you are miserable; perfectly young and alive and as if on your deathbed, somehow carrying the whole business of life as a burden, a dead weight on the heart. You are alive because you cannot do anything else. What can you do? You are alive, you have found yourself alive, so you carry it. But life is not an ecstatic phenomenon for you, you are not joyful about it, not celebrating it.

It is such a great blessing to be alive. Even for a single moment to be alive and aware is too much. A long life is given and many lives and you are not thankful, because unless you celebrate how can you feel any gratitude, any thankfulness? Perfectly young, alive, but inside you carry the misery.

Dying, a man who knows will carry the wellbeing.

Laughter will be coming from his inside, from the very core of his being.

Don't try to synthesize the opposite poles of life. Just be integrated. And when I say just be integrated I mean, whatsoever you feel in loneliness carry into the marketplace; whatsoever you feel in your meditation carry it into love – because in love the other will be present, in meditation you are alone. Sooner or later things will settle of their own accord. You need not settle them; you simply settle yourself. Get settled yourself, and things will fall into their own arrangement – they always fall, they always follow you. Once you are settled, the whole world is settled. Once you are in harmony, the whole world is in harmony. Once the inner accord is reached, there is no discord in the world.

My emphasis, total emphasis, absolute emphasis is: Get settled. Don't try to find any harmony in the opposites. You can never find it, and if you try too much you will get more and more disturbed – because it is impossible!

Another thing also you have asked about: that while with me you feel wellbeing, you feel a silence, you feel everything is possible. That too can become a dependence. Then when you are not with me, things seem to be more impossible, things seem to be not so much in accord. You are confused.

While with me you feel silence because you are less. While with me, sitting with me, for moments you become egoless, for periods you are not there, you are simply with me. The barrier is broken, the wall has disappeared. In that moment I am flowing in you. Everything seems possible. Away from me you gather your walls again. You are there. Things are not so beautiful then. So just try to understand what is happening, and carry that understanding when you go away from me. What is happening? When everything seems possible, even the final enlightenment seems possible, what is happening? You are not there. Without you everything is possible; with you everything is impossible. You are the problem.

Listening to me you forget. If you forget, *you* are not there – because your being there, the ego, is just a mental phenomenon. You have to create it every moment. It is just like pedaling a bicycle. You have to go on pedaling; if you stop for a single moment the cycle stops. There is a momentum, a little momentum; the cycle will go a few yards and then will stop. If you want the cycle to continue you have to go on pedaling. It is a continuous process. The cycle moving is not something permanent, it has to be created every moment. The ego has to be pedaled every moment – and you are pedaling it.

When you are here the pedaling stops. You are more concerned with me. Your total focus and attention moves. It is just like a small boy cycling. He is curious about everything. He looks at a tree with hundreds of parrots chattering there, and he falls from the cycle because the attention has moved. He stops pedaling, he forgets that he is on the cycle and that he has to continue pedaling it.

Small children find it difficult in the beginning to cycle just for one reason – because they are so curious about everything. No country allows driving licenses for children, only because they are so curious. They will forget. Any moment their total attention can go anywhere and they will forget that they are driving, that they have a dangerous tool in their hands and others' lives are in danger. They are unfocused. Their consciousness is flowing everywhere.

While you are here you are so much concerned with me, so much involved in it, you forget the pedaling. And for certain moments, when you forget yourself completely, silence descends on you, a bliss arises, everything seems possible. You become divine – that's why everything seems possible. Only for a god is everything possible. For a god nothing is impossible. In that moment you become godlike.

Away from me, you turn back again – your mind starts thinking, you start pedaling, and you pedal more because you have to compensate. You have not pedaled your cycle for a few moments, so you pedal more just to compensate. Intense ego comes back. You lose contact with your self.

With me, what is really happening is that you are more in contact with your self. The ego is not there. You are in deep contact with your self; your inner source is available to you, flowing. There is no block in energy. Away from me, all the blocks come back, old habits return. Then things don't seem so good. Then the whole phenomenon of being with me seems like a dream. You cannot believe it. It looks like a miracle – and you think that I may have done something. I have not been doing anything. Nobody can do anything to you. It happened because you allowed it.

When you move away from me, carry this feeling. Whatsoever you are feeling here, carry it with you. Then I will be needed less and less. Otherwise I can become a drug. Then every morning you awake and you start hankering for me. Then you are getting ready to come to me, a deep urge – then I can become a drug. Then you will become more and more dependent on me. That's not the way to reach satori, *samadhi* or enlightenment. That's not the way. If you become dependent on me I am a drug, and I am destructive then. But this is you who can convert me into a drug.

Whatsoever you feel near me, in my presence, with me, carry it with you. You must come to a point when whether with me or without me you remain the same. Then I am a help, then I am not a bondage. Then I am a freedom to you – and I must become a freedom to you. When I say I must become a freedom to you, it means you must come to a point when you are freed from me also. If it is a constant dependence and you are not freed it is not helping, it is simply postponing things. A real master will always make his disciples free of him. That is the goal. Come to me, go away from me, but carry the feeling with you. You remain the same. Move in the polar opposites always remaining the same. Then everything is possible, because you are the source of all the energies.

You have the source of all life within you. All that is happening in life is happening from the same source from which you happened. You are related to it, you are one with it. If birds can be so happy and singing, you can be, because the same source supplies them with the happiness, the singing. The same source is available to you, but somehow you have created blocks. If the trees are so green, so at home, not worried, you can be the same, because the sap that comes to the trees is coming to you. You may have forgotten it, but it is there.

All that has happened in life, all that is happening all around you, all this mystery, is your heritage. Claim it. It is wasting away unclaimed just by your side while you go on begging. The empire is there, and the empire goes on wasting and waiting and you go on begging. Claim it!

This is the way it can be claimed: remain the same while moving into opposites. This is what Krishna says in the Gita: In pain or pleasure, be the same; in success or failure, remain the same. Whatsoever happens, let it happen – you remain the same. This sameness will give you integrity.

One thing more you have asked: that I say to you to live in the world, not renounce it, and yet be completely mad and ecstatic. It seems difficult, because how can you then live normally in the world, in relationship with people? Yes, I say this to you.

One thing: renouncing the world is ugly to me, because that means renouncing the gift that God has given to you. You have not created life. You are not there because of your choice. It is a gift. Renouncing it is going against God. All renunciation is against God. It is saying no. That's why those who renounce become more egotistical. The moment you renounce you say: I am wiser than life, I am wiser than the divine source from where everything comes. When you renounce you say: I choose. When you renounce you use your will – and will creates ego.

When I say don't renounce, I am saying: Don't be a will, don't be a chooser. Whatsoever is happening is not happening because of you, so who are you to choose this or that? Let it happen. What can you do? Let it happen; don't be disturbed by it. Renunciation is just an escape. Because you get hurt, because you get disturbed, you renounce. You renounce the situation, you don't renounce the attitude that gets hurt. You don't renounce the heart that is with so many wounds that anybody can hurt it. You don't renounce the mind which is ill, which is always ready to get disturbed. You renounce the world – which is easier. You escape to the Himalayas, but all that was within you will be with you. It will not make any difference. This is a deception.

Remain integrated, remain silent, remain happy, and allow the world to happen. Who are you to renounce or not renounce? Wherever you find yourself, be there. Be integrated and silent and happy. Don't go to the Himalayas, create a Himalaya within – that's what I mean when I say don't renounce. Don't go to the hills, create that silence within, so wherever you move the hills move with you. Relationship is beautiful because it is a mirror. But there are stupid people – they see their face in the mirror and they see it is ugly so they destroy the mirror. The logic is apparent: this mirror is making them ugly, so destroy the mirror and then you are beautiful.

Relationship is a mirror. Wherever you are related with a person – a wife, a husband, a friend, a lover, an enemy – a mirror is there. The wife mirrors the husband. You can see yourself there. And if you see an ugly husband, don't try to leave your wife – the ugliness is in you. Drop that ugliness. This mirror is beautiful; be thankful to this mirror.

But stupid and cowardly people always escape and renounce; brave and wise people always live in relationship and use it as a mirror. Living with someone is a constant mirroring around you. Every moment the other reveals you, exposes you. The closer the relationship, the clearer is the mirror; the more distant the relationship, the mirror is not so clear. That's why all renouncing becomes really the renunciation of love. Wife and husband – that becomes the base for breaking the relationship, because twenty-four hours living with a person in the same house, twenty-four hours being related....

Even when a wife is not talking, not saying anything to her husband, she is mirroring. Even when the husband is just reading his newspaper, he is mirroring. The way he is putting his newspaper, the wife knows that the newspaper is just creating a wall. He is hiding behind it. He may be pretending to himself that he is reading. He may be reading the same news twice, thrice. He may not be reading at all, but just going through the words mechanically. But the way he is hiding himself behind the newspaper becomes a mirror. He is avoiding the wife, he is fed up with the wife, he doesn't want her to be here, he doesn't want to look at her, to see her. Her presence, the very presence is heavy. He wants to escape somehow.

When you are in love language is not needed. Gestures...even silence becomes eloquent. A constant mirroring goes on, and everybody is ugly because beauty is something which happens only by and by, when your inner being becomes revealed. Ego is always ugly. So only when the ego is not does one become beautiful. It is the ego that is mirrored.

Whosoever continuously reminds you that you are ugly becomes the enemy – you want to renounce. But is it wise to renounce the mirror? It is foolish. Even if nobody mirrors you, you will remain the same. You may even grow more in the same direction when nobody reminds you. The mirror is beautiful and good. It helps you. And if you are alert, by and by you can drop the ego. Then in the mirror of the other your beautiful self will be revealed.

Once you are a nothingness, a white cloud, then all the lakes of the world will reveal your whiteness, then all the lakes of the world will reveal your floating let-go. So I say there is only one thing to be renounced and that is renunciation, nothing else.

Live where God is, or the whole – if you don't like the word god, there is no problem, it is only a word. So God or the whole – wherever you find the whole has placed you, be there. The whole never places anybody in renunciation – never. The whole always throws you into relationship, because nobody is born alone, nobody can be. At least the mother, the father will be needed; a society, a family will be needed. The whole always throws you into relationship. That's why I say renunciation is going against God.

Gurdjieff has many insights. One of his insights is that all religious people are against God. This is strange but true. And I fully approve of him; he is right. All religious people are against God, because they set themselves up as judges: this is wrong, that is right; and this should be done, that should not be done; and one should move away from the world. God throws you into the world, and so-called religious preachers teach you to renounce it.

I am not that kind of a religious man. I am with God, with the whole. Wherever it leads you, move like a cloud; move with him, and give yourself totally to the whole. The only thing to remember is the opposites – the silence, the equilibrium, the balance, the integrity.

You say it will be difficult. Yes, it *will* be difficult. If you are ecstatic it will be difficult in a family which is pathological – and every family is pathological. It will be living just as if you are forced to live in a madhouse – it will be difficult, because everybody will be mad there. So what can you do? If you are thrown into a madhouse – you are not mad and everybody else is mad – what will you do? If you are really not mad, you will act madly. That's the only wise way there, so nobody comes to know that you are sane, because if they come to know they will create trouble. In a madhouse a really wise man will act more madly than any madman can do. That is the only safe state there.

So in this life where everybody is mad, what can you do? This whole planet is a madhouse, a big madhouse. Everybody is pathological, ill, diseased, abnormal, what can you do? Act! With people, when you feel, don't try to create unnecessary trouble – just act, and enjoy the act. With people, acting; for yourself, be madly ecstatic. What do I mean? I mean if somebody has died in the neighborhood, what will you do? Be madly ecstatic there? Then you will be beaten. Weep and cry, act beautifully – because that is what is needed in that whole pathological situation where death is not accepted, where death is evil. Don't create any trouble for anybody. If you are wise, act – and act so beautifully that nobody cries like you. Enjoy it! That is your inner thing. Make it an ecstasy! But for the outer, for people who are around you, act it beautifully.

Be an actor in the world. When you are an actor you are not disturbed, because then you know this is just acting. The whole of life is a great psychodrama. Be an actor there, and inside remain in your non-egoistic blissfulness.

Enough for today.

*Whatsoever
You Do,
Be Total*

CHAPTER TWELVE

Beloved Osho,
You have talked to us about total surrender to the master,
but often our minds come up with reasons
for not following the instructions literally.
We say things like: The master can't know that
the situation has changed.
Or: The master doesn't realize what
the practical conditions are in the West.
Should we follow everything the master says to the letter,
or are there times when we should use
our own discretion?

 OU SHOULD FOLLOW either absolutely, or not at all. No compromise should be made, because anything halfhearted is not only useless but harmful. Anything halfhearted divides you – that is the harm. You should remain an undivided unity.

So either surrender totally...then there is no need to think on your part; follow blindly. I emphasize the word 'blindly' – as if you have no eyes; somebody who has eyes is leading you. Then you will remain an undivided unity; and undivided, integrated, you will grow.

Or, if you feel this is impossible and cannot be done, don't follow at all. Completely follow yourself. Then too you will remain undivided. To remain undivided is the end, the aim. Both will do, the ultimate result will be the same. If you can be alone, without a master, if you can follow your own consciousness wheresoever it leads, it is the same, the result will be the same. So it depends on you.

But the mind always says: Do both. The mind says: Follow the master, but think about it. Follow only those things which you think right. Then where is the following? Where is the surrender? If you are the judge, and you are to decide what to follow and what not to follow, then where is the surrender, where is the trust? Then it is better to follow your own consciousness. But don't deceive – at least there should be no deception; otherwise you go on following yourself and you think that you are following a master.

If you are the deciding factor, if you have to choose, if you have to discard something, accept something, then you are following yourself. But you can create the impression around yourself and you can deceive yourself that you are following a master. Then nothing will come out of it. You will not grow, because through deception there can be no growth. And you will get more and more confused, because if you are to decide what is to be done and what is not to be done, if you have to choose from your master's guidance you will create a chaos, because whenever a master guides you his guidance has an organic unity about it. Every instruction is related to another. It is a compact whole. You cannot discard something and follow something; you will become a ruin, a wreck. Even if a single thing is denied, then the whole has been disturbed. You don't know how things are interrelated.

So this is my suggestion to you: Remain a unit, undivided. Decide. If you have to decide, then decide: I will follow myself. Then don't surrender – there is no need either!

This is what Krishnamurti has been saying for these forty, fifty years continuously: Don't follow. People can reach without following anybody, but the path is arduous and very long because you are not ready to accept any help or guidance which can be given to you – which *is* possible and which can cut many unnecessary difficulties on the path. This is what Krishnamurti has been saying. Nobody has done it.

This is the problem of the mind. The mind can accept: Don't follow – not because it has understood, but because it is very ego-fulfilling not to follow anybody. Nobody wants to follow anybody. Deep down the ego resists.

So around Krishnamurti all the egoists have gathered. They are again deceiving themselves. They think they are not following anybody because they have understood the fallacies of following, they have understood that the path has to be traveled alone, they have understood that no help is possible, nobody can help you, nobody can guide you; alone you have to travel. They think that they have understood this, that's why they are not following anybody. That is not the real thing – they are deceiving. They are not following because their ego won't allow. Still they go on listening to Krishnamurti. For years together they go again and again.

If no help is possible, why do you go again and again to Krishnamurti? If nobody can guide you, what is the point of listening to him again and again? It is pointless. And even this attitude, that you have to travel the path alone, is not discovered by you – it has been revealed to you by Krishnamurti. Deep down he has become your master. But you go on saying that you don't follow. This is a deception.

The same deception can happen from the reverse side. You come to me, you think you have surrendered, and still you go on choosing. If I say something that suits you, that means it suits your ego – you follow it. If I say something which doesn't suit your ego, you start rationalizing: This may not be for me. So you feel that you have surrendered, and you have not surrendered.

People around Krishnamurti think they are not following anybody, and they are following. You around me think you are following me and you are not following me. Mind is always a deceiver. Wherever you go it can deceive you, so be alert.

I say to you: You *can* reach without following, but the path will be very, very lonely, very long. It is bound to be so. One can reach, it is not impossible – people have reached. I myself have reached through not following; you can also reach. But remember that not following should not become an ego-fulfillment; otherwise you will never reach.

A master or no master, that is not the basic thing. The basic thing is the ego, *your* ego. No ego – then even without a master you can reach. With ego – even a buddha cannot lead you. Either follow totally or don't follow totally, but be total. It is for you to decide. Remain undeceived by the mind and look deep within yourself. Be aware of what you are doing. If you are surrendering, then surrender.

I remember: it happened once with a group in Gurdjieff's life. He was working with a few disciples. Absolute surrender was needed – and Gurdjieff had said that whatsoever he said, they had to follow. He was helping them to practice a certain exercise; he used to call that exercise the stop exercise. So whenever he said: Stop! you had to stop whatsoever you were doing. You were walking, one foot was above the ground, and when he said: Stop! you had to stop there. You were talking and your mouth was open and he said: Stop! you had to stop with an open mouth. You were not to change it, you were not to make your posture convenient, because that would be a deception, and you were not deceiving anybody except yourself.

One day, suddenly, in the morning when people were doing some exercise outside the camp and a few people were passing through a canal that was running by, he suddenly said: Stop! – he was inside the camp. So people stopped. Four were crossing the canal. It was dry, the water was not running, so they stopped.

But suddenly somebody opened the canal and the water started coming. They started to think: What to do? Gurdjieff is inside the tent, he doesn't know that we are standing in a canal and the canal is flowing. But they waited, because mind can wait for a moment.

When the water came up to their necks, one jumped out. He said: This is too much. Gurdjieff does not know.

Then the canal was flooded more. Two others jumped when the water came just near their noses...because now they would be drowned and the rationalization was simple and easy. You would have also done the same. They are going to die...the master is inside the tent and he doesn't know!

Only one remained. The water was flowing above his head and he was standing. Then Gurdjieff rushed out of his tent and brought him out of the canal. He was almost unconscious. The water had to be brought out of his body; he was just on the point of death. But when he opened his eyes he was another man. The old man really died. This was a transformation. He was totally different.

What happened in that moment of death? He accepted the master. He rejected his own mind and the rationalizations. He rejected his own life-lust. He rejected his own innermost biological urge to survive. He rejected everything. He said: When the master has said stop, I have stopped. Now nothing can move me.

It must have been very, very difficult – almost impossible. But when you do the impossible you are transformed. Dying, he would not allow the mind to interfere. Death was there, but he accepted death rather than his own mind and judgment.

He was never the same man again, nobody ever met the old man again. Then others realized that they had missed a great opportunity. The three who had jumped out of the canal missed a great opportunity.

This is total surrender. It is not a question of whether it is appealing to your mind or not, whether your mind says yes or not. When you surrender you have surrendered all possibility of saying no. Whatsoever the situation, you will not say no. The total yes means surrender. Difficult! That's why transformation is difficult. Not easy – that's why spiritual birth is not easy.

But I don't say that you cannot reach alone. You can reach alone and you can reach with a master; you can reach in a group, you can reach as an individual. All the possibilities are open. I am neither for this, nor for that. It is for you to decide, and decide without any deception.

Remember, it is not a question of East and West. The mind is the same deep down; all the differences are superficial. Eastern and Western – these are just surfaces...cultural, racial impressions, but they are on the surface. Deep down the human mind is the same. From where you come is irrelevant.

Surrender or remain absolutely alone, but both the paths can be traveled only by persons who are total. Alone, Buddha reached enlightenment; following Buddha, many reached the same enlightenment.

I am not partisan. I don't say, as Krishnamurti says: Only this is the way. I don't say, as Meher Baba says: Only this is the way. I know well they say: Only this is the way, to help you, because once you become aware that another can also be the way confusion starts in you. Then you start swaying – sometimes you think this, sometimes you think that. That's why masters have been saying: Only this is the way – just to make your mind unconfused. Otherwise the opposite will also attract you and you will go on changing your standpoint. To make you total, masters go on emphasizing.

But I say both are ways. Why? – because that emphasis has become old, and you have heard too much about: This is the *only* way. It has become a dead cliché. It doesn't help now. It used to help in the past; it cannot help now, because the world has become so much one. The earth has become just a global village, and every religion is known to every other religion and all the paths have become known. Now humanity is acquainted with all the paths – all the paths, all the possibilities, all the alternatives.

In the past people knew only one path, the path into which they were born. It was good to emphasize that this is the only way – to make their minds confident about it, trusting about it. But now this is not the situation at all. A Hindu reads the Koran, a Christian comes to India to seek guidance, a Mohammedan is aware of the Gita and the Vedas. All the paths have become known. Much confusion exists, and whosoever says that this is the only path is not going to help now because you know other paths are there. You also know that from other paths people have reached and are reaching. Hence I don't emphasize any path.

You can take my help if you surrender, you can take my help if you don't surrender – but you have to be clear about it. If you choose the path of surrender, then you have to follow me totally. If you choose that you are not going to surrender, then decide it. I can be a friend on the path, there is no need to make me a master.

I can be just a friend on the path – or not even a friend.

You are searching and you meet somebody absolutely unknown, a stranger, and you ask him: Where is the river? Which
path leads to the river? When he has spoken you thank him and
you move. I can be just a stranger. No need even to be a friend,
because with a friend also you get involved. You can take my help
– my help is unconditional.

I don't say: Do this, then I will help you. I don't say: Surrender,
only then will I help you. But this much I must say: Do whatsoever
you like, but do it totally. If you are total, the transformation is
closer. If you are divided, it is almost impossible.

Beloved Osho,
When Wakuan saw a picture
of the bearded Bodhidharma, he complained:
Why hasn't that fellow got a beard?
Beloved Osho, why don't you have a beard?

THE TRADITION OF ZEN is really beautiful. Bodhidharma
has got a beard, and a disciple asks: Why has this fellow
not got a beard? The question is beautiful, but only a
Zen disciple can raise it – because the beard belongs to the body,
not to Bodhidharma. That fellow is beardless, because the body is
just an abode. Apparently the question is absurd, but it is meaningful, and such questions have been asked many times.

Buddha continuously talked – morning, evening, afternoon, in
this village, in that village, moving, forty years continuously talking. One day Sariputta asked: Why have you remained silent? Why
don't you talk to us? Patently absurd! Buddha laughed and said:

You are right. And this man *was* talking – nobody has talked as much as Buddha. But Sariputta was right, because this talking happened only on the surface and Buddha did remain silent.

One Zen monk, Rinzai, used to say: This man Buddha was never born, he never walked on this earth, he never died – he is just a dream. And every day he would go to the temple and bow down before Buddha's statue.

Then somebody said: Rinzai, you are just mad! Every day you go on insisting that this man was never born, never died, never walked on this earth, and still you go to the temple and bow down.

Rinzai said: Because this man was never born, never walked on this earth, never died, that's why I go and bow down.

The questioner persisted, saying: We can't follow you. Either you are mad or we are mad, but we cannot follow – what do you mean?

And Rinzai said: The birth of this man was just a dream to him. Walking on this earth was just a dream to him. Death was not real to him – just an end to a long dream. And this man, the center of his being, remained beyond birth, beyond death.

It is said that Buddha always remained in the seventh heaven. He never came down – only his reflection was here. And this is true! This is true for you also. You have never come down, only the reflection – but you have become so identified with the reflection that you have forgotten. You think that you have come down. You cannot come down – there is no way to fall down from your being.

You can look into a river and you can see the reflection, and you can become so identified with it that you can think that you are under water. You can suffer because of it; you can feel suffocated, and you can feel now you are going to die. And you are always standing on the bank, you have never come down to the water – you cannot come!

So I say to you: Not only Buddha, nobody has come down from the seventh heaven, ever. But a few people get obsessed, identified with their reflections. This is what Hindus call the world of maya, the world of reflections. We remain in the Brahman, we remain in the ultimate reality, rooted there eternally. Nobody ever comes down. But we can get identified with the reflection, with the dream.

So you are right in asking me. This fellow is also beardless. If you look at my body, you are not looking at me. If you look at me, then you will understand. The beard cannot grow on its own. The beard can grow only on the body. And this beard is really very symbolic: soul is alive, body is half dead and half alive, beard is almost dead. Your hair is a dead part of your body. That's why you can cut it and you don't feel any pain. Cut your finger, you will feel pain. Your hair is part of your body, but if you cut it you don't feel any pain. It is dead cells of the body. So sometimes it happens that in a graveyard...if you go to a Mohammedan grave- yard and dig up a body, the man may have died beardless but there will be a beard now. Even on dead bodies beards can grow because beards are dead, just dead cells.

It is good to grow a beard, because then standing before a mir- ror you can see all the three layers of you: the completely dead, the half dead, half alive, and the absolutely alive. Beard is material, matter; body is matter and spirit meeting. The meeting is always difficult, but body is just a meeting ground of matter and spirit. Whenever the meeting breaks the balance is lost – you are dead. Matter reabsorbed in matter, spirit reabsorbed in spirit.

This fellow is also beardless.

The whole question is: Why is Bodhidharma not matter? And the answer is: Because spirit cannot be matter.

Zen disciples ask in a peculiar way. Nowhere else can such questions be asked. You cannot ask a Christian pope: Why is this fellow Jesus beardless? The very question will be thought profane; you cannot be so intimate with Jesus. You cannot call him this guy or this fellow; that will not look holy. Your behavior will look insulting. But not so with Zen. Zen says: If you love your masters you can laugh about them; if you love them there cannot be any fear, even the fear of a man who is holy. If you love them, fear disappears.

So when for the first time Christian theologians became aware of the tradition of Zen, they couldn't believe that such a religion could exist, because Zen monks go on laughing about Buddha. Sometimes they use such words you cannot believe! They can say: This stupid fellow – for Buddha! And if you ask them, they will say: Yes, he was stupid, because he was trying to say something which cannot be said and he was trying to transform us who are impossible. He was a stupid fellow – he was trying to do the impossible!

Zen masters have used terms and words that no religion can use. But because of that I say that no religion is so religious as Zen, because if you really love, where is the fear? You can joke, you can laugh, and an enlightened man like Buddha will laugh with you – there is no problem. He will not feel hurt. If he feels hurt, he is not enlightened at all. And he will not say: Don't use such profane language – because for Buddha all language is profane, only silence is sacred. So whether you call him a stupid fellow or one who has awakened, both are the same for him. Language as such is profane. Only silence is holy. Whatsoever you say is the same.

This disciple, Wakuan, is asking: Why has this fellow Bodhidharma not got a beard? Bodhidharma is the first master of Zen. Bodhidharma created this ever-flowing, ever-renewing river of Zen.

Bodhidharma went to China fourteen hundred years ago. When he entered China he was carrying one of his shoes on his head. One shoe was on his foot, one shoe was on his head. The emperor had come to receive him. He became embarrassed: What manner of man is this? He had been waiting so long, and he was thinking: A great holy man, a great saint and sage is coming – and this man is behaving like a buffoon! The emperor was disturbed, he felt uneasy. And the first opportunity he got, he asked Bodhidharma: What are you doing? People are laughing, and they are laughing at me also because I have come to receive you. And the way you have behaved is not a way to behave; you should behave like a saint!

Bodhidharma said: Only those who are not saints behave like

saints. I *am* a saint. Only those who are not saints behave like saints – and he is true, because you care about your behavior only when it is not spontaneous.

The emperor said: I cannot understand this carrying one shoe on your head; you appear like a buffoon.

Bodhidharma said: Yes, because all that can be seen is buffoonery. Only the unseen.... Your standing here like an emperor, robed in a special dress, crowned, is buffoonery. Just to say this to you I was carrying one shoe on my head. All this is acting and buffoonery. The real is not there on the periphery. Look at *me*, don't look at my body. This is very symbolic that I carry one shoe on my head. I say that in life nothing is sacred and nothing is profane. Even a shoe is as sacred as your head. I carry this shoe as a symbol.

It is said the emperor was impressed, but he said: You are too much! Just one thing I wanted to ask you and that is, how to put my mind at ease. I am so impatient, so disturbed, uneasy.

Bodhidharma said: Come in the morning at four o'clock and bring your mind with you. I will put it at ease.

The emperor could not follow. He started thinking: What does he mean, this man – bring your mind with you? When he was going down the steps of the temple where Bodhidharma was staying, Bodhidharma again said: Remember, don't come alone, otherwise who will I put at ease? Bring the mind with you. Come at four o'clock – and alone, no guards, nobody else with you.

The whole night the emperor couldn't sleep. He was thinking: This man seems to be a little crazy. When I am there, my mind will obviously be with me. So what is this insistence – bring your mind with you? Sometimes he thought: It is better not to go, because, who knows, alone this man may start beating me or something. You cannot believe...you cannot predict this man.

But at last he decided to go, because the man was really magnetic. He had something in his eyes, a fire which doesn't belong to this earth. He had something in his breath, a silence which comes from beyond. So the emperor came as if hypnotized, and the first thing Bodhidharma asked was: Okay, so you have come. Where is your mind? And he was sitting there with a big staff.

The emperor said: But when I have come, my mind has come with me. It is inside me – it is not like a thing I can carry.

So Bodhidharma said: Okay, so you think the mind is within you. Then sit and close your eyes and try to find out where it is. You just point it out to me and I will put it right. This staff is here – and I am going to make your mind silent, don't worry. The emperor closed his eyes and tried to look, and Bodhidharma was sitting just in front of him. He tried and tried and tried, and time passed and then the sun was rising and his face was absolutely silent. Then he opened his eyes and Bodhidharma, sitting there, asked: Could you find it?

The emperor started laughing and he said: You have put it right – because the more I try to find it, the more I feel it is not there. It was just a shadow, and it was there because I never penetrated within. It was just my absence. I became present inside and it disappeared.

This Bodhidharma is really a very rare being. His disciples could joke about him, laugh about him – he enjoyed it!

An enlightened person is a continuous laughter. He is not a serious man, as is ordinarily thought. Wherever you see seriousness know well something is wrong, because seriousness is part of a diseased being. No flower is serious unless it is ill. No bird is serious unless it is ill. No tree is serious unless something is wrong. Whenever something is wrong, seriousness happens. Seriousness is illness. When everything is okay, laughter arises.

Bodhidharma is continuously laughing, and his laughter is a belly laughter, an uproar. His disciples used to ask questions nobody except a Bodhidharma can answer. And I tell you: That fellow was without a beard, and this fellow is also without a beard.

Goso said: When you meet a Zen master on the road
you cannot talk to him and you cannot
be with him in silence. What are you to do?
Beloved Osho, When we meet
the master of masters on the lawn – what to do?

YES, IT IS TRUE. When you meet a Zen master on the road you cannot talk with him, because what can you talk with him about? Your worlds are so different, your languages belong to two different dimensions. What can you talk with him about? What can you ask? Is any question really worth asking? Is any question really meaningful? When you meet a Zen master, what will you talk about? All that you can talk about belongs to this world, this mundane world, the market, the house, the family. All that you can talk about, all that you are, is so futile.

It is true. When you meet a Zen master on the road...and you always meet a master on the road because the master is always moving. You never meet him anywhere else. Remember, you always meet a master on the road, because he is always moving. He is a river, never static, never standing. If you cannot move with him you will miss him. He is always on his feet. You always meet him on the road.

What can you talk to him about? And you cannot be silent either, because to be silent is almost impossible for you. You cannot talk, because the master belongs to a different world. You cannot be silent, because the world you belong to is never silent. Your mind goes on chattering. Your mind is a constant chatter-box. Consistent, inconsistent – thoughts go on and on and on and there is no end to it, they move in a wheel.

You cannot be silent and you cannot talk – then what to do? If you start talking it will be absurd. If you start being silent, it will not be possible. It is better not to decide on your part. Ask the master what to do. Tell him: I cannot talk because we belong to different worlds. Whatsoever I ask will be useless, and whatsoever you can answer I cannot question. Whatsoever I question is useless, it is not even worth answering. And I cannot be silent because I don't know what silence is. I have never known it; silence has never happened to me. I know a sort of silence – the silence that comes between two thoughts as a gap, the silence that exists between two words, just as a gap.

Our silence is just like the peace which happens between two wars. It is not really peace; it is just preparation for another war. How can that be peace which bridges two wars? The war simply goes underground, that's all. It is a cold war, it is never peace. Our silence is like that.

So tell the master: I cannot be silent and I cannot talk – so tell me what to do. Don't start anything on your own, because whatsoever you start will be wrong. Talk or silence – whatsoever you start will be wrong. Just leave everything to the master, and ask him: What am I to do? If he says: Talk – then talk. If he says: Be silent – then try to be silent. He knows, and he will ask only that which is possible for you.

Ultimately he will ask the impossible, but never in the beginning. He will ask the impossible in the end because then it will also have become possible. But in the beginning he will ask only the possible. By and by he will push you towards the ultimate abyss where the impossible happens. If he says talk, then talk. Then even your talking will be a help. But then you are not really asking, just talking as a catharsis. You are bringing your mind out, you are acting your mind out. You are opening yourself. You are not asking, but exposing. This exposure will help. You will be relieved of much burden.

When a master is near you, if you can be really frank and say all that comes to you, irrelevant, inconsistent, not bothering about yourself, not managing and manipulating it.... When a master is near you, you can say totally whatsoever comes to your mind. It will become a gibberish; if you don't manage it, it will be like a madman talking. But when a master is near you, if you are frank, honest and true and bring your mind out, the master will penetrate you from the back door. From the front door your mind is going out; from the back door the master is entering you.

So when near me on the lawn be sincere and true. Don't bring questions which are intellectual; they are useless. Metaphysics is the most useless thing in the world. Don't bring any metaphysical questions; they are not true, they don't belong to you. You may have heard about them, read about them, but they are not part of you. Bring your nonsense out, whatsoever it is. And don't try to manipulate it. Don't try to rationalize it and polish it. Let it be as raw as possible – because before a master you must be naked. You should not wear clothes and you should not hide yourself.

That is an exposure, and if you can talk as an exposure not as an inquiry – just opening your heart, not asking for anything – then silence will follow, because when you have exposed your mind and you have passed through a catharsis, silence comes to you. This is a different type of silence, not a forced silence, not a controlled silence, not a silence with any effort on your part.

When you have exposed your mind completely, released all that is there, a silence comes, descends on you, overwhelms you, a silence which is beyond understanding, and a silence which is beyond you – a silence which belongs to the whole and not to the individual. Then you can be both. Now with a Zen master on the road you can talk and you can be silent also.

Enough for today.

God Is
In Search of
You

CHAPTER THIRTEEN

Beloved Osho,
Yesterday you told us very clearly that
we need to follow the master's word to the letter.
But we cannot consult you on every detail.
How can we choose the right path
when the mind is always looking for the easy way?

THE REAL PROBLEM is not consulting the master but how to be more meditative, because the physical part of the master is not the significant thing. If you are more meditative you can consult the master every moment. The physical presence is not necessary, it becomes necessary only because you are not meditative. Because you are identified with your body, that's why in your mind the master is identified with his body. Because you think that you are a body, you also think that the master is a body. The master is not a body, and when I say this, that the master is not a body, I mean that he is not confined in time and space.

It is not a question of being in his presence. Wherever you are, if you are meditative, you are in his presence. Even when the master is dead he can be consulted. Buddha is still consulted even today – and the answers are received. It is not that Buddha is sitting somewhere and giving you the answers, but when you are deep in meditation you *are* the buddha. Your buddha-nature arises and your buddha-nature answers you, and now Buddha is no longer confined anywhere. That means, for one who is blind he is not to be found anywhere; but for one who can now see it means he is everywhere.

You can be in contact with your master wherever you are. The way is not to go to the master, the way is to go within. The deeper you reach into yourself, the deeper you have penetrated the master.

Answers will be coming, and you will come to know and feel that those answers are not given by your mind. There will be a total difference of quality. The quality changes so absolutely that there can be no confusion about it. When your mind answers you feel *you* are answering. When the mind is not there you are simply meditative; the answer comes as if from someone else, not from you. You hear it.

That is the mystery of the Koran. Mohammed thought that he heard it – and he was right. And Mohammedans are wrong if they think that God was speaking. Mohammed is right when he thinks that he heard the Koran, and Mohammedans are wrong when they think that God was speaking. Nobody was speaking. But when your mind is silent, from the very depths of your being arises the answer. And it is so deep, so beyond your so-called mind, that you feel that you have heard it. It has come to you, it has been revealed to you.

You are always identified with the surface and the answer comes from the depth. You don't know your own depth – that's why you will feel God is answering, that the master is answering. In a way you are right – because when the answer comes from your depth it is from the master.

Hindus have always been saying that your real master is within you, and the outer master is just trying to bring your inner master up, to make your inner master functional. Whenever your inner master has started functioning, the work of the outer master is done. The outer is just a representative of the inner.

I am your depth. Once your depth has started functioning I am not needed. Once I feel your depth has started answering you, I will stop answering you. All my answers are not really concerned with your questions; all my answers are concerned with how to create the response within you so your inner depth starts speaking to you, so your own consciousness becomes your master.

Be more meditative. Be more silent.

Allow more and more stillness to penetrate you.

What is to be done? How to be more meditative? In a sense,

nothing can be done directly, because whatsoever you do directly the mind comes in. If you try to be silent you cannot be, because the mind is trying. Wherever mind is, disturbance is. Mind is the disturbance, mind is the noise. So if you try to be silent, mind is trying to be silent. You will create more noise, which is now concerned with silence. Now you will try, and think, and do this and that, and you will get more and more uneasy.

Nothing can be done about silence. Silence is already there, you just have to allow it. It is just like sunlight: your windows are closed and you cannot bring sunlight into your house in bundles, in buckets. You cannot do that! If you try you will be foolish – and many are doing that. Simply open the windows, open the doors. Allow the breeze to blow. Allow the rays to come in. Invite and wait. You cannot force. Whenever you force, things go ugly. If a man forces himself to be silent his silence will be ugly, tortured, forced, artificial, just on the surface. Deep down there will be turmoil.

So what is to be done? Open your mind and wait. Look at the trees, look at the parrots screeching. Listen to them, don't do anything. Whatsoever is happening around you, just be a passive alertness. The light on the water, the river flowing, the noise, the children playing, laughing, giggling – you just be there, a passive presence, open, listening, seeing, not thinking. The birds are there in the trees, making a noise, singing.... You just listen. Don't think, don't create a second series in your mind about what is happening. Just let it happen, and sooner or later you will feel the mind has disappeared and a silence has come to you. You will actually feel it descending on you, penetrating, from every pore of the body, reaching deeper and deeper.

In the beginning it will be only for moments, because you are such a habitual thinker, addicted to thinking, like a man who is addicted to alcohol or some drug, that only for moments will there be a gap – and again you will start thinking. You may start thinking about this silence that is descending upon you. You may start thinking: Oh! This is the silence that the masters have always been talking about – and you have destroyed it. You may start thinking:

This is the silence the Upanishads say is the goal to be achieved, this is the silence that poets have been talking about, the silence that surpasses understanding – you have missed it.

The poets have entered, the masters have entered, the Upanishads have come. You have missed it, you have lost it. Now you are again disturbed; now you are not a passivity, now you are not alert. Now those singing birds are no longer there for you. Your mind has come in. Now those beautiful trees have disappeared. The sun is no longer in the sky and the clouds are no longer floating. You are not open now – closed, your windows are closed, your doors are closed.

Thought, thinking, is the way to close the mind. Non-thinking, no thought, is the way to open it. Whenever you are not thinking you are open; whenever you are thinking a wall has been raised. Each thought becomes a brick and the whole process of thinking becomes a wall. Then you are hidden behind the wall, crying and weeping – why is the sun not reaching you? It is not the sun – it is you who are creating walls around you.

Be more meditative. Whenever you have any opportunity, any space, any time, just allow things to happen around you. Look deeply, attentively, but don't be active – because activity means thinking. Sitting quietly, allowing things to happen, you will become silent.

Then you will come to know that silence is not a quality of the mind. Mind cannot be made silent. Silence is the quality of your inner soul, of your inner being. It is always there but because of the chattering, the constant chattering of the mind, you cannot hear it. Whenever you become passive, non-thinking, you become aware of it. Then you are unoccupied. In that unoccupied moment meditation happens.

So whatsoever the situation – sitting in a marketplace – don't think that the singing of the birds is a must. It is not. The humming of a marketplace is also as beautiful as the humming of the birds: people carrying on their work, talking, chattering, noise all around, you just sit there passively.

Remember this word passive, and another word, alert. Passive alertness is the key. Remain passive – not doing anything, just listening. And listening is not a doing. To listen to anything there is nothing to do, your ears are always open. To see you have to open the eyes – at least that much has to be done. To listen not even that much has to be done. Ears are always open, you are always listening. Just don't do anything and listen. And don't comment, because with commentary, thought starts. A child is crying: don't say anything inside about why he is crying. Two persons are fighting – don't say inside: Why are they fighting? Should I go and do something so that they don't fight? No, don't say anything. Just listen to what is happening. Just be with what is happening – and suddenly there is silence.

This silence is totally different from the silence which you can create. You can create silence – you can sit in your house, you can close the doors, you can take a rosary, a mala, and you can go on turning its beads. A silence will come to you, but that will not be the real silence. It will be just like a child who has been given a toy to play with, so he goes on playing and becomes absorbed in his play; then he is not mischievous.

Parents use the toy as a trick just to make the child less mischievous. He sits in a corner and goes on playing, and the parents can continue their own work without the child being a continuous nuisance. But the child has not transcended mischief; his mischief has been directed towards the toy, that's all. The mischief is there; the child is there. Sooner or later he will become fed up with the toy. Bored, he will throw it away and the mischief will be back.

Rosaries are old men's toys. Just as you give a toy to a child, children give rosaries to old men so that they are not mischievous. They sit in a corner and they go on turning their rosary. But they also get fed up; they get absorbed, but they also get fed up – then they keep changing rosaries. They go to another master and ask for another mantra because the old one is not functioning. In the beginning, they say, it functioned.

Many people come to me and say: We have been doing a

mantra; in the beginning it was helpful but it is not helping any more. Now we don't feel anything, it has become boring. We do it as a duty, but the love has disappeared. If we don't do it, we feel that we have missed something; if we do it nothing is gained.

This is what addiction means: if you do it nothing is gained; if you don't do it you feel that something is missing. This is what a smoker feels. If he smokes, he knows nothing is gained. He is doing something silly, just a stupid thing – taking smoke in and throwing it out. But that too is just like a rosary. You take the smoke in, and then you throw it out. Inhale, exhale, inhale, exhale – it becomes a rosary; you go on changing the beads. You can make it a mantra; when you inhale the smoke, say Ram; when you exhale, say Ram. It becomes a rosary!

Anything that you can repeat continuously becomes a mantra. Mantra means a repetition of a certain word, a certain sound, anything. A mantra helps the mind to be absorbed – it is a toy. For a few moments you feel good because the mischief stops, and you are so absorbed that the mind cannot function. This is a forced silence. It is pathological, it is not good. It is negative, it is not positive. This silence is like the silence that happens in a graveyard, the silence of death.

But the silence I am talking about is totally, qualitatively different. It is not a diversion of mischief, it is not a forced occupation, it is not a mantra hypnosis. It is a silence that happens to you when you are passive and alert, not doing anything, not even moving your rosary – totally passive, but alert.

Remember, passivity can become sleep. That's why I emphasize the word alertness – because you can be passive and you go to sleep. Sleep is not meditation. One quality of sleep is there, one quality, that of passivity; and one quality of waking is there, that of alertness. Relaxed as if you are asleep, alert as if you are awake. One thing is taken from sleep, unconsciousness – that should not be there, because meditation cannot be unconscious; and one thing is taken from your waking state, occupiedness, because if you are occupied then the mind is working, you are enclosed in thoughts.

While you are awake there are two things: alertness and occupiedness. While you are asleep there are two things: passivity and
unconsciousness. One thing from awakeness, one thing from sleep:
ʾassivity and alertness – they make meditation. If you take the two
other ingredients, occupation and unconsciousness, you become
mad. Those two ingredients, occupied and unconscious, make
madness, make the madman. Passivity and alertness make the
meditative man, a buddha. You have all four ingredients. Mix two
and you will become mad. Mix the other two and you will become
meditative.

Remember this: I say again and again that silence, the bliss that
pervades you when you are open, is not something to be done by
you. It is a letgo. It is a happening to you, it comes to you.

People come to me and they say: We are searching for God –
how to reach him? And I tell them: You cannot reach him and you
cannot search for him – because you don't know him. How will
you recognize that he is God? You don't know him. How will you
move? How will you choose the path? You don't know him. How
can you decide if this is his house, this is his abode? No, you cannot, you cannot search for the divine. But there is no need because
the divine is always near you, within you. Whenever you allow
him, he searches for you, he reaches you.

God is in search of you. God has always been in search of you.
No search on your part is needed. Seek and you will miss. Don't
seek. Simply remain passive and alert so whenever he comes you
are open. Many times he comes and knocks on your door but you
are fast asleep – or even if you hear the knock you interpret it in
your own way. You think: It is just the wind blowing fast and
strong. Or you think: Some stranger has knocked and he will go by
himself; there is no need to disturb my sleep.

Your interpretations are your enemies, and you are great inter-
preters. Whatsoever is, you immediately interpret it; your mind
starts functioning and grinding it and you change it immediately.
You color it; you give it a different meaning that was never there.
You project yourself into it. You destroy it.

become ends, the moment becomes eternal.

Yes, you have to follow the master totally. There may be times when you cannot consult him physically, and sooner or later the master will disappear from the body. Then there will be no possibility to consult him physically. It is better to get attuned to him non-physically; otherwise you will be crying and weeping. My body can disappear any moment. Now there is really no need to carry it – it is being carried for you. If you don't get attuned to my non-physical existence, sooner or later you will get very much depressed, sad, much anguish will be there. Then it will be very difficult to be attuned to me non-physically.

So I go on dropping physical contact with you more and more – just to make you alert and aware that you have to be attuned non-physically. You can get attuned, it is not difficult. Be more meditative and it will start happening to you.

Beloved Osho,
We have quite a few questions about female energy.
Some women say that since they've met you,
although their physical desires continue,
a mortal man is no longer satisfying enough for them.
Other women say that
since they have met you they feel more loving.
Gurdjieff is reported to have said
that a woman cannot attain except through a man.
Would you talk to us about female energy.

Y ES, GURDJIEFF HAS SAID that a woman cannot attain except through a man – and he is right. He is right because female energy differs from male energy. It is just as if someone says that only a woman can give birth to a child. A man cannot give birth to a child – he can give birth to a child only through a woman. The physical structure of the woman carries a womb; the physical structure of a man is without a womb – he can have a child only through a woman. And the same in reverse order happens in spiritual birth: a woman can get enlightened only through a man. Their spiritual energy differs also, just like their physical part.

Why? Why is this so? And remember, this is not a question of equality or of inequality – this is a question of difference. Women are not lower than men because they cannot attain directly; man is not lower than woman because he cannot give birth to a child directly. They are different. There is no question of equality or inequality, there is no question of evaluation. They are simply different, and this is a fact.

Why is it difficult for woman to attain enlightenment directly, and why for man is it possible to attain enlightenment directly? There are two ways, only two, basically only two, which lead to enlightenment. One is meditation and the other is love. You may call them Gyana Yoga and Bhakti Yoga – the path of wisdom and the path of devotion. The basic ways are only two.

Love needs another; meditation can be done alone. Man can achieve through meditation – that's why he can achieve directly. He can be alone. He is alone deep down. Aloneness comes naturally to man. For a woman, to be alone is difficult, very difficult, almost impossible. Her whole being is a deep urge to love, and for love the other is needed. How can you love if the other is not there? You can meditate if the other is not there – there is no problem.

Woman, the female energy, reaches the meditative state through love; and the male energy reaches love through meditation. A Buddha becomes a great loving force – but through meditation. When Buddha came back to his palace his wife was very angry, naturally, because for twelve years he had not shown his face. One night he had simply disappeared, not even saying anything to her. While she was asleep he escaped like a coward.

The wife of Buddha, Yashodhara, would have allowed him. She was a brave woman. If Buddha had asked she would have allowed him; there would have been no problem about it, but Buddha would not ask. He was afraid something might go wrong, she might start crying and weeping or something. But the fear was not because of her – the fear was deep down in himself. He was afraid it would be difficult for him to leave Yashodhara weeping and crying. The fear is always of oneself. It would be very cruel and he could not be so cruel, so it was better to escape while his wife was asleep. So he escaped.

After twelve years he came back. Yashodhara asked many things. One of the things she asked was: Tell me, whatsoever you have attained there, could you not attain it here living with me? Now that you have attained you can tell me.

It is said that Buddha remained silent. But I answer: Buddha could not have attained, because a man deep in love...and he *was* deep in love with Yashodhara; it was a very intimate relationship. If there had been no relationship with Yashodhara, if she had simply been a Hindu wife, no love relationship, then Buddha could have attained even living with her. Then really there is no problem. The other is there on the periphery, you are not related. If you are not related, the other is not – only a physical presence moving on the boundary.

But Buddha was in deep love. And it is difficult for a man to attain meditation when he is in love – this is the problem. Very difficult, because when he is in love, whenever he sits silently, the other arises in the mind; his whole being starts moving around the other. That was the fear, that's why Buddha escaped.

Nobody has talked about it before, but Buddha escaped from that house, from the wife, from the child, because he really loved. And if you love a person, then whenever you are occupied you may forget him, but when you are unoccupied the other will come to the memory immediately, and then there is no gap for the divine to enter. When you are occupied, working in a shop, or.... Buddha was on his throne and looking after the affairs of the kingdom, then it was okay – he could forget Yashodhara. But whenever he was not occupied, there was Yashodhara – the gap was filled by Yashodhara and there was no passage for the divine to enter.

Man cannot attain to the divine through love. His whole energy is totally different from female energy. First he should attain to meditation – then love happens to him. Then there is no problem. First he must reach the divine, then the beloved also becomes divine.

After twelve years Buddha comes back. Now there is no problem, now the god is in Yashodhara. Before, Yashodhara was too much and it was difficult to find the god. Now the god is totally there, there is no space left for Yashodhara.

Totally the opposite happens to a woman. She cannot meditate because her whole being is an urge towards the other. She cannot be alone. Whenever she is alone she is in misery. So if you say: To be alone is bliss, to be alone is ecstatic, a woman cannot understand it. This emphasis on being alone has existed all over the world because of too many seekers who are men – a Buddha, a Mahavira, a Jesus, a Mohammed. They all went into loneliness, and they only attained in loneliness. They created the milieu.

A woman, whenever alone, feels anguish. If there is a lover, even in her mind, she is happy. If someone loves, if someone is loved – if love exists around a woman, it nourishes her. It is a nourishment, it is a subtle food. Whenever a woman feels that love is not there she is simply starving, suffocating; the whole being shrinks. So a woman can never think that loneliness can be blissful.

This female energy has created the path of love and devotion. Even a divine lover will do – there is no need to find a physical lover. Krishna will do for Meera, there is no problem, because for Meera the other exists. He may not be there, Krishna may just be a myth; but for Meera he is, the other exists – and then Meera is happy. She can dance, she can sing, and she is nourished.

The very idea, the very notion, the very feeling that the other exists and there is love, and a woman feels fulfilled. She is happy, alive. Only with this love will she come to a point when the lover and the beloved become one. Then meditation will happen.

For female energy, meditation happens only in the deepest merger of love. Now she can never be alone. Then she can be alone, then there is no problem; the beloved has become merged, it is within. Meera or Radha or Teresa, they all achieved through a lover – Krishna, Jesus.

This is my feeling, that whenever a male seeker comes to me he is interested in meditation, and whenever a female seeker comes to me she is interested in love. She can be made interested in meditation if I say that love will happen through it. But her deep desire is for love. Love is God for a woman.

This difference has to be understood, deeply understood, because everything depends on it. Gurdjieff is right. Female energy will love, and through love will flower the meditative state, the *samadhi*. Satori will come, but deep down in the roots will be love and satori will become the flower. For male energy satori will be in the roots, samadhi will be in the roots, meditation will be in the roots, and then love will flower. But love will be a flowering.

When female seekers come to me it is bound to happen: they will feel more love, but then a physical partner will be less satisfying. Whenever there is deep love a physical partner will always become unsatisfactory, because the physical partner can fulfill only the periphery, he cannot fulfill the center. That's why, in ancient countries like India, we never allowed love – we allowed arranged marriages. Once love is allowed, the physical partner is going to be unsatisfactory sooner or later, and then there will be frustration.

Now the whole West is disturbed. Now there will be no satisfaction at all. Once you allow love, then an ordinary man cannot fulfill it. He can fulfill sex, he can fulfill the superficial, but he cannot fulfill the deep, the depth. Once the depth is functioning, once you have disturbed the depth, only God can fulfill – nobody else.

So when female seekers come to me, their depth is shocked.

They start feeling a new urge, a new love arising. Now their husbands or their boyfriends, their partners will not be able to satisfy it. Now this can be satisfied only by a much higher quality being. This is going to be so.

So either your boyfriend, your husband, has to become more meditative, create higher qualities of being...only then will he be fulfilling; otherwise the relationship will break. The bridge cannot remain; you will have to find a new friend. Or if it is impossible to find a new friend – as it would have been for Meera – difficult, then you have to love the divine. Then just forget the physical part – now it is not for you.

The same happens to male seekers in a different way. When they come to me they become more meditative. When they become more meditative, the bridge between their old partners is broken, becomes shaky. Now their girlfriend or their wife has to grow; otherwise the relationship is on the rocks, it cannot be maintained.

Remember this, that all our relationships, so-called relationships, are adjustments. If one changes, the adjustment is broken – for the better or for the worse, that is not the point. People come to me and they say: If meditation brings higher qualities, then why is the relationship broken? That is not the question. The relationship was an adjustment between two persons as they were. Now one has changed, the other has to grow with them; otherwise there will be trouble, things will become false.

Whenever a man is here, he becomes more meditative. The more meditative he is, the more he wants to be alone. The wife, the beloved, will be disturbed by it. If she is not understanding then she will start creating trouble – this man wants to be more alone. If she is understanding then there is no problem, but that understanding can only come to her if her love grows. If she feels more loving then she can allow this friend to be lonely, alone, and she will protect his aloneness. She will try to see that it is not disturbed – this will be her love now.

And if this man feels...if Buddha feels that Yashodhara is protecting, safeguarding, seeing, caring, that his meditation is not disturbed, that his silence is helped, then there is no need to escape from this Yashodhara. But this happens only if Yashodhara's love grows.

When a man's meditation is growing, a woman's love should grow. Only then can they keep pace, and a higher harmony will arise and it will go on, higher and higher. And a moment comes when the man is totally in meditation and the woman is totally in love – then only the perfect meeting, then only the real, supreme orgasm between two persons. Not physical, not sexual – total. Two existences meeting into each other, dissolving. Then the lover becomes the door, the beloved becomes the door, and they both reach the one.

So whosoever comes to me should come perfectly aware that it is dangerous to be near me. Your old arrangements will be disturbed. And I cannot help it – I am not here to help your adjustments. That is for you to decide. I can help you grow – grow in meditation, grow in love. To me, both words mean the same, because they reach the same end.

Enough for today.

Both
Are
Needed

CHAPTER FOURTEEN

Beloved Osho,
You said every child is born a god,
yet my two children were very different right from birth.
One is very serene and god-like,
but the other seemed disturbed
before she was influenced by any conditioning.
How should we deal with the difficult one?

THIS RAISES A VERY BASIC QUESTION. Existence itself is divine; then from where does the evil come? From where does the bad, the immoral, the unacceptable come? The good is okay because we have made it synonymous with God – good means God. But from where does the bad come? This has puzzled humanity for centuries. As far back as we can go, this problem has always been there in the mind of man.

The logical solution, the solution that the mind can find, is to divide existence, to create a duality, to say that there is God, which is good, and there is evil, the devil, Beelzebub, Satan, which is bad. Mind thinks the problem is solved – so all that is bad comes from the devil, and all that is good comes from God. But the problem is not solved; the problem is only pushed back a little. The problem remains the same. You have pushed it back a step, but nothing is solved – because from where does the devil come? If God is the creator, then he must have created the devil in the beginning, in the first place, or God is not the supreme creator. The devil has always been there, just as an enemy, the antagonistic force – then both are eternal. If the devil is not created then the devil cannot be destroyed, so the conflict will continue eternally. God cannot win, the devil will always be there disturbing.

This is the problem for Christian theology, Mohammedan theology, Zoroastrian theology, because all these three theologies have followed the simple solution that mind suggests. But mind cannot solve it. There is another possibility which doesn't come from the mind and will be difficult for the mind to understand. That possibility has arisen in the East, particularly in India, and that possibility is that there is no devil, there is no basic duality – only God exists, there is no other force. This is what *advait* – the non-dual philosophy – means: only God is. But we see the evil is there!

Hindus say that the evil exists in your interpretation, not in itself. You call it bad because you cannot understand it or because you are disturbed by it. It is your attitude that makes it bad or appear bad. There is no evil. Evil cannot exist. Only God exists, only the divine exists.

Now I will take your problem against this background. Two children are born – one is good, one is bad. Why do you call one good and why do you call the other bad? Is it really reality or your interpretation? Which child is good, and why? If the child is obedient the child is good; if the child is disobedient the child is bad. One who follows you is good, one who resists is bad. Whatsoever you say, the one accepts it. If you say: Sit silently – the one sits. But the other tries to disobey, tries to be rebellious – the other is bad. This is your interpretation. You are not saying anything about the children, you are saying something about your mind.

Why is the obedient one good? In fact, the obedient ones have never been brilliant, have never been very radiant, they have always been dull. No obedient child has been a great scientist or a great religious man, or a great poet – no child who is obedient. Only disobedient ones have been great inventors, creators; only the rebellious one transcends the old and reaches to the new and into the unknown.

But for the parents' ego the obedient one feels good, because it helps your ego. When the child follows you, whatsoever you say, you feel good; when the child resists and denies you, you feel bad.

But a really alive child *will* be rebellious. Why should he follow you? Who are you? Why should he follow you just because you are a father? What have you done to be a father? You have been just a passage – and that too very unconscious. Your sex is not a conscious act, you have been pushed by unconscious forces to move into it. The child is just an accident. You were never expecting, you were not consciously aware to whom you were giving an invitation to come. The child has suddenly come as a stranger. You have fathered it, but you are not the father.

When I say you have fathered it, it is a biological thing. You were not needed, even a syringe can do that. But you are not a father because you are not conscious. You have not given the invitation, you have not asked a particular soul to enter the womb of your wife, your beloved. You have not worked for it.

And when the child is born, what have you been doing to it? When you say the child should follow you, are you confident enough that you know the truth that he should follow you? Are you confident enough, certain that you have realized something that the child should follow?

You can force yourself on the child because the child is weak and you are strong. That is the only difference between you and your child. Otherwise you are also childish, ignorant; you have not grown, you are not mature. You will get angry just like the child, you will get jealous just like the child, and you will play with toys just like the child. Your toys may be different, a little bigger, that's all.

What is your life? Where have you reached? What wisdom have you gained so that the child should follow you and should say yes to you whatsoever you demand? A father will be conscious of it; he will not force anything on the child. Rather he will allow the child to be himself, he will help the child to be himself. He will give freedom to the child, because if he has known anything, he must know that only through freedom does the inner grow. If he has experienced anything in his life, he knows well that experience needs freedom. The more freedom, the richer is your experience. The less freedom...there is no possibility to experience. If there is no freedom at all then you can have borrowed experiences, imitations, shadows, but never the real thing, never the authentic.

Fathering a child will mean giving him more and more freedom, making him more and more independent, allowing him to move into the unknown, where you have never been. He should transcend you, he should go ahead of you, he should surpass all the boundaries that you have known. He must be helped but not forced, because once you start forcing you are killing, you are murdering the child.

The spirit needs freedom – it grows in freedom and only in freedom. If you are really a father you will be happy if the child is rebellious, because no father would like to kill the spirit of the child.

But you are not fathers. You are ill with your own illnesses. When you force a child to follow you, you are simply saying that you would like to dominate someone. You cannot do it in the world, but this small child – at least you can dominate him, possess him. You are being a politician to the child. You want to fulfill some unfulfilled desires through the child – domination, dictatorship. At least you can be a dictator to the child; he is so weak, he is so young and helpless, and he depends on you so much, that you can force anything on him. But by forcing you are killing him. You are not giving birth to him, you are destroying him.

The child who follows will look good – because he is dead. The child who is rebellious will look bad because he is alive.

Because we have missed life ourselves, we are against life. Because we are already dead, dead before death, we always want to kill others. Subtle are the ways. In the name of love you can kill. In the name of compassion you can kill. In the name of service you can kill. Beautiful names we find – deep down, the murderer is sitting.

Realize this, then you will not think in these terms – that this child is good and that child is bad. Don't interpret. Every person is unique, every person is different. The divine creative force is such that it never repeats.

So only say this much, that this child is different from that child. Don't say this is good and that is bad. You don't know what is good and what is bad. This child is obedient, that child is disobedient; but no one knows what is good.

And don't force. If this child by his own spontaneity is obedient, then it is good. This is his nature – help it to grow. And if that child is rebellious, disobedient, this is his nature – help him to grow. Let one grow to be a deep yes-sayer; let the other grow to be a deep no-sayer. But don't interpret, because the moment you interpret you start destroying. This is his nature to say yes, and that is his nature to say no. Both are needed.

Life will be very flat and dull if there is nobody to say no. If everybody is a yes-sayer, it will be absolutely dull and stupid. The no-sayer is needed, that is the polar opposite. Obedience will be meaningless if there is nobody to rebel. Don't choose, simply feel the difference and help. And don't force yourself on them, don't be violent.

Every father is violent, every mother is violent, and you can be violent because you are violent in the name of love. Nobody is going to criticize you, because you say you love your child so much that you have to beat him, you love him so much that you have to put him right. You say because you love him that's why you are trying to put him right – he's going wrong. Are you certain what is wrong and what is good? Nobody is certain, nobody can be certain – because the phenomenon is such that a thing which is good this moment becomes bad the next; the direction that seems bad in the beginning turns out to be good in the end. Life is a flux, every moment changing.

So a real father or a real mother will give his or her children only awareness, not morals, because morals are dead. You say: This is good, follow! But the next moment the thing becomes bad, and what is the child supposed to do? The next moment life changes. It is changing, it is a continuum of change, and your morals are fixed – you say *this* is good, *this* has to be followed. Then you become dead. Life goes on changing and you go on, fixed with your morals. That's why religious persons look so dull, their eyes vacant, superficial, with no depth – because depth is possible only if you move with the river of life.

So what should a father or a mother give as a gift to their children? Only awareness. Make the children more aware. Allow freedom and tell them: Be alert and move with freedom. Even if you have to err, don't be afraid, because life learns through errors also. One becomes alert through errors also – so don't be afraid. It is human to err.

If you err with alertness only one thing will happen: you will not commit the same mistake again and again. Once you commit the mistake you will experience it, you will become alert about it and it will disappear. It will make you richer and you will go ahead, unafraid. Just remember one thing, that whatsoever you pass through, be more conscious. If you say yes, say it consciously. If you say no, say it consciously.

Don't get hurt when a child says no – because who are you to fix a child? He comes through you, you are just a passage. Don't become a dictator. Love never dictates, and if you never dictate then this goodness and badness will disappear. Then you will love both. Your love will flow unconditionally. That's how God's love is flowing to this world – unconditionally.

I have heard.... Somebody said to Junnaid, a Sufi mystic: A very evil man comes to listen to you and you allow him so much closeness and intimacy. Throw him out, he is not a good man.

Junnaid said: If God does not throw him out of existence, who am I to throw him out? If God accepts him...I am not superior to God. God gives him life, God helps him to be alive; and that man is still young and fresh and he will live long, longer than you. So who am I to decide? God is showering on both, the good and the bad.

The situation is absolutely clear, crystal-clear – that for God there is no good, no bad. When I say God, I don't mean a person sitting somewhere up in the sky. That is an anthropocentric attitude: we conceive of God in our own image. There is nobody sitting there. God means the whole, the totality of existence. A bad man breathes as beautifully as a good man; a sinner is as accepted by existence as a saint. Existence makes no differentiation. But because of dualistic thinking – Christian, Mohammedan, Zoroastrian – we think in terms of conflict.

There is a story: There was a town, Sodom, in old Israel. The people were very perverted in that town, sexually perverted – homosexuals. So it is said that God destroyed the town. The whole town was destroyed. A great fire descended and everybody was killed.

After many, many centuries, one Hassidic saint, one Hassidic mystic, was asked: When God destroyed Sodom there must have been at least a few good persons in the town? – all were destroyed. So the questioner said: We can accept that the bad were destroyed because they were bad – but why the good?

Now look at the cunning mind. The Hassid thought it over and said: He destroyed the good also so that they could be witnesses that these bad people were bad. This is a cunning calculation, this is just saving face. The real thing is that for God there is no good, no bad. When he creates he creates both; when he destroys he destroys both – unconditionally.

This is really foolish, this attitude of good and bad. A person smoking cigarettes becomes bad, a person enjoying alcohol becomes bad, a person who has fallen in love with somebody else's wife becomes bad. We think God is sitting there and calculating: This man smokes, this man is an alcoholic, this man has fallen into adultery, let this fellow come and I will see. This is foolish if God is calculating about such trivial things! This is our tiny mind.

For existence there is no interpretation and no division. Good and bad are human conceptions, not divine. Every society has its own conceptions of good and bad, every age changes and has its own conceptions of good and bad. There is no absoluteness about good and bad. Good and bad are relative – relative to society, to culture, relative to us. God is absolute; for him there is no distinction. And if you are deep in meditation where thoughts disappear, then there is no distinction – because good and bad are thoughts. When you are silent, what is good and what is bad? The moment the idea arises: This is good, that is bad, the silence has been lost. In deep meditation there is nothing – no good, no bad.

Lao Tzu is reported to have said: A hair's distinction, and heaven and hell are set apart. In the mind of a meditator, if even a slight distinction arises then the whole world is divided.

Meditation is non-distinction, no distinction. You simply look, and you see the whole and don't divide it. You don't say: This is ugly, that is beautiful; this is good, that is bad. You don't say anything. You simply are. You don't say anything, you don't make any division. The non-dual is there.

In meditation you become God. People think in meditation they will see God. This is wrong; there is nobody to be seen. God is not an object. In meditation you become God, because all distinctions disappear. In meditation you become one with the whole, because in meditation you cannot divide yourself from the whole – all divisions have fallen. You are so silent that no boundary is there. Every boundary is a disturbance. You are so silent there is no I, no thou. You are so silent that all boundaries have blurred and disappeared. One exists, unity exists. This is what Hindus call the Brahman – the one, the unity, the ultimate unity of existence.

It is mind that divides, makes distinctions, says this is this, that is that. In meditation there is isness, undivided. You are God when you are in meditation, and only in meditation will you come to know unconditional love.

If you are a father, both your children will be just children – strangers coming from an unknown world, moving into an unknown existence, growing, maturing. Out of your love you give to them; you share your life, your experiences, but you never force anything. When you don't force, then who is obedient and who is disobedient? When you don't force, how can you decide who is good and who is bad?

Now I come to the last point. When you don't force, how can one be obedient and another disobedient? The whole phenomenon disappears. Then you accept the other – the child, the wife, the husband, the friend – as he is, as a fact. If we can accept each other as facts, without any oughts, shoulds, without any good and bad, life will become paradise this very moment.

We reject. Even if we accept somebody, we accept in part. We say: Your eyes are good, but everything else is just dirty. Is this acceptance? We say: This act of yours is good, but all else is bad, cannot be accepted, and I accept only that which is good. That means: I accept only that which is according to me.

You may not know how you are destroying each other, because whenever the parents say to the child: We accept only this part, not anything else – when a wife says to the husband: I accept only this in you, not the other – what are you doing? You are creating a division in the other's mind also.

When the father says: Don't do this, I don't accept this, I am angry about this – when he punishes a child because he thinks he has done something wrong, what is he doing? When he appreciates the child, gives him a toy, brings flowers for him, sweets, and says: You have done well, you have done something good which I approve – what is he doing? He is creating a division in the child. By and by the child will also reject the part that the parents have rejected, and he will be divided: he will become two I's.

You may have observed little children – they even punish themselves; they even say to themselves: Bobby, this is not good. You have done a bad thing. They start rejecting the part that has been rejected by their parents. Then a division is created. The rejected part becomes the unconscious, the suppressed part; and the accepted part becomes the conscious, the conscience. Then their whole life will be a hell, because the rejected and the accepted will go on fighting; continuously there will be a turmoil.

The rejected cannot be destroyed. It is you, it is there. It is always working within you – you may have put it in the dark, that's all. But once you put part of you in the dark that part becomes more forcible, because it works through darkness and you cannot see it, you cannot be aware of it and it takes its own revenge. Whenever there is a weak moment and your conscious part is not very strong, it will come out. You may be good for twenty-three hours, but for one hour, when the conscious is tired, the unconscious asserts itself.

So even saints have their sinner moments, even saints have to give leave to their sainthood. They are on holiday, sometimes they have to be. So if you catch a saint on his holiday don't be too disturbed: everybody has to have a holiday. Everybody gets tired – unless one is whole. Then there is no tiredness because there is no other part which is constantly fighting, creating trouble, asserting itself, taking revenge.

So we have two words: one is saint, the other is sage. The saint always has the sinner hidden within him; the sage is the whole. The sage cannot be on holiday because he is always on holiday – there is no rejected part; he lives as a whole totality. He moves moment to moment as a whole; he never rejects anything. He has accepted himself completely.

But this rejection is created by the parents, by the society. A small child is always a great discoverer, and of course he begins his discovery with his own body; that is the nearest existence to him. He cannot go to the moon, he cannot go to Everest; they are very far away. Some day he may go, but right now the nearest part is his own body. He starts discovering it. He touches his body, he enjoys it.

Observe a little child touching his toes – happy, happy as you can never be even if you go to the moon. He has discovered his body! He touches his toe, enjoys it, brings it to his mouth, because these are the ways he discovers. He will taste it, smell it, touch it. But when he comes to his sexual parts, parents become disturbed. That disturbance is in the parents, not in the child. He does not make any distinctions; the toe or the sexual organ are the same. There is no division in his body up to now. The whole body is there: fingers, eyes, nose, sexual organs, toes, are one flow. There is no division of lower and higher.

Hindus have a division; all over the world all the cultures have divisions. Hindus say: Never touch below the navel with your right hand, because that part below the navel is dirty. Touch below the navel with your left hand; touch above the navel with your right hand. The body is divided, and the division has gone so deep in the mind that by right we mean good – we say: You are right – by left we mean bad. So if you want to condemn somebody, just say he's a leftist, a communist. The left is bad.

A child doesn't know which is left, which is right. The child is whole, he is a unity. He doesn't know which is lower, which is higher – the body is an undivided flow. He will come to discover his sexual parts, and parents become disturbed. Whenever a child, boy or girl, touches the sexual organs, immediately we say: Don't touch! We remove the hand. The child is shocked. You have given an electric shock to him. He cannot understand what you are doing.

And this will happen many times. You are hammering into the child that something in his body has to be rejected – the sexual part of the body is bad. Psychologically, you are creating a complex. The child will grow, but he will never be able to accept his sexual organs. If you cannot accept your body in its totality there will be problems, there will be trouble, because the child will make love, he will move into the sexual act, but there will be guilt: something wrong is going on, something basically wrong is happening. He is condemning himself. Making love, the most beautiful thing in the world, he is condemning and is guilty. He cannot make love totally, he cannot move totally into the other, because he is holding back. Half is moving, half is being controlled. This creates a conflict and love becomes a misery.

This happens in all dimensions of life. Everything becomes miserable because in everything the parents have created a division: this is good and that is bad. This is why you are miserable – because of your parents, the society. Don't do the same to your children. It will be very difficult. Because you are divided, you would like to divide the child – it is unconscious!

But if you become alert...if you are really meditating you will become alert. Don't create the same schizophrenia in your child; don't divide, don't make a split. You have suffered enough; don't create the same suffering for your child. If you really love you will not divide him, because division creates suffering. You will help him to remain whole, because wholeness is holy, and wholeness gives ecstatic possibilities, opens doors for the peak experiences.

How can you help a child to remain whole? One thing: remain alert so you don't divide him unconsciously. Don't condemn a thing. If you feel it is harmful, tell the child that this is harmful but don't say this is bad – because when you say harmful you are stating a fact; when you say bad you have brought a valuation into it.

Parents have to say many things to children, because children don't know. You have to say: Don't go near the fire – but say: This is harmful. If you get burned you will suffer, but then still it is up to you. Say: This is my experience, that whenever I was burned, I suffered. I tell you my experience, but even if you want to do it you can do it. This is harmful.

Say what is harmful, say what is beneficial, but don't say good and bad. If you are alert, you will drop the words good and bad from your vocabulary – because with good and bad you are bringing your valuation to things. Say harmful – and still allow freedom, because your experience cannot become the children's experience. They will have to experience themselves. Sometimes even harmful things will have to be done; only then can they grow. Sometimes they will have to fall and get hurt; only then will they know. They have to pass through things, get hurt and scarred, but that is the only way one grows.

If you protect the child too much he will not grow. Many people remain children, their mental age never grows beyond that of a child. They become old – they may be seventy, but their mental age remains nearabout seven, because they have been so protected. Look at very rich families: their children are protected so much they are not allowed any freedom to err, to experience, to go astray, to go off the road. Almost every moment somebody is following them – the servants, the tutor, the governess; they are never left alone. Then look what happens to them: almost always rich families produce mediocre children, stupid, silly. Great minds have never come from rich families – it is difficult. Innovators never come from them, adventurers never come from them – they cannot. They are so much protected, they never grow.

For growth unprotectedness is needed, protectedness is also needed – both are needed. Look at a gardener working with his trees: he helps them, he protects them, but still he gives them freedom to move in the sun, in the rains, in the storms. He will not take those trees inside the house to protect them from the storm and from the sun and from the dangers that are always there outside. If you take the tree inside it will die. A hothouse plant is unnatural, and we all become hothouse plants because of over-protective parents.

Don't protect the children, don't leave them unprotected. Follow them like a shadow. Look after them, be careful and create a balance, so whenever it is so dangerous that they may die you protect them; but whenever you feel that it is not going to be so dangerous you allow them. The more they grow, the more you allow. By the time a child becomes sexually mature you should give him total freedom – because nature has made him a man now. Now no need to be so worried. Sometimes accidents will happen, but they are worth it.

Give the child a wholeness. Make him infectious to your awareness. Love him, tell him what your experience is, but don't try to make him follow your experience. Don't force. If he follows of his own accord, it is good; if he doesn't follow, wait – there is no hurry.

It is difficult to be a father or to be a mother, the most difficult thing in the world. And people think it is the easiest.

I have heard: One woman was coming in a taxi to her home from the market, and the taxi driver was just crazy. He was going zigzag; any moment there would be an accident. And he was going so fast...the woman was very, very nervous, sitting on the edge of the seat, and many times she said: Don't go so fast, I'm scared. But he wouldn't listen. Then she said: Listen! Twelve children are waiting for me at my house. If something goes wrong, what will happen to the twelve children?

So the driver said: And you are telling me to be alert!

Difficult to follow it? He is saying: You have given birth to twelve children – you were not alert, and you are telling me to be alert in driving!

It is easy to give birth to many children; there is no problem, animals do it easily. But to be a mother is very difficult, the most difficult thing in the world. To be a father is even more difficult – because to be a mother is natural, to be a father is not so natural. Father is a social phenomenon. We have created the father; it doesn't exist in nature. To be a father is still more difficult, because there is no natural instinct for it. It is difficult because this is the most creative act, to create a human being.

Be alert. Give more freedom. Don't make distinctions of good and bad; accept both, and help both types to grow. Soon this helping the children to grow will become a deep meditation for you – you will also grow with them. And when your child flowers into a yes-sayer, or a no-sayer...because there have been beautiful no-sayers: Nietzsche is a no-sayer – but beautiful! His genius to say no is such a wonderful and beautiful phenomenon that the world would not be so rich if there were not people like Nietzsche. He cannot say yes. It is difficult for him. No is his whole being.

Buddha is a no-sayer. He said: There is no Brahman, there is no soul, there is no world. You cannot find a greater no-sayer. He left nothing. He says: There is nothing. He goes on saying no, goes on eliminating. It is very difficult to find a yes from him – impossible. But what a beautiful being evolved out of that no! That no must have been total.

There have been yes-sayers, the devotees – the *bhaktas:* Meera, Chaitanya or Jesus or Mohammed, these are yes-sayers. And there are two types of religion, of course: one which is around a no-sayer, the other religions which are around a yes-sayer. You also will belong to one or the other. If you are a no-sayer, then Buddhism will be a great help to you. If you are a yes-sayer, then Buddhism cannot help you at all; it will be destructive. Christianity can help, Hinduism can help.

Both are needed. When I say this, I mean they always exist in a proportion, just like men and women – almost always the number is the same. The whole world is divided – half men, half women. And how nature keeps this proportion is a miracle. In every other dimension the same proportion is maintained: always half no-sayers and half yes-sayers in the world, always half who can follow the path of knowledge and half who can follow the path of love. Love is yes-saying, knowledge is always no-saying. And this proportion is maintained by nature always.

So if you have got two children, one is a yes-sayer and the other is a no-sayer, this is the proportion! This is good that you have got both in your home. You can create a harmony out of them. Don't try to destroy the no-sayer, don't try to push and help only the yes-sayer. Create a harmony between the two. These two children are representative of the whole world, the yin and yang, the opposites, the poles. Create a harmony between them and your family will really be a family, a unit, a harmonious unit.

But don't interpret, don't condemn, don't be moralistic. Just be a father, a mother. Love them and accept them and help them to be themselves. This is the base of all love: to help the other to be himself. If you want to pull, manipulate, you are not in love, you are destructive.

Beloved Osho,
In the West, most of our growth methods tend to be
group-oriented like encounter groups and psychodrama.
In the East, although there are ashrams where seekers live
together, the stress seems to be on the individual.
Would you tell us about the two approaches.

T here are two types of growth methods. You can pursue your spiritual growth alone, or you can work through a group, through a school. Both types have always existed even in the East. Sufi methods are group methods. In India also group methods have existed, but were never so prevalent as in Islam or Sufism. But this is a new phenomenon as far as quantity is concerned – that the West is totally group-oriented. Never before have there been so many group methods alive, and so many people working through them, as exist now in the West.

So in a way we can say that the East has remained with individual efforts, and the West is now growing towards group methods. Why is this so and what is the difference? And why this difference?

Group methods can exist only if your ego has come to a point where it is a burden to carry it. When the ego has become so burdensome that to be alone is to be in anguish, then group methods become meaningful, because in a group you can merge your ego.

If the ego is not very evolved then individual methods can help you. You can move to a mountain, you can be isolated, or even living in an ashram with a master you work alone: you do your meditation, others do their meditation, you never work together.

In India, Hindus have never prayed in groups. With Mohammedans, group prayer entered India. Mohammedans pray in groups; Hindus were always praying alone; even if they went to the temple, they would go alone. It is a one-to-one relationship – you and your God.

This is possible if the ego has not been helped to grow to a point where it becomes a burden. In India it has never been helped to grow – from the very beginning we have been against the ego. So you grow in ego, but the ego remains vague, blurred; you remain humble, you are not really an egoist. It is not a penetrating peak in you, it is flat ground. You are egoistic, because everybody has to be, but not absolute egoists. You always think it is wrong and go on pulling yourself down. In certain situations you can be provoked and your ego becomes a peak – but ordinarily it is not a peak, it is flat ground.

In India the ego is just like anger – if someone provokes you, you become angry; if nobody provokes you, you are not angry. In the West the ego has become a permanent substance. It is not like anger, it is now like breathing. There is no need to provoke it – it is there, it is a constant phenomenon. Because of this ego, a group becomes a very helpful thing. In the group, working with a group, merging yourself in the group, you can put your ego aside easily. That's why not only in religion, but in politics also, a few phenomena can exist only in the West. Fascism, for example, could exist, could become possible in Germany, which is the most egoistic country in the West, the most Western. There is nothing like the German ego all over the world. That's why Hitler could become possible – because everyone is so egoistic, everybody is in need of merging.

Nazi rallies, millions of people marching – you can lose yourself, your self need not be there. You become the march, the band playing, the music, the sound, the hypnotizing Hitler, a charismatic personality. Everybody looking at Hitler, the whole mass around you like an ocean – you become just a wave. You feel good, you feel fresh, you feel young, you feel happy. You forget your misery, your anguish, your loneliness, your alienation. You are not alone. Such a great mass is with you and you are with it. Your individual private worries drop. Suddenly there is an opening – you feel light, as if you are flying.

Hitler became successful not because he had a very meaningful philosophy – his philosophy was absurd, it was childish, immature – not because he could convince the German people that he was right...that was not the point. It is very difficult to convince

German people, one of the most difficult things, because they are logicians, they have logic in their minds, rational in every way. It is difficult to convince them, and to have been convinced by Hitler would have been impossible. No, he never tried to convince them. He created a hypnotic group phenomenon; that convinced them.

It was not a question of what Hitler was saying; it was a question of what they were feeling when they were in the group, in the mass. It was such an unburdening experience that it was worth it to follow this man. Whatsoever he was saying – wrong or right, logical, illogical, foolish – it was good to follow him. They were so bored with themselves that they wanted to be absorbed by the mass. That's why fascism, nazism and all types of group madness, became possible in the West.

In the East only Japan could follow, because Japan is the counterpart of Germany in the East. Japan is the most Western country in the East. The same phenomenon was there, so Japan could become an ally to the Hitlerite madness. The same is happening in other fields also – in religion also, in psychology also. Group meditation is happening, and only group meditation will happen for a long period to come. When a hundred people are together – you will be surprised, particularly those who don't know the Western mind will be surprised – just holding hands, one hundred people sitting just holding hands, feeling each other, and they feel elated.

No Indian will feel elated. He will say: What nonsense! Just holding hands with a hundred people sitting in a circle, how can it be an elation? How can you become ecstatic? You can feel at the most the perspiration of the other's hand. But in the West a hundred people holding hands are elated, ecstatic. Why? – because even holding hands has become so impossible because of the ego. Even wife and husband are not together. The joint family has disappeared. It was a group phenomenon. Society has disappeared. In the West now, no society exists really. You move alone.

In America – I was reading the statistics – everybody moves within three years to another town. Now, a man in a village in

India remains there – not only he, his family has remained there for thousands of years. He is deeply rooted in that soil. He is related to everyone, he knows everybody, everybody knows him. He is not a stranger, he is not alone. He lives as part of the village, he always has. He was born there, he will die there.

In America, every three years on average people move. This is the most nomadic civilization that has ever existed: vagabonds – no house, no family, no town, no village, no home really. In three years how can you get rooted? Wherever you go you are a stranger. The mass is around you but you are not related to it. You are unrelated, the whole burden becomes individual.

Sitting in a group, in an encounter group or in a growth group, touching each other's bodies, you become part of the community. Touching each other's hands and holding each other's hands, just lying near each other, or lying on top of each other in a pile, you feel oneness, a religious elation happens. A hundred people dancing, touching each other, moving around each other, become one. They merge, the ego is dissolved for a few moments. That merger becomes a prayerful thing. Politicians can use it for destructive ends, religion can use it for very creative phenomena – it can become a meditation.

In the East people are in the community too much, so whenever they want to be religious, they want to go to the Himalayas. Society is too much around. They are not fed up with themselves, they are fed up with the society. This is the difference. In the West you are fed up with yourself and you want some bridge, how to be communicative with the society, with others; how to create a bridge, how to move to the other so you can forget yourself. In the East people are fed up with the society. They have lived with it so long, and the society is all around so much, that they don't feel any freedom. So whenever somebody wants to be free, to be silent, he runs to the Himalayas.

In the West you run to the society, in the East people run from the society. That's why lonely methods, individual methods have existed in the East; group methods are in existence in the West.

What am I doing? My method is a synthesis. In the first steps of Dynamic Meditation you are part of the group; in the last part the group disappears, you are alone. I am doing this for a particular reason...because now East and West have become irrelevant. The East is turning towards the West; the West is turning towards the East. By the end of this century there will be no East and no West – one world. This geographical division has existed too long; this cannot exist any more.

Technology has already dissolved it, it is already out of existence, but because of a habitual attitude in the mind it continues. It continues only as a mental phenomenon; actually it is no more. By the end of this century there will be no East, no West – just one world. It is already there. Those who can see, can see it already there. A synthesis will be needed – group and individual both. You work in a group in the beginning; in the end you become totally yourself.

Start from society and reach to yourself. Don't escape from the community – live in the world but don't be of it. Be related but still remain alone. Love and meditate, meditate and love.

Whatsoever happens before is not the question; whatsoever follows is not the question. Meditate and love if you are a man, love and meditate if you are a woman – but don't choose. Love plus meditation is my slogan.

Enough for today.

Share
Through
Your Being

CHAPTER FIFTEEN

Beloved Osho,
You said to us this week
that we should not concern ourselves with others.
But most of us from the West have friends and relatives
with whom we would like to share what we've found.
What should we tell them about sannyas?
What should we tell them about you?
How can we explain the unexplainable?

THERE ARE THINGS which cannot be told, you cannot share them verbally. But there is a way to share them and that is through your being. Be a sannyasin; that is the only way to tell others what sannyas is. If you are a sannyasin your whole being will say that which cannot be said. Then your whole way of life will tell stories which cannot be conceptualized.

Language is impotent. It cannot say that which is alive, it can say only dead things. You can say something about sannyas, but it will not be true. How can you say anything about sannyas? It is an inner flowering, it is an inner freedom, it is an inner ecstasy, a benediction. You can share it of course, but the sharing will be through your being, through your very being – the way you walk, the way you sit, the way you look, your eyes, your body, your very breath. The silence that surrounds you, the bliss that goes on and on being thrown all about you, the vibrations of you – they will tell and only they *can* tell. Be a sannyasin; that is the only way. And what is sannyas? It is a freedom from the mind. It will be difficult to understand sannyas if you don't understand what mind is.

Mind is the accumulated past. All that you have experienced, all, that you have known, all that you have lived through is accumulated in the memory. That accumulated past is the mind. So mind is always dead because it belongs to the past. Mind is always dead, never alive. Whenever a thing has become dead it becomes part of the mind. It is just like dust that a traveler gathers. You are here and now, and mind is always in the past. Mind is your shadow that follows you.

Sannyas is getting free from the past, living in the moment – not carrying the past in the head, not being burdened by it. Moment to moment, die to the past as if it never existed, as if you are born anew. Every moment be fresh and young. Put aside the past. Don't gather the dust. If you gather the dust you will get duller and duller every day. Your consciousness will be covered, your mirror-like being will not be able to mirror anything. The longer you have lived with the past, the more the mirror will be covered. It will not reflect. You will become less and less sensitive. This is what has happened.

Sannyas means a breakthrough. Looking at the past, understanding that it is useless because it is no more, understanding that it is useless, a burden, you put it aside. Then you are here and now this very moment, in the present, in the plenitude of the present.

Sannyas means living without time: not being influenced by the past, and not being carried by the future – no burden of the past, and no desire in the future. Sannyas is a goalless, purposeless life.

If somebody says that sannyas is a means to achieve God, he is talking nonsense. Sannyas is not to achieve anything. Sannyas is to live in such a way as if you have achieved everything. It is not a desire, because it makes no difference whether you desire wealth, power, prestige, or you desire God, *moksha* – it makes no difference. The basic mechanism remains the same: you desire. And whenever you desire, the future comes in. Whenever the future is there, it is nothing but a projection of the past. Whenever the future is, it is nothing but the modified known. It is never the unknown. How can you desire the unknown? That which you don't know, how can you desire it?

God cannot be desired. If you desire, it is something else. God is the unknown, how can you desire it? God is the unexperienced, how can you desire it? You can desire sex, you can desire power, you can desire the ego, because you have known them. You have known them for many, many lives. But how can you desire God? How can you desire love? How can you desire ecstasy? You have never known them; desire is impossible. That's why all the scriptures and all the buddhas say: God happens to you when you are desireless. Moksha comes to you, you never go to moksha. You cannot go because you don't know. Nirvana happens to you when you are desireless.

Sannyas is desirelessness, and desirelessness means living in the now. And remember, now is not part of time; now is beyond time. Time comes in only when you think in terms of the past, in terms of the future. This very moment is not part of time. This very moment is not recorded on your watch, because the watch is always moving in the future. It is always moving in the future, never here and now. It is coming from the past and moving into the future.

The watch is representative of your mind: it is never here! The moment you say it is here, it has moved. The moment you see where it is, it has become past. From past to future it is jumping. If you look minutely at your watch, you will see it is not moving, it is jumping. The minute hand looks as if it is moving because the jump is very slow, but the hand that records seconds, you can see it is jumping. It jumps from the past to the future, it is never here and now. And this is the way of the mind.

Now is beyond time, it is timeless – or you can call it eternal. You never leave it, it is always there. You never go into it, you never come out of it – it is there. If you can live in such a way that your whole life is surrounded by the now, you are a sannyasin, you are desireless – you don't desire even God.

The moment you desire God, you have made God into a commodity. Then you will be exploited by the priests, because they sell that commodity. Then you will be exploited by temples and churches and mosques, because those are the shops where that commodity is sold. A sannyasin has nothing to do with temples and churches, because God is not a commodity.

What happens when you are not desiring? It doesn't mean that you kill yourself, suppress yourself; it doesn't mean that you kill your desires. The point has to be understood deeply, because this has happened.

Scriptures say that those who have known say: When you are desireless, the divine happens to you. Then the mind jumps, just like a cat jumping on a mouse, catches hold of this desirelessness and says: Okay, if God can be attained through desirelessness, then I will desire desirelessness. Now this becomes the desire, and again you have missed. Then sannyasins try to be desireless, so this state of desirelessness becomes the thing to be achieved in the future.

So what can you do? You can kill desire and think that you are desireless. Desirelessness is not the death of desire, because when desire dies, you are also dead. This will look very subtle and difficult: if there is no desire, if you have killed all desire, you will also be dead. That is not the way for desirelessness to happen. It is not the death of desire but a transformation of the desire. Desire moving into the future is one way of desire; desire remaining here and now and enjoying the present is another way of desire. The second way is desireless, because it is not moving into the future.

A man who is desireless is not dead. He is more alive than you because his desire is concentrated here and now. If he is eating his food, you cannot even conceive how happy he is – eating his ordinary food, just bread and butter. His whole being is here: he is not just throwing things inside.

A man who lives in the future never eats well. He is just throwing food inside. He is not concerned with eating because his mind is concerned with the future. He lives in ambition. He cannot eat well; he can think of what he will eat tomorrow, but he cannot eat this moment. He can imagine what type of foods, where he is going to eat tomorrow, but today is vacant and empty. And every tomorrow, unfortunately, becomes today – he will miss his whole life.

While he is making love he doesn't feel anything, he is frustrated – but he thinks of other women that he is going to capture in the future. And the same will happen again with every woman, with every man, because the meeting is here and now and the mind always moves. He will not be able to make love, he will not be able to eat well, he will not be able to enjoy the bliss that nature gives, continuously showers all around you. As in autumn when leaves are falling down from a tree silently, bliss is showering every moment silently without making any noise around you. Everything is beautiful, everything is a benediction – but you are not present.

So a sannyasin doesn't mean a man who has killed his desires. A sannyasin means a man who has brought all his desiring force here and now. He lives totally. Whatsoever he is doing he is totally absorbed in. Nothing is left standing behind. He is not divided. While eating he becomes eating, while making love he becomes love, while moving he becomes movement.

Buddha has said – and very few have understood what he means – that when you move only movement exists, not the mover; when you talk only talking exists, not the talker; when you listen only listening exists, not the listener; when you observe only observation exists, not the observer. This is what a sannyasin is. The activity becomes so total that the actor is lost in the activity. There is nobody standing behind – no division. You have moved completely; you have flowed into the activity, whatsoever the activity. Then enjoyment becomes perfect.

So a sannyasin, a man who is desireless, is not a man with dead desires. He is a man whose desiring forces, all the energies that can desire, have turned upon the present moment. They are not running in the future, they have turned upon the present moment. His desires are concentrated here and now. He has become a world. Everything moves back into him. Nothing goes into the future because future is false, it is nonexistential.

If your desires move into the future, it is as if a river is moving into a desert: it will be lost, it will never reach the sea, it will never enjoy the ecstasy that comes to a river when it meets the sea. When a river reaches an ocean the orgasm is felt all over the river, the dance, the ecstasy, the blessing. It will not come if a river moves into a desert and is lost. It will evaporate, it will die. There will be no communion with existence. When desire moves into the future, the river of desire has moved into the desert. Future is nowhere; it is always the present. Future is a creation of the mind – it is false, it is a dream. A sannyasin lives in the reality, not in the dream. He enjoys the reality.

So remember this: I insist again and again that a sannyasin is not a man who is against life; really, he is the man who is for life. And a sannyasin is not a man who has killed all his being and desires and has become a dead thing. He is life in abundance, he is a great source of aliveness.

What happens? – because this is subtle – what happens? What will the difference be? You feel hunger, you start thinking about food. You never feel the hunger in its totality; otherwise it has its own beauty. A person who cannot feel hunger is already dead. When hunger is there, hunger is in the present, but you start thinking about food. When food is there, you start thinking about some other food that you are going to get tomorrow.

A sannyasin, a man who lives in the present, enjoys hunger when hunger is there. He is totally hungry, he becomes hunger. Every cell of the body waiting for food as if it has not rained for many days and the earth is waiting for the rains. Every pore praying, waiting, inviting; the whole body waiting, inviting, enjoying the hunger. Then food is there. Then he enjoys the food and satisfaction comes to the whole being, spreads all over the body and mind and soul. He enjoys this contentment.

One Zen master was asked: What is meditation?

He said: When I am hungry I am hungry, and when I feel sleepy I fall asleep.

The questioner could not understand. He said: I am asking about meditation, not about you.

The master said: This is all that we know meditation to be. When I feel hungry I feel hungry; there is no division. When I eat I eat, and when I feel sleepy I go to sleep. No fight with life, no resistance – surrender, floating, becoming a white cloud.

A sannyasin is a white cloud moving in the blue sky, enjoying every moment that God has given, enjoying every grace that comes to him. If this is possible...and this *is* possible – this has happened to many, this can happen to you; only a deep understanding is needed – then no karma is accumulated. Then you don't accumulate anything. You eat, you love, you do everything – but you do it so totally that there is no ego to accumulate any memory out of it. You never say: *I* did this – how can you? When the doing was there you were not there, so who can say: I did this?

If you say to a sannyasin: You were hungry and you have taken your food, he will say: I was not hungry, I have not taken the food. Hunger was there and the hunger has taken the food; no action on my part, I was not there. If you are not there, if the actor is not there, who will accumulate karma?

That's what Krishna says to Arjuna: Do whatsoever happens to you. Whatsoever the situation demands, do it, and forget the doer. Don't think: I am doing; rather think: God is doing through me. This is another way of saying the same thing: God is doing through me. I am just a *nimitta* – an instrument, a passage, a vehicle. I am just a flute, hollow within, nothing substantial. God goes on singing and bringing new tunes, creating new songs. I am just a passage, a bamboo flute. A sannyasin is a bamboo flute, a passage. He is not there. Much happens around him, much happens through him, but he is not there.

Become a sannyasin, because this...this is beautiful!

This must come to your mind, that you have to share. You are here; your mother will be waiting at home – your wife, your husband, your children. And love always shares.... You will go back. You will not be taking any visible thing with you – not a present to your mother or your wife, some ornaments or something from this country – you will be taking something invisible. This invisible cannot be talked about, because you are not taking a philosophy with you. I am not giving you a philosophy, I am not giving you any ideology, I am giving you a different type of life, a way of being.

It will be difficult to tell them. If they ask directly it will be difficult. Don't try to say anything, because that will not be of any help, that may create more problems. Rather, be open to them so they can share. Rather, be vulnerable. Be with them – laugh, enjoy, eat, meditate, and tell them to share your being, a new way of life that has happened to you. Your very presence, your being which is laughing, enjoying, will become infectious – it becomes, and they will feel it.

This will take time. It will not be easy, it will be difficult. So before you go, be prepared. Be ready to share. They will not always understand. In the beginning there is going to be misunderstanding, more possibility of misunderstanding, because they have never thought about it. This is something unknown, and whenever the unknown knocks at the door the mind feels scared, because the mind cannot categorize it, the mind cannot tackle it. It is shattering and shocking. Mind always feels happy if it can categorize a thing, put it into a corner and say: This is this – label it and be finished. Mind is always happy if it can analyze a thing – divide it, cut it, look into it, and be finished with it.

But sannyas cannot be categorized. It is not a category. It is such an altogether different quality of being that there exists no category for it. It cannot be analyzed, it cannot be broken into fragments. It is not a mechanism; you cannot break it, take the pieces apart and put them together again. No, it is an organic unity. If you analyze it, it is no longer there; and you can never put it back together again, it is impossible. Sannyas is a live force – organic, just like a flower. Analyze the flower, take each petal away, break it, look inside it, be satisfied that you have inquired, then try to put it back together. By that time the flower is gone, the petals are dead, and they can never be put back again in the same way, because it was an organic unity, it was not a mechanism.

Sannyas is a flowering, a flowering of human consciousness – just as flowers coming on a tree show the tree has come to a completion and sooner or later fruits will follow. Flowers are just indications that the tree is ready to give fruits. The tree is ready, it is fulfilled. Flowers are just the ecstasy of the tree before it starts giving fruit – because fruit means the fulfillment. The tree has come to its peak, its climax; it has achieved the crescendo of its being. It is happy, it enjoys it – its life has not been futile; now fruits are going to come. The tree is ecstatic and gives flowers.

Sannyas is a flowering, and moksha is the fruit. Sannyas means now your inner being, your inner tree, has come to a point where the jump, where the explosion is going to happen. Before it happens, the whole being enjoys it. You are fulfilled. It has not been a waste. Many, many lives you waited – and it has come now. So long a waiting, so much patience...but it has been meaningful. Now you have achieved, you have reached. The whole being flowers.

Hindus have chosen red, orange, ochre, as the color of sannyas because of flowers. Green and red are the basic colors in nature. Green is the tree, red is the flower. Your being has come to a flowering. Soon the fruits will follow. Soon the seeds will be coming. Take this flowering with you.

It is good that you think how to share with loved ones, with friends, with wife and husband, with the family – how to share it? It is beautiful, it is good. It is virtuous to think of sharing such a beautiful thing. But you can share only if it has happened to you. If you have been only listening to me, thinking about flowers and you have not flowered, you cannot share. If you take my words they will not be real flowers, because words cannot be real – they will be plastic flowers. You can carry them, you can give them to your friends, but there will be no fragrance in them. They will not say what I have been saying to you, they will not convey anything. There will be no communication through them.

So if you want to share sannyas, meditation, be meditative, become more and more deeply involved in this way of life. Desireless, still enjoy every desire when it comes. Whatever happens, keep enjoying it as a gift, as a grace, but never asking for it, never demanding it, never planning for it, never thinking about it.

Live totally, and not through thought.

Thought is the corrupting force. It corrupts everything and corrupts absolutely, because thought is cunning – it is cunningness personified. The more you think the more you will become cunning. You will think it is cleverness, you will think it is intelligence. It is not, because if there is intelligence, then thought is not needed. Intelligence is enough; thought is not needed. You need thought because intelligence is not there. If intelligence is there then you respond moment to moment. You need not think about what you should do next, because when the next moment comes intelligence will be there and you will respond. A mirror never thinks: When another man comes in front of me, what am I going to do? There is no need. The mirror is there, so it mirrors. If intelligence is there you never think about the next problem, because when the problem is there the intelligence will respond. You can rely on it.

Because we don't have intelligence, we think about it. Thinking is a substitute. Greater intelligence, less thinking. When intelligence is perfect, no thinking. A buddha never thinks – there is no need. Whatsoever life brings before him, he responds. You think because you cannot rely on your intelligence, so you have to plan beforehand. When the moment comes then you will follow the blueprint that you prepared in the past. What type of living is this? You live out of the past. That's why so many errors are unnecessarily committed and everything goes stale and dead – because you always act out of the past. Life goes on, new every moment, riverlike, changing. The change never stops, but you have stopped in the past. You carry a blueprint. Whenever life gives you a problem you look in your memory – the blueprint, the planning – and then you act out of it. You have missed. Life is always new, blueprints are always old.

Life is just like birds flying in the sky: they never leave any mark. There is no path. When they have flown, the sky is as vacant as it was before. It is not like earth where people walk, and through their walking, through their footprints, paths are created. Life is like the sky – no paths are created.

A sannyasin is like a bird flying in the sky, following no foot-prints, following no paths, because no paths exist. He moves moment to moment through his present intelligence, not through his past memory.

Look: we have done something quite the contrary – we have made everything a planning. Even a husband coming back from his office, from his work, thinks how he has to meet his wife; he plans inside, talks with himself. He will say this, he will touch her hand this way, he will give her a long kiss – or something. What is the need to plan it? Don't you have any love?

If love is not, then planning is needed because you cannot rely on yourself; you may completely forget. If you have not planned it beforehand, you may reach home and you may completely forget that your wife has been waiting the whole day – preparing food for you, washing your clothes, just surrounded by you, by your love. She has been waiting and waiting and waiting and getting impatient. And now you have come, and you don't even look at her. You sit in your chair and you start reading your paper, or you put on your radio or tv as if the wife does not exist. You are afraid of this, you can't do this, so you plan. You make it a point to remember. You have to remind yourself how to behave with your wife, with your beloved. What type of love is this which can-not respond without planning? If love is there, there will be no thinking about it.

The same is true about intelligence: if intelligence is there, there will be no thinking about it. Thinking is a substitute. Thought is very clever and cunning. It can create the illusion of the real – that is the cleverness. You can smile without smiling. A smile comes to your lips but it is only on the lips, just a painted smile, not related to you at all. There is no bridge. It is not bubbling from the center of your being. It has not come from you; you have just put it on, it is a mask. Thought can do that; and then by and by you go on becoming more and more false. Cunningness means creating a pseudo-life around yourself.

A sannyasin is real. If he smiles his smile comes from his being.

If he is angry anger comes from his being. If he loves he loves from his being. He is not pseudo, he is not a phony. He is real and authentic. You can rely on him. If he loves, he loves. If he is a friend, he is a friend. If he is not, you can rely on him – he is not. But he is not deceptive.

This is what I mean by a really virtuous man – authentic, reliable. Whatsoever is, is really there. He wears no masks, he uses no false faces. He lives with the real. And remember: you can come to the real only if you *are* real. If you are false you can never come to the real. If you are unreal then the world that you see is going to be unreal, because the unreal can be connected only with the unreal. You are unreal; that's why the world is illusory, a maya. If you are real the world disappears; it becomes divine, it becomes real.

The word maya is beautiful. It means that which can be measured. Maya means that which can be measured. Mind is the measuring phenomenon. Mind goes on measuring things, mapping out, analyzing. Mind tries to measure everything. That's why Hindus have called the world maya – that which can be measured by the mind.

What is your science? Nothing but measuring. Hindus call science *avidya*. They call it not knowledge but anti-knowledge; it is not real knowing, because that which is real cannot be measured. It is immeasurable, it is infinite. It has no beginning and no end. The real is immeasurable, the unreal is measurable. And with measure comes reason, logic; with the immeasurable, logic drops, reason drops. Mind is very clever and cunning: it has created the world of illusion.

Then what is a sannyasin? He is not a mind; on the contrary, he is innocence. He is innocent like a child just born – with no past, with no idea of the future. A sannyasin, every moment, is a child just born. This is the process: every moment he dies to the past. Whatsoever has passed he throws away, he renounces it, because it is a dead thing, dust; no need to carry it. He cleanses himself; his mirror becomes again fresh. He goes on cleansing the mirror. This cleansing I call meditation.

People ask me: When will we be able to drop meditation? You will not be able to drop it. It will drop one day when you are not, but you will not be able to drop it, because you will need cleansing. You become continuously dirty, every moment the dirt gathers – it's the nature of life. Every moment you need a bath, a cleansing. When you are not there, then nothing – there is no problem because there is no one who can get dirty. But you *are* there, so meditation has to be continued. It is an effort to remain innocent.

Look: if you are innocent, there is nothing you are lacking. If you can look with innocent eyes towards the sky, you become the sky. With mind you start measuring. You say: This is beautiful or not beautiful, or: Today's sky is clouded, or: Tomorrow's sky will be better, or: Yesterday's sky was more beautiful. You start measuring.

But if you are innocent, not a mind but just a being looking at the sky, there is nothing to say, nothing to think. The sky is there, and you are also like a sky. The inner and the outer meet. Both the spaces become one and there is no boundary. The observer becomes the observed. That's what Krishnamurti goes on saying: the observer becomes the observed. The outer and the inner lose their boundaries, become one.

If you look at a tree with innocence, with no mind measuring, what happens? There are not two, the tree and you; somehow the tree has entered you and you have entered the tree. Only then do you come to know what a tree is. You look at the stars, you look at a river, you look at a line of birds flying against the blue sky.... Boundaries go on merging. All differentiation is lost, all distinction is lost. Unity arises. It is not a unity put by thought, it is not a unity of philosophers, it is a totally different unity. You don't think that it is one, you suddenly *know* that it is one. You don't say inside your mind: This is one because the Upanishads have said so, because the Vedas have said so. It *is* one.

If the Vedas are in your mind and the Upanishads, you are not innocent, you are cunning. Measurement is continuing. You are measuring, applying mind and thought, comparing. You are clever and cunning, you are not intelligent, and howsoever clever you are, a clever mind is mediocre. Intelligence is needed. A child is born intelligent, not clever. He looks at the world with clear eyes; his perception is absolutely clear, unclouded.

When I say innocence is sannyas, I mean your perception should be clear, with no thoughts to become barriers. You should look – you should become the look. You should observe, but there should be no observer behind you manipulating. This innocence is possible, and only this innocence goes beyond time and space. Only this innocence reaches to the ultimate, to moksha, the absolute freedom. Become a sannyasin – an innocent one, reborn, cleansing, moving moment to moment into the unknown. Then you will be able to share.

The whole process of human education, culture, conditioning, is just the opposite: it teaches you how to be cunning and clever. It teaches you the mind, it never teaches you innocence. It teaches you automatization – this word has to be remembered – it makes you more and more automatic, because if you are more and more automatic you are more efficient.

You learn driving: in the beginning it is difficult. The difficulty is not in the driving or in the car or in anything else – the difficulty is in you, because you have to be alert. In the beginning you have to be alert; the danger is there. You have to be continuously conscious of what you are doing. You have to be alert to the traffic, to the people passing, to the mechanism; you have to be alert to the clutch, to the gears, to the wheel and everything. You have to be alert to so many things that your mind cannot continue its routine inner chattering. It has to be alert. That creates the trouble.

Later on, after a few days, you become automatic. Now the hand goes on working, the legs go on working, the car and you have become one mechanism, and your mind can continue its inner chattering. There is no problem, your mind is not needed. This is what I mean by automatic. Now your body is a mechanism, it functions. You will be needed only in certain rare cases.

If there is going to be an accident, suddenly you will be needed. Then your thinking process will have to stop. Suddenly there will be a shock, your whole body mechanism will shiver, and you will have to be there, you will have to be alert. But these are rare moments. Otherwise you can continue: you can smoke, you can sing, you can even talk with somebody, you can listen to the radio or you can continue your inner talk, the inner dialogue – there is no need to be there. You have become automatic.

But this is more efficient, because if you need to be continuously aware you cannot be very efficient, you cannot go very fast – because you don't know how to be aware. Because of this factor, because people are not aware, they live unconscious lives. Society has learned a trick: make everybody more and more automatic. The whole of schooling is nothing but making you automatic. Language, mathematics – everything becomes automatic. You can do it without being worried about it. It becomes mechanical.

When I say become innocent, it means a de-automatization. It means whatsoever you do, do fully conscious. If you are driving a car, then drive only – become driving, don't do anything else; don't continue the inner talk. Just become so deeply involved and alert that there is no driver – only driving, fully conscious. It will be difficult – that's why societies have not bothered about it. Only individuals can pass through such an arduous path. Do everything consciously. By and by your body-automatism will dissolve, you will become de-automatized. Then innocence will flower.

A child is innocent because nothing is automatic yet. He has not learned anything, he is not conditioned yet. Sooner or later we will condition him. He will learn things; then more and more mind will be there and less and less he himself. Less and less being and more and more mind will be there. Then he will become just an automaton, a mechanism – efficient, working well, serving the society, but dead.

Serve, help the society work, but don't become automatic. As you have already become automatic, de-automatize yourself. By and by, bring more and more consciousness. Whatsoever you are doing, bring more consciousness, because whatsoever you are doing, if you are less conscious it becomes automatic. That is the way of automatization: being less and less conscious, doing things like a mechanism.

More and more conscious doing, not like a mechanism but a presence – then innocence will flower in you. And that innocence is the greatest thing that can happen to a human being.

Innocent, you are divine. Innocent, you have become gods.

Enough for today.

About
The Author

MOST OF US LIVE OUT OUR LIVES in the world of time, in memories of the past and anticipation of the future. Only rarely do we touch the timeless dimension of the present – in moments of sudden beauty, or sudden danger, in meeting with a lover or with the surprise of the unexpected. Very few people step out of the world of time and mind, its ambitions and competitiveness, and begin to live in the world of the timeless. And of those who do, only a few have attempted to share their experience. Lao Tzu, Gautam Buddha, Bodhidharma...or more recently, George Gurdjieff, Ramana Maharshi, J. Krishnamurti – they are thought by their contemporaries to be eccentrics or madmen; after their death they are called 'philosophers'. And in time they become legends – not flesh-and-blood human beings, but perhaps mythological representations of our collective wish to grow beyond the smallness and trivia, the meaninglessness of our everyday lives.

Osho is one who has discovered the door to living his life in the timeless dimension of the present. He has called himself a 'true existentialist', and has devoted his life to provoking others to seek this same door, to step out of the world of past and future and discover for themselves the world of eternity.

Osho was born in Kuchwada, Madhya Pradesh, India, on December 11, 1931. From his earliest childhood, his was a rebellious and independent spirit, insisting on experiencing the truth for himself rather than acquiring knowledge and beliefs given by others.

After his enlightenment at the age of twenty-one, Osho completed his academic studies and spent several years teaching philosophy at the University of Jabalpur. Meanwhile, he traveled throughout India giving talks, challenging orthodox religious leaders in public debate, questioning traditional beliefs, and meeting people from all walks of life. He read extensively, everything he could find to broaden his understanding of the belief systems and psychology of contemporary man. By the late 1960s Osho had begun to develop his unique dynamic meditation techniques. Modern man, he says, is so burdened with the outmoded traditions of the past and the anxieties of modern-day living that he must go through a deep cleansing process before he can hope to discover the thought-less, relaxed state of meditation.

In the early 1970s, the first Westerners began to hear of Osho. By 1974 a commune had been established around him in Poona, India, and the trickle of visitors from the West was soon to become a flood. In the course of his work, Osho has spoken on virtually every aspect of the development of human consciousness. He has distilled the essence of what is significant to the spiritual quest of contemporary man, based not on intellectual understanding but tested against his own existential experience.

He belongs to no tradition – "I am the beginning of a totally new religious consciousness," he says. "Please don't connect me with the past – it is not even worth remembering."

His talks to disciples and seekers from all over the world have been published in more than six hundred volumes, and translated into over thirty languages. And he says, "My message is not a doctrine, not a philosophy. My message is a certain alchemy, a science of transformation, so only those who are willing to die as they are and be born again into something so new that they cannot even imagine it right now...only those few courageous people will be ready to listen, because listening is going to be risky.

"Listening, you have taken the first step towards being reborn. So it is not a philosophy that you can just make an overcoat of and go bragging about. It is not a doctrine where you can find consolation for harassing questions. No, my message is not some verbal communication. It is far more risky. It is nothing less than death and rebirth."

Osho left his body on January 19, 1990. His huge commune in India continues to be the largest spiritual growth center in the world attracting thousands of international visitors who come to participate in its meditation, therapy, bodywork and creative programs, or just to experience being in a buddhafield.

Suggested
Further
Reading

HEARTBEAT OF THE ABSOLUTE
Discourses on the
Ishavasya Upanishad

IN THESE DISCOURSES Osho gave during a Mount Abu meditation camp, sutras from ancient Hindu scriptures are transmuted into stunning insights that can open the reader's eyes to his own inner reality. Osho speaks on issues that touch the heart of every intelligent individual – on love, possess- iveness, God as another name for existence, our investment in forgetting the phenomenon of death, karma, the nature of the mind, and meditation. In addition, he gives practical suggestions about how to prepare for meditation and how to derive the most from meditation techniques.

THE TANTRA EXPERIENCE

DISCOURSES ON 'The Royal Song' of Saraha, the founder of Tantric Buddhism, a lineage which bears fruit to this day in Tibet. "Saraha is one of my most loved persons; it is my old love affair. You may not have even heard the name of Saraha, but Saraha is one of the great benefactors of humanity. If I were to count on my fingers ten benefactors of humanity, Saraha would be one of those ten. If I were to count five, then too I would not be able to drop Saraha."

THE MUSTARD SEED
Commentaries on the
Fifth Gospel of Saint Thomas

ESSENTIAL FOR THOSE brought up in a Christian environment. Osho brings to life these excerpts from a scroll found at Nag Hammadi, Egypt, contributing a new understanding to these little-known sayings of Jesus – the man he calls "a revolutionary of the inner world."

No Water No Moon

Osho breathes new life into many familiar Zen stories.
"I found *No Water No Moon* one of the most refreshing, cleansing and delightful books I could imagine," wrote the renowned violinist Yehudi Menuhin. "It is a book which will never cease to be a comforting companion."

Finger Pointing to the Moon
Discourses on the Adhyatma Upanishad

These seventeen talks were given at a meditation camp at Mount Abu, Rajasthan. In this beautiful series on the seeds of wisdom, the Upanishads, Osho says, "This Upanishad is a direct encounter with spirituality. There are no doctrines in it; there are only experiences of the fulfilled ones.... In it there is no discussion of that which is born out of curiosity or inquisitiveness, no; in it there are hints to those who are full of longing for liberation, from those who have already attained liberation...."

THE HEART SUTRA

DISCOURSES ON Gautam Buddha's Prajnaparamita Hridayam Sutra highlight both Osho's and Buddha's essential teachings: the merging of negative and positive, the non-existence of the ego and the buddha-nature of mankind. In addition, Osho speaks on the seven *chakras* and the corresponding facets in man – the physical, psychosomatic, psychological, psycho-spiritual, spiritual, spiritual-transcendental and transcendental.

JOURNEY TO THE HEART
Discourses on the Sufi way

THIS IS A JOURNEY towards the heart, on the path of the Sufis. Here Osho speaks on some of the ancient teaching stories of the Sufi mystics, including those of Bayazid, Bahauddin, Dhun-Nun and Maruf Karkhi. This is the path of love: the lover and the beloved. The search for the beloved, the godliness that is within us all.

"Sufism is *the* religion. Whenever a religion is alive it is because Sufism is alive within it."   *– Osho*

The Hidden Harmony

ACCORDING TO OSHO, if Heraclitus had been born in India rather than Greece, he would have been recognized as not simply a philosopher but as a mystic. Further, Osho says that if Heraclitus had been accorded his rightful status, the whole course of Western history would have been totally different.
Though only fragments remain of his words, Osho finds in them a poetry that is refreshing in its simplicity and clarity. Through this series of eleven discourses, Osho acts as a via media to this mystic of twenty-five centuries ago.

In Search of the Miraculous
Volume 2

GUIDING THE READER through the seven bodies and their corresponding chakras, Osho talks on psychic phenomena, dreams, telepathy, hypnosis, color therapy, Dynamic Meditation, Kundalini, gurus and the Tantra dimensions of sex. "I am talking about very scientific things," he says, "not something belonging to religious superstitions."

MEDITATION:
THE ART OF ECSTASY

EMPHASIZING THE 'festive dimension' of meditation, Osho suggests a variety of techniques specially designed for today's seeker. He also provides detailed descriptions of each stage of Dynamic Meditation.

Included is an appendix highlighting Osho's radical meditation techniques, as well as other meditative and traditional therapies.

THE SEARCH
Talks on the Ten Bulls of Zen

THE TEN PAINTINGS that tell the Zen story about a farmer in search of his lost bull provide an allegorical expression of the inexpressible. Originally Taoist, they were repainted by the 12th century Chinese Zen master, Kakuan. Osho examines the deeper layers of meaning behind each painting, as well as answering questions from disciples and other seekers, in this special selection of discourses.

Osho
Commune
International

THE OSHO COMMUNE INTERNATIONAL in Poona, India, guided by the vision of the enlightened master Osho, might be described as a laboratory, an experiment in creating the 'New Man' – a human being who lives in harmony with himself and his environment, and who is free from all ideologies and belief systems which now divide humanity.

The Commune's Osho Multiversity offers hundreds of workshops, groups and trainings, presented by its nine different faculties:

Osho School for Centering and Zen Martial Arts
Osho School of Creative Arts
Osho International Academy of Healing Arts
Osho Meditation Academy
Osho Institute for Love and Consciousness
Osho School of Mysticism
Osho Institute of Tibetan Pulsing Healing

Osho Center for Transformation
Osho Club Meditation: Creative Leisure

All these programs are designed to help people to find the knack of meditation: the passive witnessing of thoughts, emotions, and actions, without judgment or identification. Unlike many traditional Eastern disciplines, meditation at Osho Commune is an inseparable part of everyday life – working, relating or just being. The result is that people do not renounce the world but bring to it a spirit of awareness and celebration, in a deep reverence for life.

The highlight of the day at the Commune is the meeting of the White Robe Brotherhood. This two-hour celebration of music, dance and silence, with a discourse from Osho, is unique – a complete meditation in itself where thousands of seekers, in Osho's words, "dissolve into a sea of consciousness."

For
Further Information

M ANY OF OSHO'S BOOKS have been translated
and published in a variety of languages
worldwide. For information about Osho, His medi-
tations, books, tapes and the address of an Osho
meditation/information center near you, contact:

Osho International
24 St James's Street, St James's,
London SW1A 1HA, U.K.

Osho Commune International
17 Koregaon Park
Poona 411001, India

Chidvilas Inc.
P.O. Box 3849, Sedona
AZ 86340, U.S.A.